DRAWING *from* THE MODERN

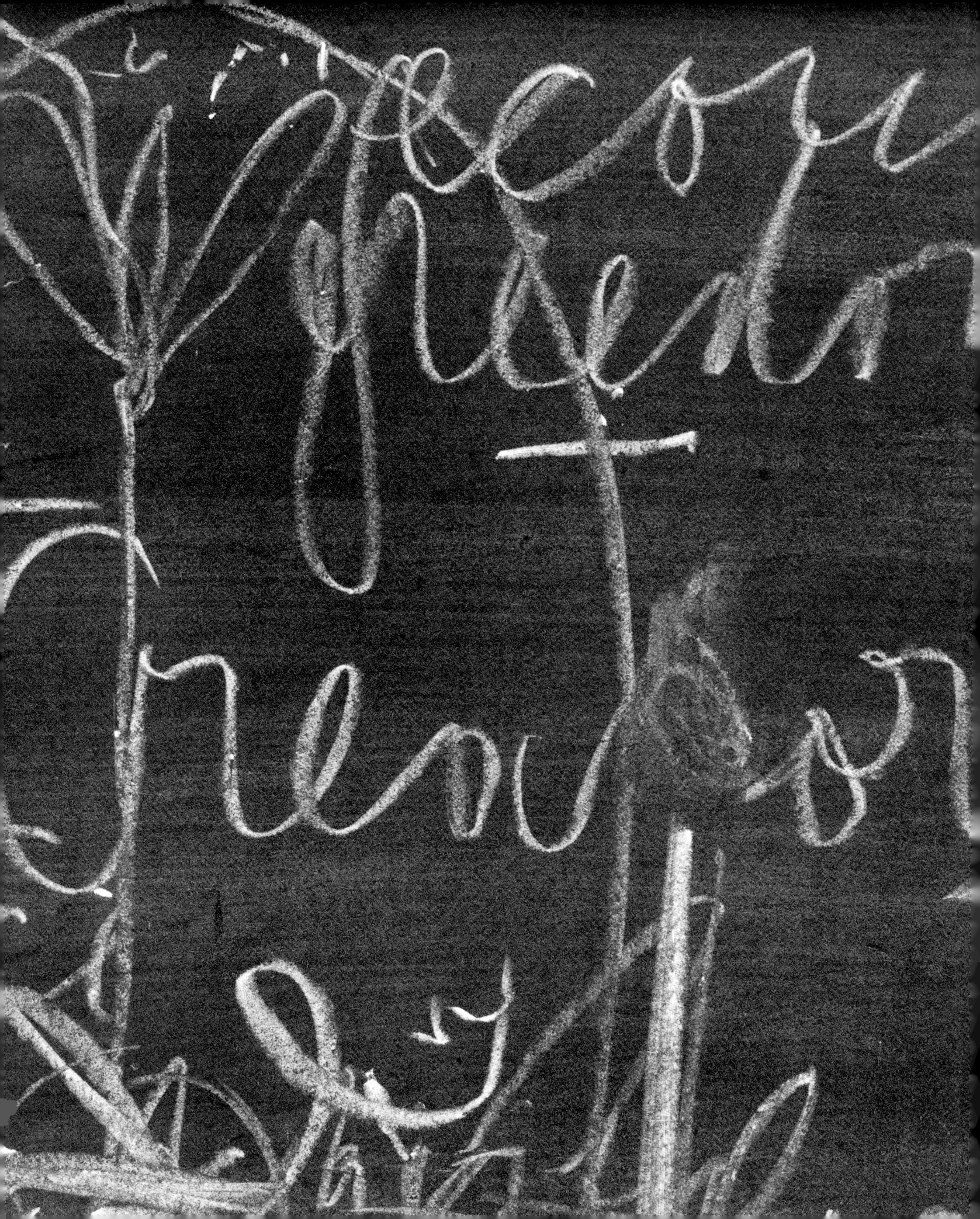

Gary Garrels

DRAWING *from* THE MODERN
1945–1975

THE MUSEUM OF MODERN ART, NEW YORK

Published on the occasion of the exhibition *Drawing from the Modern, 1945–1975*, The Museum of Modern Art, New York, March 30–August 29, 2005, organized by Gary Garrels, The Robert Lehman Foundation Chief Curator of Drawings, and Curator, Painting and Sculpture. This is the second of a three-part exhibition presenting 125 years of works on paper from the collection of The Museum of Modern Art.

This series of publications is made possible by Kathleen and Richard S. Fuld, Jr., Donald B. and Catherine C. Marron, Mr. and Mrs. Henry R. Kravis, and Ronald S. and Jo Carole Lauder.

Produced by the Department of Publications
The Museum of Modern Art, New York
Edited by Libby Hruska
Designed by Amanda Washburn
Production by Elisa Frohlich
Typeset in Apex
Printed and bound by CS Graphics Pte Ltd., Singapore

Front cover: **JACKSON POLLOCK**
Untitled (detail), (c. 1950)
Ink on paper, 17 1/2 x 22 1/4" (44.5 x 56.6 cm)
Gift of Jo Carole and Ronald S. Lauder in honor of Eliza Parkinson Cobb, 1982

Printed on 150 gsm Phoenix Motion Xenon

Library of Congress control number: 2005920375
ISBN: 0-87070-664-0

Published by The Museum of Modern Art
11 West 53 Street, New York, New York 10019-5497
www.moma.org

Distributed in the United States and Canada by D.A.P./Distributed Art Publishers, Inc., New York

Distributed outside the United States and Canada by Thames and Hudson, Ltd., London

Printed in Singapore

Frontispiece: **JOSEPH BEUYS**
Untitled (Sun State) (detail), (1974)
Chalk on painted board with wood frame, 47 1/2 x 71 1/8" (120.7 x 180.7 cm)
Gift of Abby Aldrich Rockefeller and acquired through the Lillie P. Bliss Bequest (by exchange), 1984

CONTENTS

FOREWORD

Among the first works to enter The Museum of Modern Art's collection seventy-five years ago was a drawing. In October 1929, Paul J. Sachs, one of the Museum's earliest supporters and a professor at Harvard specializing in the history and connoisseurship of drawing, offered a portrait by George Grosz titled *Anna Peter*. A simple and straightforward pencil drawing showing none of what we think of as modernism's radical experimentation and swaggering transgression, the elderly and seemingly tight-lipped *Anna* nonetheless speaks loudly about MoMA's commitment to drawing. As part of a group of initial acquisitions, the work confirms the centrality of drawing right from the Museum's beginnings. Moreover, the acquisition of the work, which was completed only two to three years before MoMA's founding (it is dated 1926–27), demonstrates the Museum's dedication to collecting and exhibiting art of its own time.

Since the acquisition of *Anna Peter*, the notion of drawing has changed enormously—from the adoption of unconventional media like paper ephemera and botanical products to the extension of the support far beyond the sketchbook-size sheet. As our understanding of what constitutes a drawing has expanded, so has drawing's role within the Museum. Originally acquired to enhance viewers' understanding of the Museum's primary collection of painting and sculpture, drawings soon began to be collected for their own sake and as independent works. In establishing a separate Department of Drawings in 1971, with its own exhibition program and, eventually, galleries, the Museum renewed its commitment to collecting drawings and showing their crucial role in telling the history of modernism. Since MoMA's first drawing exhibition in 1947, which drew from a group of only 227 objects, the collection has expanded almost thirty-five-fold to include more than seven thousand works.

As new galleries open once again, *Drawing from the Modern* highlights masterworks from what is arguably the world's preeminent collection of modern and contemporary drawing. The exhibition, presented in three sequential parts, surveys 125 years of modern drawing, and illuminates, in particular, shifts in drawing strategies—how artists have deployed a diverse range of media to transform a blank support. The review of the department's holdings that such an exhibition necessitated has reinforced for us the collection's unparalleled strengths—a true embarrassment of riches. Rather than just sitting back and enjoying the view, the range of these treasures has only provoked a desire to look even deeper. Committed to telling modernism's varied and varying stories and using drawings as a window onto the working out of pictorial and thematic problems, the department's curators continue to develop and refine the collection: finding new ways to understand the activities of the late-nineteenth- and early-twentieth-century avant-gardes, reassessing the postwar years by looking at global developments, and, perhaps most importantly, staying actively involved in—and actively collecting—art of our own time.

Glenn D. Lowry
Director, The Museum of Modern Art

ACKNOWLEDGMENTS

While the collection of The Museum of Modern Art has long been acknowledged for its outstanding quality, the staff of the Museum deserves equal public recognition. Their professionalism and commitment to the highest standards are matchless, across departments and at every turn. I deeply appreciate the dedication and camaraderie of everyone who has contributed to this project in both large and small ways, and their unflagging passion about the pleasure and importance of art.

A number of colleagues have made a crucial difference to the success of this exhibition and publication, and I especially want to thank the following individuals and departments: Glenn D. Lowry, Director, first invited me to join the Museum staff and welcomed my ambitions for the Department of Drawings. Bringing new works into the collection and making the collection more broadly available to the public through this project has been a shared mission. Jennifer Russell, Deputy Director for Exhibitions and Collections Support, never ceases to astonish me with her care for the most quotidian of tasks and her vision about where these tasks are leading us.

To mount an exhibition requires innumerable steps to shift works from the storerooms to the walls of the galleries in order to transform vision into reality, and I am honored to be part of the team that makes such dreams possible: in Paper Conservation, Karl Buchberg, Senior Conservator, Erika Mosier, Associate Conservator, Scott Gerson, Assistant Conservator, and Lee Ann Daffner, Andrew W. Mellon Foundation Conservator of Photographs; in the Department of Registration, Ramona Bannayan, Director of Collections Management and Exhibitions Registration, Allison Needle, Senior Registrar Assistant, Pete Omlor, Manager of Art Preparation and Handling, and the preparators; in the Department of Exhibition Design and Production, Jerome Neuner, Director, Hope Cullinan, Assistant to the Director, Peter Perez, Framing Conservator, and the entire staff—John Martin, William Ashley, Cynthia Kramer, Karen Van Wart, and Tina Gauthier; and in the Department of Graphic Design, Ed Pusz, Director, Claire Corey, Production Manager, and Burns Magruder, Senior Designer.

To publish a book that brings these works beyond the walls of the Museum and to give them public presence for years and decades to come requires equal effort and imaginative skills. Here I would like to thank: in the Department of Publications, Michael Maegraith, Publisher, Marc Sapir, Production Director, Elisa Frohlich, Associate Production Manager, Christina Grillo, Associate Production Manager, David Frankel, Managing Editor, Cassandra Heliczer, Associate Editor, Libby Hruska, Associate Editor, and Amanda Washburn, Senior Book Designer, as well as Lawrence Allen, Bryan Stauss, and Rebecca Zimmerman; and in Imaging Services, Erik Landsberg, Head of Collections Imaging, Thomas Griesel, Collections Photographer, Paige Knight, Collections Photographer, John Wronn, Collections Photographer, and Roberto Rivera, Administrative Assistant.

To sustain ideas, flow of information and knowledge, communication both with and between the curators and the public, an exceptional understanding of how the realms of art and reality can meet is required. To make this possible, I especially thank: in the Department of Education, Deborah Schwartz, Deputy Director for Education, Sarah Ganz, Director of Education Resources, David Little, Director of Adult and Academic Programs, Laura Beiles, Assistant Educator of Adult and Academic Programs, and Sara Bodinson, Assistant Educator; Ruth Kaplan, Deputy Director for Marketing and Communications, Kim Mitchell, Director of Communications, Daniela Carboneri, Manager of Communications, and Kim Donica, Publicity Coordinator, Department of Communications; in the General Counsel's office, Stephen Clark, Associate General Counsel, and Jane Panetta, Manager; in the library and archives, Milan R. Hughston, Chief of Library and Museum Archives, Jennifer Tobias, Librarian, Ian Goulston, Assistant Librarian, Michelle Elligott, Museum Archivist, and Tom Grischkowsky, Archives Specialist; and in Collection and Exhibition Technologies, Eliza Sparacino, Manager, Gaël Anne Lelamer, Senior CEMS Assistant, Susanna Ivy, CEMS Assistant, and Steven Wheeler, CEMS Assistant.

I am especially thankful to curatorial colleagues who offered their support: Deborah Wye, Chief Curator, Prints and Illustrated Books, and in the Department of Painting and Sculpture, Lilian Tone, Assistant Curator, and María José Montalva, Curatorial Assistant. For many years before I joined the curatorial staff at the Museum, I was inspired and educated by colleagues who preceded me in the Department of Drawings; Margit Rowell and Magdalena Dabrowski have been no less generous since I have taken my post here, and I especially want to thank Bernice Rose, whose model of scholarship, connoisseurship, and openness to new art and ideas has set the standard to which I constantly aspire.

My colleagues in the Department of Drawings, individually and as a team, have intellectually prodded and nurtured me, attended to innumerable tasks, buoyed my spirits and shared my excitement. Each of them brings consummate professionalism, endless curiosity and commitment, and indefatigable energy to any and every objective. To look at and talk about works of art with them opens my eyes and my thinking. I cannot thank them enough for their assistance and their friendship: Miriam Basilio, Curatorial Assistant; Kathleen Curry, Assistant Curator, Research and Collections; Jodi Hauptman, Associate Curator; Jordan Kantor, Assistant Curator; Maura Lynch, Administrative Assistant; David Moreno, Preparator; Tricia Paik, Curatorial Assistant; Luis Enrique Pérez-Oramas, Adjunct Curator; Francesca Pietropaolo, Curatorial Assistant; John Prochilo, Department Manager. The interns who have worked through various stages of this project met every request with conscientious, thorough, and unflagging good cheer: Elena Carratala, Ingrid Greenfield, Jack McGrath, Jess McIntosh, and Elisabeth Sherman. Francesca Pietropaolo brought her unassuming but acute intelligence, vivid passion, and indispensable grace to every aspect of both the exhibition and the publication, tirelessly working and protecting me from my mistakes and making this project always a pleasure. For their essays for the book I am enormously grateful to Miriam Basilio, Jodi Hauptman, Jordan Kantor, Tricia Paik, Luis Enrique Pérez–Oramas, and Francesca Pietropaolo.

Outside the Museum, for their assistance in facilitating the publication of photographic material in this book, I would like to acknowledge Michele L. Agosti and Kimberly Davis, LA Louver; Gregg Burchard, Andy Warhol Museum; Deanna Cross, The Metropolitan Museum of Art; Anita Duquette, Whitney Museum of American Art; The Over Holland Collection; Ryan Jensen, Art Resource, New York; Sarah Kessler, P.S.1 Contemporary Art Center; Sandi Knakal, Ellsworth Kelly Archives; Janie C. Lee; Josefina Manrique, Fundación Gego; Trina McKeever, Richard Serra Archives; Laura Muggeo, Ronald Feldman Fine Arts; Dianne Nilsen,

The University of Arizona, Tucson; Michael Randazzo and Amy Eshoo, Werner H. Kramarsky Collection; Anna Marie and Robert Shapiro, Dr. Reiner Speck; Meredith D. Sutton, Jack S. Blanton Museum of Art, Austin; Sarah Taggart, Jasper John Archives; Gordon VeneKlasen and Asha Agnish, Michael Werner Gallery; and Kathleen Mylen-Coulombe, Yale University Art Gallery.

For their generosity in lending works that are fractional and promised gifts to the Museum and letting these works be taken from the walls of their homes to be shared with the public over several months, I am deeply indebted to Sarah-Ann and Werner H. Kramarsky, Anna Marie and Robert Shapiro, and Joel Wachs, and to those lenders who wish to remain anonymous. Without the support of Kathleen and Richard S. Fuld, Jr., Donald B. and Catherine C. Marron, Mr. and Mrs. Henry R. Kravis, and Ronald S. and Jo Carole Lauder this publication would not have been possible. I am deeply grateful to them for their extraordinarily generous gift and for their sustained commitment to the Department of Drawings.

Finally, I thank Richard Hoblock, who allows me to think out loud, offering critique and support, shares anxieties and discoveries with equal attention, and maintains humor and balance at all times.

Gary Garrels
The Robert Lehman Foundation
Chief Curator of Drawings
Curator, Painting and Sculpture

PREFACE

To celebrate the seventy-fifth anniversary of the founding of The Museum of Modern Art and the opening of its new and renovated building complex, the Department of Drawings has organized an exhibition in three sections, on view in new permanent collection galleries over the course of one year. *Drawing from the Modern*, along with an accompanying set of three catalogues, offers an introduction to the Museum's preeminent holdings of works on paper and a reconsideration of modern and contemporary drawing. Part one explores the variety of challenges to drawing traditions that emerged beginning in the late nineteenth century through the first half of the twentieth. Part two looks at developments in the post–World War II period, 1945 to 1975, examining, in particular, the crucial role of abstraction. Part three will present developments in contemporary drawing practice from 1975 to the present, a period in which works on paper have become, for many artists, a primary form of expression.

Because drawings are sensitive to light—media may fade, papers can yellow or become brittle over time—and in order to preserve them for future generations, they may be exhibited only periodically and for very limited periods of time. Usually, any presentation of drawings at the Museum is on view for no more than three or four months. This constraint has its benefits, forcing constant renewal and reconsideration on the part of the curators while giving viewers, over multiple visits, a variety of possibilities and contexts in which to consider the collection. While the first presentations in the newly opened building are chronological, subsequent selections may concentrate on thematic, stylistic, or cultural issues, or mix historical and contemporary works. The extraordinary depth and diversity of MoMA's collection offers opportunities for reconsideration that few other museums' holdings would allow.

The philosophy of the department proposes that no single history or defining canon of great works can adequately account for developments in modern and contemporary art. Likewise, no single collection can provide a comprehensive overview; these exhibitions thus reflect the particular collecting practices of this institution (a history described in detail in John Elderfield's introduction to his 1983 book, *The Modern Drawing*). Rather than offering an encyclopedic survey—many gaps remain to be filled, many artists are yet to be represented—our approach in these presentations, even within a chronological unfolding, has been to form groupings, or constellations, of works around periods, movements, styles, associations of artists, and/or geographic centers to allow new appreciations and critical reappraisals of artists and works both well known and less recognized. Drawings that are inarguably masterworks—incisive distillations and reflections of an artist's thinking and technique—are included. But because drawing is often the laboratory by which new ideas and techniques are developed and new materials and processes explored, many important works reflect moments of discovery rather than summary.

The richness of MoMA's collection reflects the sustained commitment of many individuals over the last seventy-five years, beginning with Alfred H. Barr, Jr., the Museum's first director, and Paul J. Sachs, a founding trustee whose first gift inaugurated the drawings collection. The trustees who have served as chairmen of the Committee on Drawings, Lily Auchincloss, Ronald S. Lauder, June Noble Larkin, Richard Salomon, and now Kathleen Fuld, as well as the vice chairmen, Robert L. B. Tobin and now Werner H. Kramarsky and Michael Lynne, have provided crucial vision and leadership to move the department and the collection forward. Their colleagues on the Committee on Drawings—whose current membership is listed on page 220—have been among the most devoted to the collection. Past members to whom we owe special thanks include Walter Bareiss, H.R.H. Prinz Franz von Bayern, Charles B. Benenson, Mrs. Carroll L. Cartwright, Agnes Gund, Patricia Orden, and Carol O. Selle. William Lieberman, John Elderfield, and Margit Rowell have, in turn, headed the Department of Drawings, and each brought distinctive and important new works into the collection. Bernice Rose, Magdalena Dabrowski, and Laura Hoptman, and now Kathleen Curry, Jodi Hauptman, Jordan Kantor, and Luis Enrique Pérez-Oramas, as curators in the department, have also played key roles in expanding the collection.

Above all, the extraordinary generosity of artists, collectors, and patrons of the Museum have enhanced the department's holdings with gifts of works of art and funds for acquisitions, often sustained over a period of years. Numerous bequests and gifts of private collections have either broadened the reach or deepened the holdings in particular areas of the Museum's collection. Among the most significant benefactors and collections are Lillie P. Bliss, Abby Aldrich Rockefeller, the Katherine S. Dreier Bequest, John S. Newberry, Blanchette Hooker Rockefeller, The Sidney and Harriet Janis Collection, The Joan and Lester Avnet Collection, James Thrall Soby, Philip Johnson, The Riklis Collection of McCrory Corporation, the Ruth Vollmer Bequest, The William S. Paley Collection, the Nina and Gordon Bunshaft Bequest, Robert L. B. Tobin, Werner and Elaine Dannheisser, the Louise Reinhardt Smith Collection, The Ian Woodner Family Collection, The UBS Collection, Jo Carole and Ronald S. Lauder, and Sarah-Ann and Werner H. Kramarsky. Other important works and their donors are not represented here, but on behalf of the curatorial staff who now have the pleasure and privilege of working with these drawings, I extend my deepest gratitude to each person who has helped shape this extraordinary collection.

Gary Garrels
The Robert Lehman Foundation
Chief Curator of Drawings
Curator, Painting and Sculpture

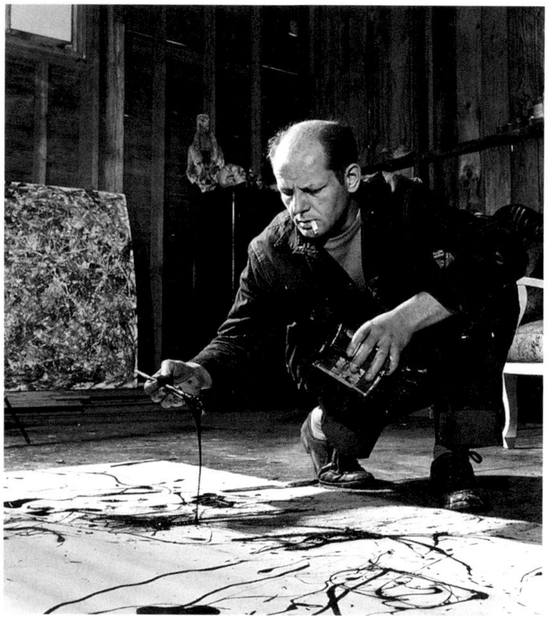

Jackson Pollock at work, 1949. Photograph taken by Martha Holmes for a 1949 *Life* magazine article

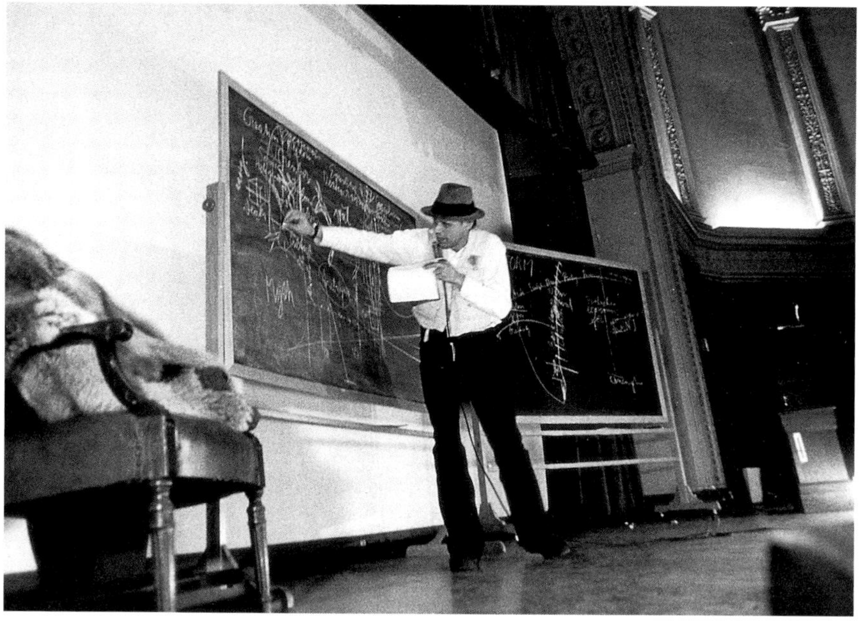

Joseph Beuys lecturing at the Art Institute of Chicago, 1974

Gary Garrels

DRAWING *from* THE MODERN

THE RESILIENCE *of* IMAGINATION

REAPPRAISAL OF MEANING

Throughout the twentieth-century and continuing today there have been various attempts to define and bracket what properly can be considered modern or advanced art. Artists and the public, as well as critics and scholars, however, grow impatient and uneasy with such limitations. The very best works of art frustrate reductive, proscriptive interpretation. The more manifold the potential of a work may be, the greater its claim for our attention, for relevance, for meaning. The more scrutiny a work can sustain, the more varied the arguments that can be made about it and the greater its capacity for significance.[1]

The understanding or the appraisal of the meaning of a work of art always springs from a discourse between the object itself and the ideas surrounding it. Artworks are neither produced nor viewed in a vacuum without intellectual underpinnings. The more we know about a work of art the better we may be able to appreciate its character and significance, its meanings and value. Yet it is actual artistic production that propels critical discourse, theory, and art history. Understanding best begins with a consideration of what is actually there. Having the works of art available, in our view, in front of our eyes, seen in a set of relationships, prompts reconsiderations of understandings and evaluations.

Art inevitably is sheathed in values, pronounced by the artists themselves as well as their critics, exemplifying moral and ethical standards. Nouns and adjectives are applied. The values of modernism and the avant-garde give special weight to certain characteristics—freedom, boldness, and individuality but also complexity, nuance, and self-consciousness. Abstraction has been held in higher regard within critical and theoretical arguments than figuration.[2] Art that advances discovery rather than retraces the known has been given priority in modernism.

Today what constitutes aesthetic advancement is questioned. It is no longer possible to see the development of art as a straight line, or with synchronicity between cities and continents. Rather, what we now can witness in retrospect are eruptions and constellations, rivalries and conversations, and the intensity of individual achievements that more properly mirror the complexities of cultures and lives in a rapidly changing world rather than a coherent intellectual program.

Visual art in the period following World War II, from the mid-1940s to the mid-1970s, witnessed enormous transformations. Abstract Expressionism affected a fundamental shift in the character and potential of visual art as well as a geographical one—particularly from Europe and the so-called School of Paris to the United States and what has been termed the New York School. Pop art, Minimal art, and Conceptual art followed, and generally have been set within a frame that until relatively recently gave precedence to the development of new work in New York.[3] Much work internationally was absorbed within this American paradigm, not always comfortably, and movements based in other countries, such as Arte Povera in Italy, Neo-Concretism in Brazil, and Gutai in Japan, for example, were marginalized in American accounts.[4] But over the last twenty years, the idea of the primacy of a single center of production for art has eroded. The renewed sense of identity in European nations, the rise of globalism, and the pervasiveness of media—photography, film, video, and other moving or time-based images—along with other influences, have forced a reconsideration of the history and development of postwar art.

Drawing, in an unexpected way, provides an astonishingly powerful and vigorous device for reexamining the art of this period, for renewing appreciation of the extraordinary achievements of well-known artists and for discovering others. Despite being among the most traditional of mediums and the radical departures and shifts of art during this time, drawing continued to play a crucial role in the work of almost all of the most significant artists. Like the concept of modernism, drawing, too, remained resilient and resistant to being summarized, confined, and proscribed. Artists did not abide by past assumptions but readdressed materials, practices, and subjects. Drawing allowed relationships between imagination and observation, perception and physicality, the mind and the hand. Its intimacy and directness, its provisional and exploratory character, and its relative mobility and lack of expense to produce made it the perfect laboratory by which to reinvent art's possibilities.[5] Drawing by its very nature provided a means for accepted understandings to be pried open, values to be reappraised, knowledge and even truth itself to be reconsidered.

Through the postwar period The Museum of Modern Art focused more intently both in exhibitions and acquisitions on new work being made in the United States, particularly New York, than in any other part of the world. Certainly this reflects the widely held judgment that New York had become the creative center for the visual arts, and there is no question even today that from the mid-1940s through the mid-1970s New York was home to an extraordinary number of exceptionally important artists. However, viewing art history through the lens of a particular collection only makes the limitations of an ostensibly objective view onto that history more apparent. Certain areas of postwar art in which drawing and works on paper are important are largely absent at this point from the Museum's collection. What is at hand begins to influence and shape our view, our understanding, the arguments and conclusions that we make.

The collection, however, is exceptionally rich and varied. Many important additions have been made in the last few years that both deepen and broaden the representation of individual artists and movements, and many of these works have not been previously on view or published. What follows then is one view of some of the major developments in drawing from the perspective of the Museum's collection and some arguments about the role of drawing within postwar art. A relatively small number of artists and works will be discussed to raise general points about the development of drawing through this period and to frame out distinctions. The comments and voices of numerous other authors have been included to introduce the richness of analysis and insight around the subject of postwar drawing and to encourage readers to use this text as a jumping-off point for further consideration of the artists, the drawings, and the issues around them. The fundamental importance of drawing for art in this thirty-year period will be recognized as indisputable.

ABSTRACTION: THE HAND AND THE BODY

Jackson Pollock and Willem de Kooning were the two leading artists of the Abstract Expressionist movement, and from the mid-1940s until Pollock's death in 1956 their work was in an extended dialogue. As noted critic Thomas Hess wrote, "Pollock and de Kooning were good friends; they also competed. Both wanted to paint masterpieces. They looked at each other's work. They were involved in the same race."[6] Drawing was essential for both artists, and no clear line can be made between their drawing and their painting. Bernice Rose, former curator of drawing at The Museum of Modern Art, has written of Pollock: "His mature style was formed out of an obsessive preoccupation with line—with drawing on any level—that led to a radical synthesis of drawing and painting."[7] And as Hess has written of

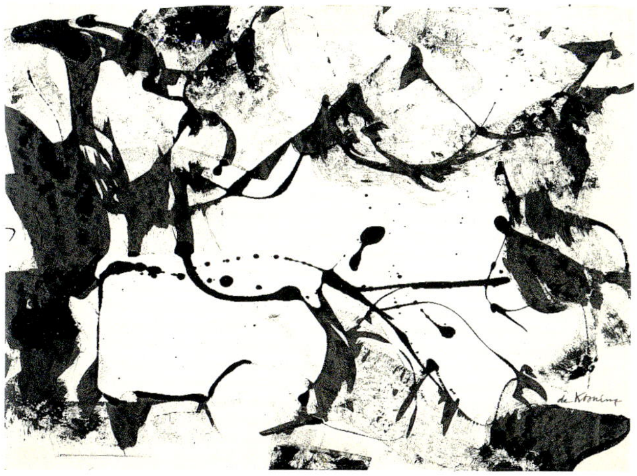

Fig. 1 **WILLEM DE KOONING**
Landscape, Abstract, c. 1949
Oil on paper mounted on board, 19 x 25½" (48.3 x 64.8 cm)
Whitney Museum of American Art, New York.
Gift of Mr. and Mrs. Alan H. Temple

GESTURE Drawing is a primary gesture. The artist's hand moves across the surface of the paper, leaving traces of thoughts and unveiling fragments of the subconscious in the form of marks. The creative process, in both its physical and conceptual aspects, is thus made visible. Such is the immediacy of drawing.

In the second half of the twentieth century, a new mode of drawing was explored. Jackson Pollock transformed the medium from within by means of a deliberately induced "accident": gesture itself. By the late 1940s, Pollock was pouring and dripping ink onto paper, working from above in large, flowing motions in a tension between control and chance effects (plate 5). Gesture became the center of a new form of abstraction. Transforming the automatic movement of the Surrealist's hand into something radically new, Pollock blurred the boundaries between painting and drawing. With this fluid, expansive gesture, process is literally made visible, as if unmasked. For the first time in the history of drawing, process *is* the image.

Parallel to Pollock, in the late 1940s Lucio Fontana began exploring drawing as gesture by piercing the surface of the paper. By the late 1950s he was also creating works in which he slashed the sheet. Challenging the notion of flat ground traditionally associated with drawing, he incorporated the space behind the surface, suggesting a dimension beyond, a new, infinite space. Constellations of punctures and swirling lines animate these works, which the artist called Spatial Concepts, as he employed drawing as a means to attain a newly conceived "spatial art." While Pollock's gesture results in spatial expansiveness and overall flatness, Fontana's act of destructive rupture, which is nevertheless highly controlled, explores a space between physicality and immateriality. The play of light and shadow accentuates the tension between the surface and the world behind it (as seen more dramatically in photographs of the drawings in various lighting arrangements, taken under the artist's guidance). Drawing is to Fontana a space of matter, light, and movement at once. Interestingly, he also explored new possibilities to animate his drawn Spatial Concepts by merging drawing with the new media of his time, such as television, in a vision of utopian quality.

In the late 1950s and early 1960s a new generation of European and American artists, chief among them Piero Manzoni, came to terms with the legacy of the Abstract Expressionist gesture. Playing with the idea of drawing as touch, Manzoni subverted the very myth of the authorial role. He did so with immense irony and levity in *Thumbprint* (1960; plate 97), where the physical and the conceptual meet: as the artist imprints the paper with his inked finger he seems to reduce gesture to its most essential, minimal quality, questioning the ideas of self-expression and originality in art and the very tradition of drawing as the primary medium of the authorial gesture.

—F. P.

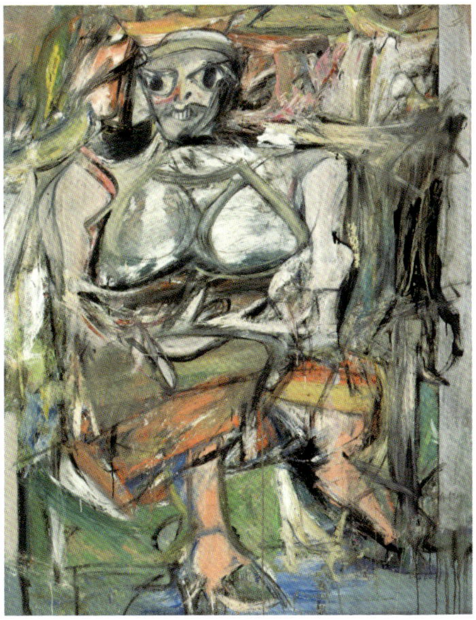

Fig. 2 **WILLEM DE KOONING**
Woman, I, 1950–52
Oil on canvas, 6' 3⅞" x 58" (192.7 x 147.3 cm)
The Museum of Modern Art, New York.
Purchase, 1953

de Kooning: "Drawings are so intimately meshed into his creative procedures that to discuss them apart from his paintings is misleading....This eluding of categories and definitions is a major aspect of the content of de Kooning's art—his refusal to be pinned down, his insistence on keeping his art and his mind open."[8] In the work of both of these artists, line is dominant and its meanings are multiple: it functions as the trace of **gesture**, as contour suggesting form and subject, and as an independent graphic, visual element. The balance between spontaneity and control, delicacy and ferocity, playfulness and will and between figure and ground, positive and negative space, open and closed form is taut. There can be no resolution between such antipodal qualities, giving these works resilience and imaginative power.

Between 1947 and 1950, Pollock made what are among the most resolutely abstract works in the history of art (plates 4 and 5). De Kooning in this same period made his first extended series of what are predominantly abstract works (fig. 1). Much has been written and theorized about the significance of their work of this period for the development of advanced art, and Pollock, de Kooning, and other artists of the Abstract Expressionist group are credited with giving art a new freedom from descriptive function, an exhilarating liberation from tradition. Part of the achievement of their work was the emphasis on pure optical sensation as well as what artist and critic Donald Judd, in writing of Pollock, observed as the "tension between emotion and sensation."[9] For both artists, however, the tension between abstraction and figuration was fundamental and drove their work forward. Pollock enmeshed figurative references within his work from 1951 and de Kooning episodically ricocheted between abstraction and recollections of the figure and landscape throughout his career (figs. 2 and 3).[10]

What is clear about the work of both Pollock and de Kooning is its intense physicality. The distinction between the work of art as an observed, reflected object and as an extension of the artist's very being has collapsed. Art historian Richard Schiff, in writing of de Kooning, has noted, "De Kooning sought to disconnect perception (what the hand could feel) from preconception (what the eye would

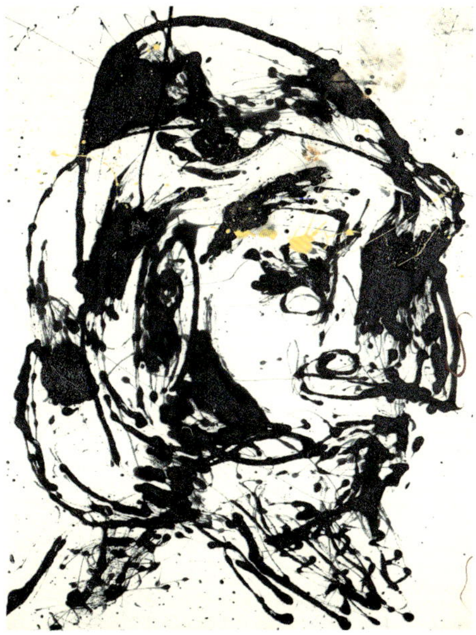

Fig. 3 **JACKSON POLLOCK**
Number 7, 1952
Enamel and oil on canvas, 53⅛ x 40" (134.9 x 101.6 cm)
The Metropolitan Museum of Art, New York.
Purchase, Emilio Azcarraga Gift, in honor of
William S. Lieberman, 1987

BODY In his much-anthologized 1952 essay "The American Action Painters," critic Harold Rosenberg detailed an increased attention to the artist's body in the making of works that would come to characterize much art of the postwar period. Referring to figures such as Willem de Kooning and Jackson Pollock, Rosenberg described how "at a certain moment the canvas began to appear to one American painter after another as an arena in which to act—rather than as a space in which to reproduce, re-design, analyze or 'express' an object, actual or imagined. What was to go on the canvas was not a picture but an event." The "event" that Rosenberg saw in the oversize works of these artists was an encounter of the artist's body with the canvas or sheet of paper; indeed, more than merely rendering space, Pollock's drips and de Kooning's muscular strokes recorded the arc of a swinging arm.

The artists of the next generation extended this engagement with the body as a subject of their work to become more self-conscious, as they moved from a body inferred though gesture to one literally foregrounded in the work. For example, Jasper Johns's monumental drawing *Diver* (1962–63; plate 43) not only has the artist's handprints and footprints as its only recognizable imagery, its dimensions are defined by the life-size arm span of the diving figure. Many of Richard Serra's early drawings are as tall as he could reach—implicating the body of the viewer in relation to them as much as representing an index of the artist's own physicality. In a similar strategy, a sculptural work by Serra was the result of throwing molten lead into the seam where the wall and floor meet. Bruce Nauman, too, deployed this kind of bodily literalism in both drawing and sculpture, often using the mold of his body to give form to works such as *Storage Capsule for the Right Rear Quarter of My Body*, 1966, the drawing for which is illustrated here (plate 112).

By the end of the 1960s, artists' uses of the body reached one of their logical conclusions, when, in the oeuvres of figures like Carolee Schneeman, Vito Acconci, and Chris Burden, the body became both palette and canvas (Burden literally took a shot in the arm in the cause of his work). For these artists, the arena opened by the so-called action painters two generations prior had redefined the parameters for art-making, and they plunged headlong—body and all—into the new, expanded field. —J. K.

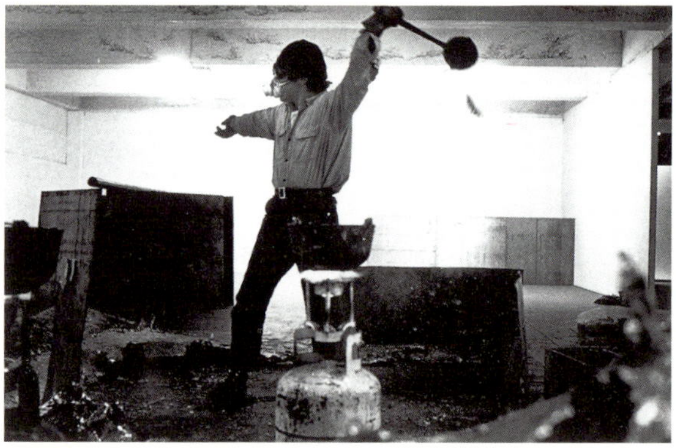

Richard Serra throwing lead, Castelli Warehouse, New York, 1969

automatically measure against as an existing standard, counteracting the effect of chance and the skill that produced it)."[11] The work of art becomes a palpable surrogate for the body of the artist as well as the mind. Bernice Rose, writing of Pollock, concluded: "Automatic drawing released the images in his imagination to his hand, and enabled his hand to free him from dependence on those images."[12] Pollock said about his own work, "Painting is a state of being.... Painting is self-discovery. Every good painter paints what he is."[13]

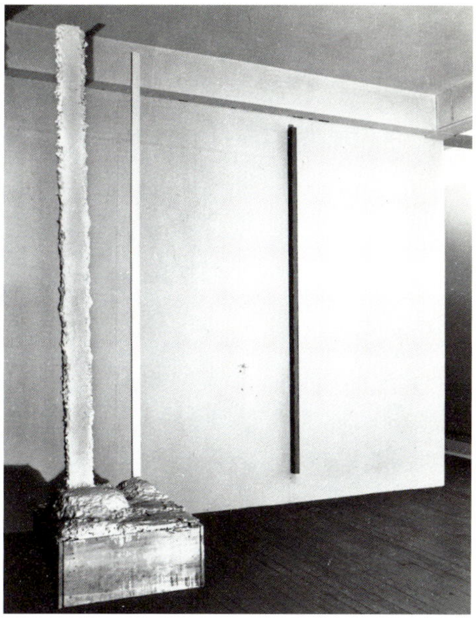

Fig. 4 Barnett Newman's ***Here I*** (left), 1950, and ***The Wild***, 1950, as installed at the Betty Parsons Gallery, New York, during Newman's second one-artist exhibition, April–May 1951. Photograph by Hans Namuth

Barnett Newman's work, although of a very different character, spans many parallels with Pollock and de Kooning. For Newman, too, drawing was crucial: "Yet I know that if I have made a contribution, it is primarily in my drawing.... Instead of using outlines, instead of making shapes or setting off space, my drawing declares the space. Instead of working with the remnants of space, I work with the whole space."[14] He considered his painting an extension or amplification of what he was able to work out and achieve through drawing. Like Pollock and de Kooning, Newman declared freedom from description and his work stands as an autonomous, sensual, and intellectual experience, albeit one that is more metaphysical. This does not mean, however, that for Newman the body is absent in the work itself or in the way that an observer should be absorbed by the work. Newman developed what he called the "zip," a generally vertical band that forcefully articulates and breaks through the picture plane of a drawing or painting (fig. 4; plate 9). As curator Brenda Richardson has observed, the zip is "a carrier of authority, dignity, presence, and vivacity commonly believed to be inherent only in animate beings."[15] Expanding on this idea, she writes, "It is the drawings that reveal the interplay of imagination, analysis, and resolution. They make tangible the conduct of intellect, the thousand decisions that comprise the essential activity of art-making. And in the drawings, too, there is a quality which is not readily evident in the majesty of the paintings—the eloquence of vulnerability."[16]

Philip Guston shared concerns with his fellow artists about the release of line from shape, the contrast between surface and space, and the tension between movement and form. The resulting work, however, is more suggestive of a state of consciousness than of a physical activity. In his ink drawings, as observed by writer Dore Ashton, Guston created spaces that "corresponded to the vast dislocations that occur in dreamlike mental conditions."[17] Floating, disembodied, finely calibrated marks, less of the body than in the mind, distinguish Guston's work of this time (plate 11).

DESKILLING

While processes of "deskilling" have a long history in modernist art, the term has been in use in an art context for only a relatively short period of time. In one of the first published instances, in 1981, artist and critic Ian Burn used the term to refer to a very specific kind of practice in which an artist delegated control of the technical making of the object to "skilled" workers, such as in the industrial fabrication of Minimalist sculpture. Recently, the term's usage has grown to include a broader range of artistic activity, including the more widespread strategies of artists willfully renouncing learned, or traditional, habits of making in works that they produce themselves. Like drawing with the left hand if right-handed, deskilling is meant to inhibit both repetition and easy elegance, and reliance on practiced abilities. A method of intentionally setting roadblocks in the studio, deskilling is one of a number of classic modernist operations intended to circumvent the often overly determined ways in which art is made and received, as well as to critique the romantic idea of the all-knowing, all-controlling genius artist.

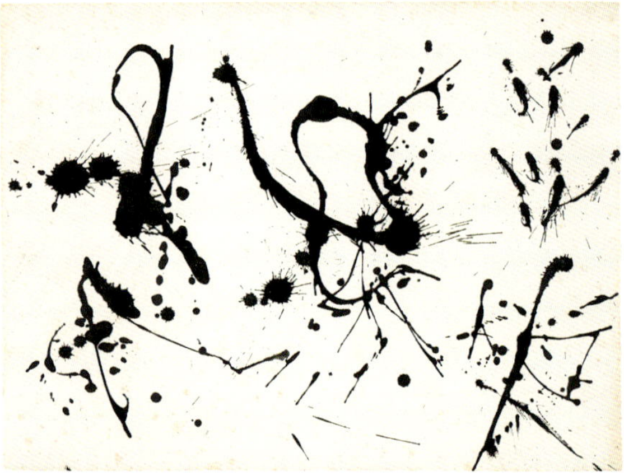

JACKSON POLLOCK
Untitled, c. 1950
Ink on paper, 18 7/8 x 24 7/8" (47.9 x 63.1 cm)
The Museum of Modern Art, New York.
The Joan and Lester Avnet Fund, 1983

One exemplary figure in this practice was the Abstract Expressionist Jackson Pollock, whose unorthodox method of painting and drawing struck at traditional ideas of what art was thought to be and how it was supposed to operate. The idea of dripping paint, and inviting such elements as gravity and chance into the process of making a work of art, seemed to undermine all conventional ideas of artistic skill—which historically had, in part, lent art its legitimacy. That is, traditional definitions of art in Western culture rested on the notion that an artist—a controlling subject and designated seer—bracketed the world into intelligible pieces, executing skilled works to be consumed by the viewer. Deskilled works, as art historian Benjamin Buchloh has recently argued, perversely disrupt these fundamental models of artistic production and reception and throw into question what a work of art is as well as the whole apparatus around which it enjoys a privileged status in society. By providing a way to circumvent some of the commonly accepted "rules" of art, deskilling has long proven a fertile means for artists to redefine what art can be. —J. K.

Even as the Abstract Expressionists broke with earlier modern precedents, particularly as one looks at Cubism and Surrealism, drawing nevertheless enables linkages to be perceived and shared issues to be clarified. Art historian Jack Flam has written with extraordinary perceptiveness about the position of drawing growing out of modernism: "One of the greatest innovations in twentieth-century drawings involves the degree to which they make visible things that cannot be seen—states of mind, ideas, and processes. As their focus shifted from the depiction of things to mental and emotional states, their technical emphasis also moved away from skills related to creating the illusion of three-dimensional space. As a result, the aesthetic criteria applied to drawing also changed. Notions such as authenticity, or psychological truth, or conviction replaced criteria based upon mimetic representation of the real world or the imitation of nature."[18] While control and nuance remain fundamental, they are achieved through nontraditional means and for nontraditional ends. The Cubists introduced collage, the Surrealists cultivated chance operations, such as frottage, and the Abstract Expressionists liberated line's potential through **deskilling**.

Yet the distinctions between the art of the first half of the century and what followed after World War II are no less fundamental than the shared continuities. The art that was being created in New York during this period undoubtedly reflected the particular situation of the United States in the postwar period. Richard Schiff has noted that at this time, "American art and social critics alike linked material presence to the value of direct experience, the means to liberated expressiveness in an era felt to be one of social conformity and subtle political repression."[19] In Europe, a different approach prevailed. Thought and language were salient, as alternatives to the descriptive and formal antecedents of earlier art and to the American emphasis on experience.

The work of the German artist Joseph Beuys is a touchstone for the distinction between American and European work after World War II. Although Beuys is usually identified as a sculptor, as with the American artists previously discussed drawings were fundamental to his work. Curator Ann Temkin has written that he "referred to them as the source of all his ideas, and as catalysts to his work in all mediums."[20] Bernice Rose has elaborated, "Drawing for Beuys is a process of opening thought beyond the habitual patterns imposed by speech; it gives form to what is impossible to say—for Beuys believes that to think is to create form."[21] From the mid-1940s to the early 1960s Beuys made thousands of drawings with a wide array of materials,

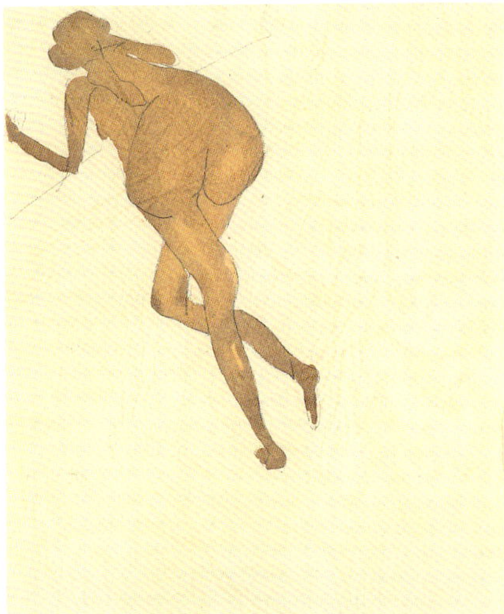

Fig. 5 **JOSEPH BEUYS**
Untitled (Hare Woman), 1952
Beize and pencil on transparent paper, overall 26¾ x 19⅝" (68 x 49.8 cm)
The Speck Collection, Cologne

CALLIGRAPHY

Critics and art historians often make an analogy between drawing and writing and employ the terms "calligraphy" or "calligraphic" to describe a type of line made typically with ink, using a pen or pointy brush, and resembling (at least for a Western viewer) Chinese, Japanese, or other Asian-language characters. A number of artists from Europe and the Americas, including León Ferrari, Brice Marden, and Henri Michaux, made the link themselves, pointing to calligraphy as an inspiration or touchstone for their work.

Alluding to the form of writing but without resolving into actual letters, the calligraphic line of Western art is rarely a means of direct communication or a text that can be literally read. That is not to say that this type of drawing lacks meaning. Rather, the significance of these marks is displaced from the legibility of the "letters" to their making, from imprint to gesture, from brush to body. In such works, Roland Barthes tells us, "writing…appears…as the very surplus of its own function; the painter helps us understand that writing's truth is neither in its messages nor in the system of transmission…but in the hand which presses down and traces a line, i.e., in *the body which throbs*…."

At various points in the twentieth century, gesture has been put in the service of expression, resulting in the existential distortions and unease of German painting, the spiritual possibilities of Kandinsky's abstractions, and the raw emotional power of the Abstract Expressionists' large canvases. In releasing gesture from expression, the calligraphic line sets the artist down a different path, offering a mode of rendering based on writing, forms rooted in the shapes of characters, and a process that reflects the actions of hand and body. While writing provides a kind of methodological frame, it is far from limiting. Readable text—a slave to legibility, linked to speech, always communicating—struggles to depict the irrational and extraordinary while the calligraphic line, working within the realm of metaphor and echoing the body, realizes the ineffable: essence, desire, faith, and, in Barthes's words, "the utopia of the Text." —J. H.

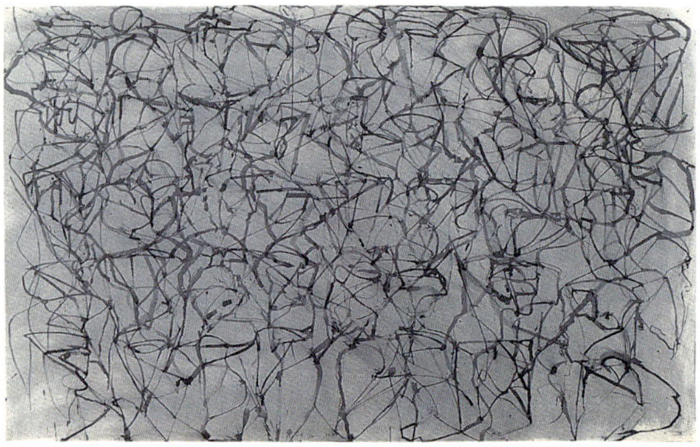

BRICE MARDEN
Muses Drawing 5 (Mnemosyne), 1989–91
Ink and ink wash on paper, 26 x 40 5/8" (66 x 103.2 cm)
The Museum of Modern Art, New York. Fractional and promised gift of Sarah-Ann and Werner H. Kramarsky, 2004

including pencil, ink, charcoal, watercolor, dirt, metallic particles, lampblack, and a variety of collaged elements, as well as two mediums distinct to his work—an iron compound called *beize* and an oil called *braunkreuz* (fig. 5). In this period, the drawings are private, intimate, exploratory—a working out of ideas and forms solely for personal understanding. The drawings may be viewed as alchemical, registering energy transformation, and as allegorical, conveying moral principles. While his untitled work from 1947 and the 1970s might be viewed as delineating "small forms of marine life along a stream—some sort of subvisual life as seen through a microscope," the overall metaphorical character of the drawing suggests the tracking of a journey, transformation from inchoate form into luminous recognition, what Rose has described as the evolution of "an ethical concept, honoring each thing in its individuality, while also acknowledging its connectedness in the over-all scheme" (plate 21).[22]

Many artists in the 1940s and 1950s developed the concept of drawing as a kind of **calligraphy** or abstract writing as a direct manifestation of the mind. Delicate and inward-focusing, these works are more meditative and ethereal than physical, but the intention and the effect can be sharply contrasting. While the American Mark Tobey has been linked to Abstract Expressionism, he lived in Seattle rather than New York, sometimes traveling and staying in Europe. He preferred to work in small scale and on paper, with skeins of lightly overlapping lines creating hovering, indeterminate, vaporous forms (plate 25). Tobey hoped to express continuity and seamlessness between the mind of man and the universe, an aspiration in line with American Transcendentalists such as Emerson and Thoreau. The French artist Henri Michaux also made fields of intimate markings but without metaphorical or metaphysical intent (plate 24). Rather, they are intended to be the most immediate and direct transcription of both the mind and the hand, a direct descendent of the self-conscious, materialist mind first posited by seventeenth-century philosopher René Descartes. Beginning in the 1940s Michaux made drawings while under the influence of mind-altering drugs, particularly mescaline, in which the intensity of the mind's activity is directly translated into agitated, viscous whorls. In an interview, Michaux said of these drawings, "The spectacle of my own mind at work somehow made me more conscious of my mind."[23]

Writing of the American artist Cy Twombly, French philosopher Roland Barthes characterized Twombly's work as "reversing the usual relationship in classical technique, one might say that strokes, hatching, forms, in short the graphic events, are what allow the sheet of paper or the canvas to exist."[24] Thus, as in Abstract Expressionism, Twombly's work highlights its physicality and, as with Pollock and de Kooning, the division between drawing

GRAFFITI Modern artists have engaged the notion of graffiti to explore a wide range of expressive possibilities. From Joan Miró to Jean Dubuffet, from Cy Twombly to Jean-Michel Basquiat, graffiti (from the Greek *graphein*, to write) has been broadly appropriated as a source of inspiration and a means for artistic reinvention. Historically, graffiti denotes the intrusion of private marks into public sites. To inscribe a text or a drawing on public walls is to subvert the terms of a dominant culture, as a playful scrawling or a destructive attack on the surface, as a gesture of political and social commentary or as a confession of unconscious desires.

Graffiti celebrates the idea of an endlessly generating, open-ended process, overwriting as it erases, simultaneously deconstructing and building new meanings. Graffiti can ultimately be seen as a metaphor for the modern desire to start from scratch, to invent a new artistic vocabulary, a means for the artist to "unlearn" how to draw and paint. Subverting given ideas of beauty, the language of graffiti is based on line as scrawl rather than as contour: it is incised in, immersed in the ground to evoke a formless image. In a return to the "ground" treated as unbounded field, speedy graffiti-like marks let the image emerge from within. This mindless scrawling responds to the need to reach back to a primordial stage before rationalization, where all that counts is the tactility of touch and the body, the impasto.

It is precisely in this sense that the apparent graffiti-like quality of Cy Twombly's work can be described. Appropriating a line from poet and critic John Crowe Ranson, Twombly has written in pencil in his drawing *Untitled (Studio Note)* (c. 1990): "The Image cannot / be dis possessed of a / primordial / freshness / which IDEAS / CAN NEVER CLAIM." Moving from an automatism of gesture to one of texture, Twombly achieves a provocative synthesis of drawing and painting. His work from the mid-1950s onward is animated by an impulsive attack on the surface: in a kinship with graffiti, he draws with a pencil or a stylus *into* rich creamy fields of off-white house paint. In an unresolved tension between diaristic intimacy and movement outside the self, his mark is tactile and sensuous. In works like *The Italians* (1961), schematic geometric forms, numbers, and organic pictograms invade the surface treated as a profusely marked wall, evoking Twombly's Italy with lyricism. The artist's marks, both playful and violently transgressive, turn the absolute flatness of the wall into a sensual floating landscape of the mind in a tension between disclosure and hermetic self-absorption. —F. P.

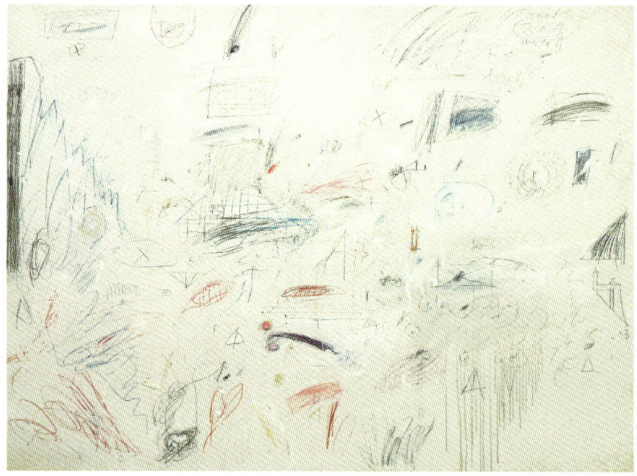

CY TWOMBLY
The Italians, 1961
Oil, pencil, and crayon on canvas, 6' 6 5/8" x 8' 6 1/4" (199.5 x 259.6 cm)
The Museum of Modern Art, New York. Blanchette Hooker Rockefeller Fund, 1969

and painting is blurred. Calligraphy and graffiti are given life within the sensuality and expansiveness established by Abstract Expressionism (plates 18 and 19). Beginning in 1951 Twombly traveled to and lived in Europe, settling in Italy in 1957, where he has since maintained his primary residence, and the European preoccupation with memory and history are embedded in Twombly's work. Traces of lived experience and the chronicled experiences of the past are fused. The impossibility of adequately articulating or describing these experiences—inevitable elisions, suppressed and erased facts, forgotten and overlooked incidents—is given voice. The body, the hand, and the mind each have equal, palpable presence.

PERSISTENCE OF IMAGES

Despite the momentum of abstraction from the mid-1940s forward, images continued to preoccupy many artists. Portraiture, the human form, the places and situations of personal encounter simply would not cease to engage the imagination, and that was particularly true in Europe after the war. The traditions of figurative art had been exploded, opened up, and renewed by modernism, and we can see the diversity of the results, for example, in works by Pablo Picasso (fig. 6), Lucian Freud, Alberto Giacometti, and Henri Matisse (plates 28, 29, and 31), among scores of others.[25] While these drawings reveal close examination of the physical world, the inner consciousness of each artist is nevertheless forcefully expressed. The observation of art historian David Rosand holds true here: "Through the drawing we can only know the draftsman, through whose vision we may believe we see the world."[26]

By the late 1940s and early 1950s a new generation of artists was emerging for whom Abstract Expressionism as well as modernism as it had developed before World War II were springboards to leap from as well as obstacles to be surmounted. In New York the leaders of these new developments were Robert Rauschenberg and Jasper Johns. For both artists the trace and gesture of the hand, the abstract mark, were joined to instantly recognizable images lifted out of the ebb and flow of daily life.

Rauschenberg initiated the shift, inspired by the intellectual and creative environment of Black Mountain College, where he enrolled in 1948.[27] Wide-open experimentation was encouraged, and from the beginning Rauschenberg explored the boundaries between painting, sculpture, drawing, printmaking, and photography.[28] By the

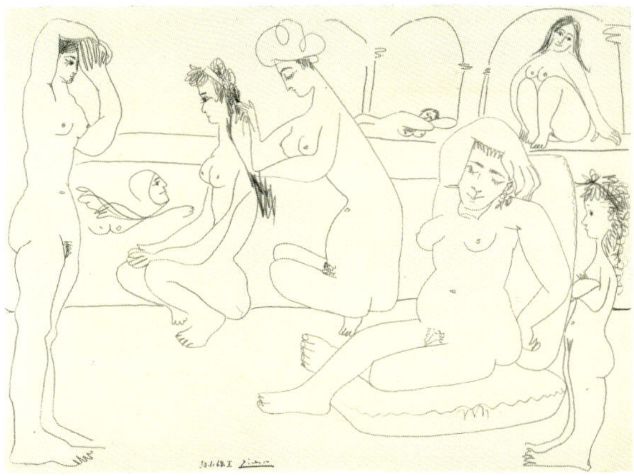

Fig. 6 **PABLO PICASSO**
The Pool, 1968
Pencil on paper, 23 x 30 5/8" (58.2 x 77.8 cm)
The Museum of Modern Art, New York.
The Joan and Lester Avnet Collection, 1978

TRANSFER While many artists have used the technique of "transfer"—the process of borrowing a found image and repositioning it, in reverse, on a new ground—the term is closely associated with the work of Robert Rauschenberg. During a trip to Cuba in 1952 Rauschenberg began experimenting with transferring printed images from magazines and newspapers to blank pieces of paper. The artist would apply a chemical solvent to an illustration, place it facedown on a blank sheet and rub the back with an empty ballpoint pen. With striations and burnishings left by the rubbing fully in evidence, these mirror images are both recognizable (in their quotidian ordinariness) and allusive (in their atmospheric haze).

Based as they are on collection and juxtaposition and made through the act of rubbing, these works are rooted in the collage practices of the early part of the twentieth century—think of Kurt Schwitters's detritus and Pablo Picasso's and George Braque's *papiers collés*—as well as Surrealist techniques to access the unconscious mind, from the "marvelous" encounters of unrelated objects seen in Joseph Cornell's box constructions to the ordinary environment made strange in Max Ernst's frottages. Rauschenberg's most important—and most extended—foray into the transfer process are his illustrations for Dante's *Inferno* (plates 38 and 39). Over the course of thirty-four works, each relating to a canto of Dante's text, we see a variety of players—politicians, athletes, astronauts—and locales—an Olympic podium, a racetrack.

To get at the function of transfer we might turn to historian Leo Steinberg's famous description of Rauschenberg's reorientation of the work of art to the horizontal "flatbed picture plane" on which "anything reachable-thinkable would adhere." Steinberg explains that the artist's great invention was "a pictorial surface that let the world in again." This surface opens up art's possibilities. In transferring—moving or conveying—bits and pieces of the world into the realm of art and allowing them to bump up against one another, Rauschenberg did not transform them into something else—a piece of newspaper, for example, does not become a wine glass. Whether in a drawing or a combine painting, these objects remain just what they are: a hymnal book, a clock, a goat, pictures of John F. Kennedy.

The achievement of the transfer is thus to put objects and images into tension. As with two mirrors that endlessly reflect one another, the transfer's collision of art and life generates an infinite series of related oppositions engaged in perpetual dialogue: culture and nature, public and private, instantaneity and memory, contemplation and distraction, found and made.

—J. H.

early 1950s he had developed a new technique to **transfer** printed photographic images, using a solvent to moisten the paper and then rubbing the image with a hard tip against another sheet of paper. The process leaves both the markings of the hand and the photographic fragment—simultaneously floating and embedded on the sheet—creating a seamless collage (plate 37). More markings would then be directly added with a variety of materials. For Rauschenberg, the images might be historical or contemporary in source, from art or media. In the extended series of thirty-four sheets titled *Dante's Inferno*, Rauschenberg followed the structure and narrative of Dante's epic poem but using the surfeit of imagery that inundates the contemporary world (plates 38 and 39).[29] The sum effect is an expansive and playful immersion within a continuum of time but from a contemporary vantage point.

Jasper Johns in his early work, in contrast, would select a single, recognizable image, isolated and iconic, and render it with a dazzling array of markings, layered and built up, again freezing the image outside the contingencies of time. The prime example, and one of his first drawings, is *Flag* (1955; plate 40), a highly finished work made after his painting of the same subject (fig. 7). Johns's early work exploits an insistent ambiguity between the work of art as an object itself and as a representation of an object, the flatness of the support surface and the illusion of that representation. For Johns, his choice of an identifiable and potentially charged subject, like de Kooning's choice of the woman, is a structure for considering the myriad marks of the hand and abstraction—"each interpretation contradicting while enriching the other," as Hess has noted of de Kooning.[30] Johns, like de Kooning, is a prime example of an artist whose work continued to change and elude stylistic or critical summary. In his enormous drawing *Diver* (1962–63; plate 43), made in the early 1960s, Johns used his own handprints to depict an abstract figure in a swan dive that also recalls a crucifixion with the image of a skull at its base. This hauntingly emotional, elegiac drawing also extends a central issue of Johns's work, as articulated by curator Nan Rosenthal: "The imprint of his hand registered in charcoal or ink proposes the general 'subject' of an artist's hand as representative of his personal style. Yet at the same time, this manner of making a mark might be understood as negating the idea of artistic expressiveness, since we know that Johns did not invent the form of his handprint but borrowed it from his body."[31]

Parallel to Rauschenberg and Johns, Ellsworth Kelly was working in Paris, developing works in which

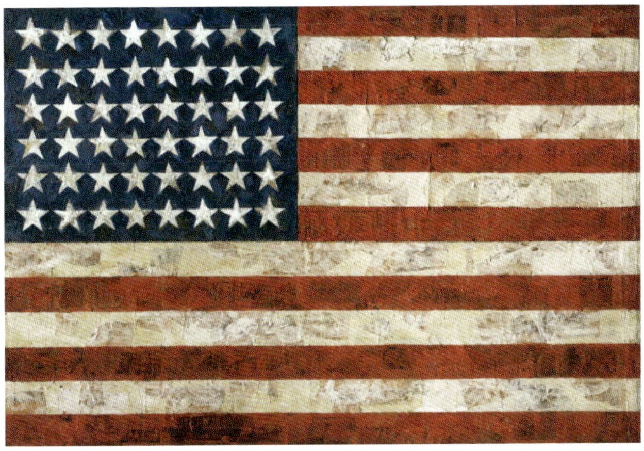

Fig. 7 **JASPER JOHNS**
Flag, 1954–55
Encaustic, oil, and collage on fabric mounted on plywood, three panels, 42 1/4 x 60 5/8" (107.3 x 153.8 cm)
The Museum of Modern Art, New York.
Gift of Philip Johnson in honor of Alfred H. Barr, Jr., 1973

POP The term "Pop art" was introduced by critic Lawrence Alloway in addressing the aesthetic challenge posed in the late 1950s to postwar Europe by American industrial culture—a condition taken up by British artists, architects, and writers known as the Independent Group. In 1957 Richard Hamilton referred to Pop as "popular (designed for a mass audience)," "transient (short-term solution)," "expendable (easily forgotten)," "young (aimed at youth)," "witty," and "sexy." If Pop art in Europe conjured an American consumer culture as seen through the lens of the postwar experience, in the United States in the early 1960s the phenomenon acquired a vernacular character of its own.

While a wide range of encounters with popular culture animates the history of modernism, it is Pop that for the first time engages it simultaneously as a source for a new subject matter and for a new artistic strategy. Paraphrasing Andy Warhol, Pop is as simple and subversive as unconditional "liking." This radical approach, borrowed from the very logic of consumer culture, allows Pop artists to insinuate "low" signifiers into "high" discourse. Inspired by the Duchampian readymade, they turned to comic books, graphics, fashion, movies, advertising, and commercial design for inspiration, treating such sources as found objects. Often drawing on a background in graphic design, Pop artists would take a found image, blow it up, edit it out, and reorganize the composition to sharpen the essential and to avoid anecdote. These works attain clarity through a pure linearity of interlocking shapes, refined sense of composition, and high stylization. If Jackson Pollock was interested in "unmaking" the image, Pop artists became pure "designers" of the image—as figure and as object—often exploiting the tension between the hand-drawn line and the mechanical quality of the printed source. The result is a poetics of the utterly banal, of displaced ordinariness, as seen in Lichtenstein's painting *Drowning Girl* (1963) and Warhol's drawing *Roll of Bills* (1962; plate 48)—works inhabited by images frozen in time and space and turned into iconic presences.

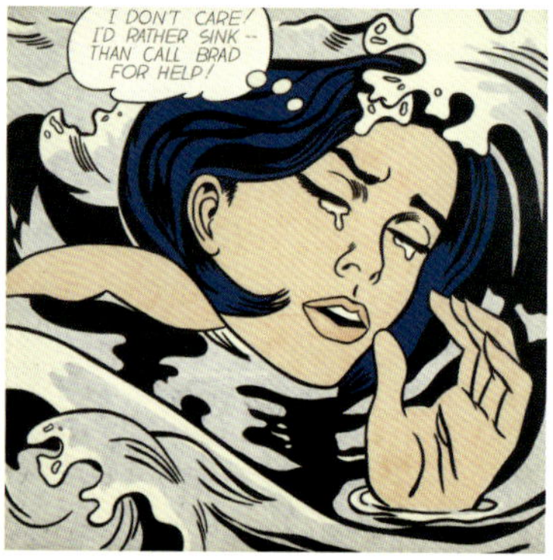

ROY LICHTENSTEIN
Drowning Girl, 1963
Oil and synthetic polymer paint on canvas, $67\frac{5}{8}$ x $66\frac{3}{4}$" (171.6 x 169.5 cm)
The Museum of Modern Art, New York. Philip Johnson Fund (by exchange) and gift of Mr. and Mrs. Bagley Wright, 1971

Rediscovering René Magritte, Pop enacts a form of modern estrangement. Lichtenstein, for instance, introduces a voluntary distance between the 1962 comic strip he adopts as his source for *Drowning Girl* (a panel from "Run for Love!" in *Secret Hearts*) and its final rendition: he turns the found object into an image of his own by selecting certain details over others, focusing on the figure of the woman, enlarging her image, and rendering it in a simplified vocabulary. Belying a penchant for objectivity, the manipulation of the original source nevertheless reveals the distinct presence of the artist's hand. Lichtenstein then pushes this idea further by taking his cue from the art world itself: One step removed from the physicality of the Abstract Expressionists, he freezes the flowing gesture of Action painting in *Brushstrokes* (1966–68; plate 52), a witty play on the author's own mark-making. —F. P.

image and abstract form are merged. The elegant line drawings and paper cut-out collages of both Henri Matisse and Jean Arp serve as touchstones, with contour and form derived either from close observation (as with Matisse) or chance operations (as with Arp). His study for *Window, Museum of Modern Art, Paris* (1949; plate 32) hovers between being a portrait of a specific place and a carefully calibrated, autonomous abstraction, read simultaneously as a whole and the sum of its parts. Collages, by contrast, result from random compositional procedures. In an extended series of plant drawings, begun in the late 1940s, Kelly defines form with a crisp, confident line, often in a very few strokes (plate 35). As Kelly has described these works: "They are exact observations....Nothing is changed or added: no shading, no surface marking. They are not an approximation of the thing seen nor are they a personal expression or an abstraction" (fig. 8).[32] They are renderings of a way of seeing, the finely distilled essence of an observed fact.

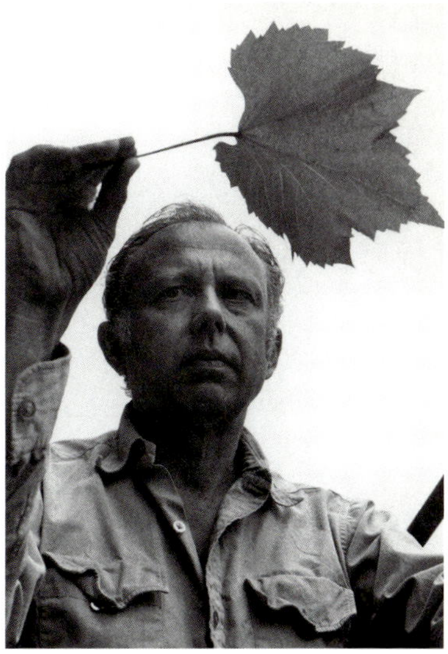

Fig. 8 Ellsworth Kelly, Chatham, New York, 1973

By the late 1950s the tension and balance between image and abstraction began to break down. The movements labeled Pop and Minimal art are at best attempts to bring focus and coherence to this split, and they both stand as figureheads for parallel strands that generally oppose but occasionally cross over one another. Both Pop art and Minimal art share an attempt to distance themselves from the expressive hand of the artist, to be reductive, to pare art back to its essentials. But finally, in both, style and authorship are present, the personality of the artist as evident to the attentive viewer as in any other works of art where self-conscious, careful decision-making takes place.

Roy Lichtenstein and Andy Warhol were the quintessential Pop artists in New York, taking cues from Rauschenberg and Johns to focus on images culled from everyday, contemporary life to make an art that is indelibly and inseparably of its time (fig. 9). Comics, advertising, and illustration are referenced as primary sources for their art. The development of their mature styles was relatively late (Lichtenstein was older than Rauschenberg and Warhol older than Johns), and both had careers in the 1950s as graphic designers, with Warhol exceptionally regarded in the design community in New York. Despite the cool, so-called mechanical look of much of their work,

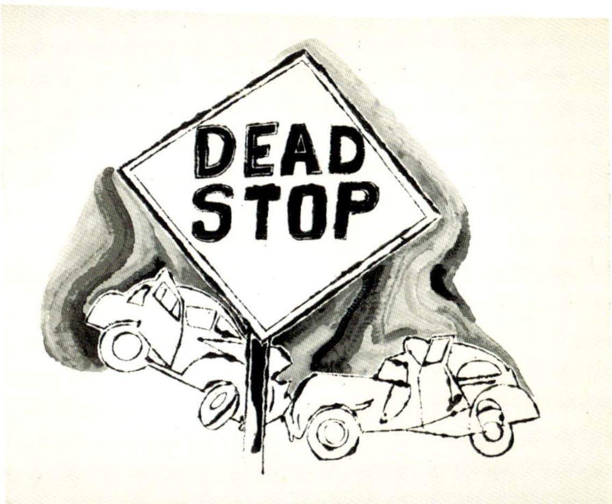

Fig. 9 **ANDY WARHOL**
DEAD STOP, 1954
Ink on paper, 19 x 23" (48.3 X 58.4 cm)
The Andy Warhol Museum, Pittsburgh. Founding Collection, Contribution The Andy Warhol Foundation for the Visual Arts, Inc.

SIGNS

The faculty of language allows us to represent the world around us. In order for it to do so, signs, which refer to objects, actions, or circumstances, are necessary. A sign is, therefore, a minimum unit of signification that stands for something else under specific conventions of collective understanding. In one of the most ancient reflections on language, the dialogue titled *Cratilus*, Plato observes that there is no natural link between the sign and the thing signified by it, other than the arbitrary accord that makes possible the signification process. This explains why the same thing can be signified by different words in countless languages.

Not all signs, however, are verbal. A classic analysis, elucidated by the semiologist Charles Peirce, distinguishes three main types of signs: symbols, which include words and mathematical characters; icons, which represent objects through visual resemblance to them; and indexes, which reflect a physical link with the thing they represent, as in the case of an animal's tracks, a reflection in a mirror, or the smoke that indicates a fire. As Peirce points out, each one of these typologies can contain elements of the other two. A written word is a symbol that can also function as an index of the hand that wrote it. An icon resembles its object but may also have a symbolic dimension, as does the cross for Christians. An index can have an iconic association with an object, as seen in an impression of a hand. Any symbol can also function as an image, when included in a work of art, just as any index can function as a symbol. A brushstroke, for example, could be a symbol of pictorial art.

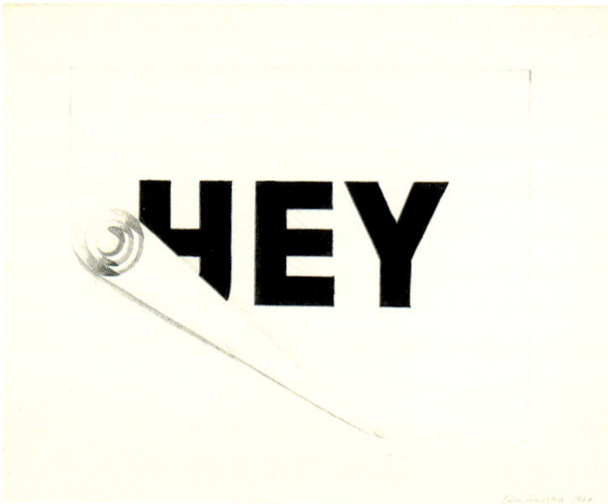

EDWARD RUSCHA
Hey with Curled Edge, 1964
Ink and powdered graphite on paper, 11 5/8 x 12 1/2"
(29.5 x 31.8 cm)
The Museum of Modern Art, New York. Gift of the artist, 1999

This layering of meaning is what allows signs to play such a versatile a role in the visual arts. Though words are not traditionally associated with modern visual art, many artists have in fact incorporated them into their works. In Edward Ruscha's work titled *Hey with Curled Edge* from 1964, for example, image and sign are intertwined so the word acts as a pure signifier that calls for an action—as in the exclamation "Hey"—while the image represents the materiality of its own support—the curled edge of the virgin paper. The inclusion of signs in modern and contemporary art challenges the very idea of the autonomy of visual forms, reminding us that the process of signification is complex and multifaceted. —L. E. P. O.

drawing—the autograph and authority of the hand, the selection of lines to form an image—was essential to it. Warhol and Lichtenstein both made drawings of objects that can also function as **signs**, often as playful and amusing perceptual games but also as a pointed and economic means to focus attention on essential issues of life: identity, work, love, and mortality.

A group of four drawings on blue mimeograph paper—simplified, iconic images based on commercial design—particularly reveal Warhol's approach (plates 46 and 47). Initially, Warhol had intended that copies be made from them, but upon realizing this could not be done without destroying the originals he abandoned the project. The ambiguity of the figure-ground relationship seen here is especially characteristic. Warhol's interest, like Johns's, is in the way our recognition and understanding of an image change as the image itself is altered through formal changes. Lichtenstein's most famous work is based on cartoons or comic strip images. A small study drawing precedes each painting, in which decisions about elimination of detail, relative scale, and overall composition are resolved (plate 49). It is only in the drawings that the clarity and rigor of his decisions are immediately evident, and that the charged emotional content still simmers.

In Los Angeles, Edward Ruscha and English émigré David Hockney took Pop art and gave it space and physicality, albeit that of props and stage sets. Light—its presence, absorption, or absence—distinguishes form. An exquisite craftsmanship with smooth but tactile surfaces and a finely modulated line sets their drawings apart from their New York counterparts. Ruscha most typically works with language as his ostensible subject, though images based on photographs also episodically appear (plates 53 and 54). Hockney consistently renders people, interiors, and places (plate 58). In the case of both artists, potential vignettes can be projected onto their works and an incipient poignancy may stir beneath the surface, belying the aloofness of New York Pop and suggesting narrative and story.

Even within New York Pop art, very different styles and attitudes were evident. Claes Oldenburg, rather than simplifying and clarifying images, added texture and deleted color (plates 63, 64, and 65). His art is not the clean, sharp, stylized aesthetic of Warhol and Lichtenstein, but rather is tactile and fleshy, dense and mottled; it reflects gritty urbanism, the appetites of the body, and the undertow of unconscious desire. Oldenburg is a masterful draftsman, his line and shading more in the tradition of European old masters than cartoonists or illustrators (plate 66). Yet his wit and playfulness is in the spirit of Pop art, while again evidencing a gravity far below the surface. As writer Adam Gopnik has observed, "The radical idea of satire is uppermost here, in the Swiftian sense that by making familiar things alien, we get outside our conventions and achieve a critical objectivity about our society."[33]

PANDEMONIUM

In late 1961, "Pandemonium," a manifesto in poster form signed by the German artists Georg Baselitz and Eugen Schönebeck, was plastered on the walls of West Berlin. It announced an exhibition of their work, which opened in a rented studio on November 10, 1961, three months after the Berlin Wall went up. The manifesto, comprising scrawled text and drawings spread across the page, demanded an art that would not ignore abjection, disorder, and suffering—"the sacrifice of flesh, bits of food in the drain, evaporation from the bedclothes, bleeding from stumps and aerial roots … gristle, negative shapes, spots of shadow, drops of wax, parades of epileptics, orchestrations of the flatulent, warty, mushy and jelly fishy beings, bodily members … gristly growths in a desert landscape." The paintings and drawings produced by Baselitz and Schönebeck during their short-lived collaboration (1961–62) could not be categorized as mimetic figuration, concrete abstraction, or Informalism. Rather, as with the Argentine group Otra Figuración, they employed a repertoire of expressive means to render figurative works that convey anguish, violence, and despair. Failed heroes, torture victims, bodily members not recognizable as human appear in the heavily worked canvases and drawings.

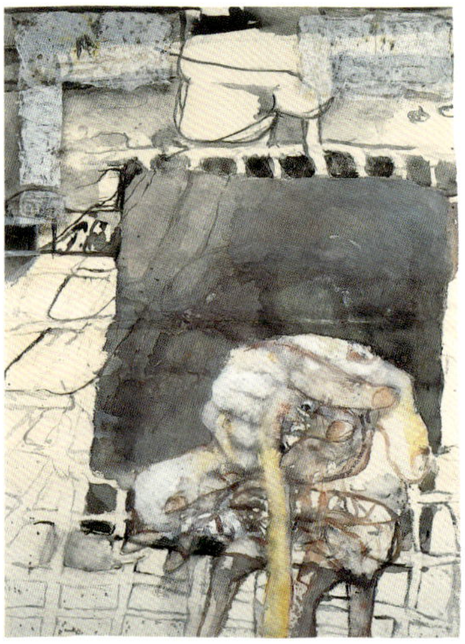

GEORG BASELITZ
Untitled, 1963
Watercolor, gouache, collage on paper, 34 1/4 x 24 1/4" (85.5 x 61.5 cm)
Courtesy Michael Werner Gallery, New York and Cologne

Like their Argentine contemporaries, Baselitz and Schönebeck called upon the ambivalent and transformative potential of chaos to confront horror in both art and life. In the second Pandemonium manifesto of spring 1962 they expressed their disgust at both artistic and political utopias: "On a foray into the crematorium, I found I had set out into my own bloody nose, navel oozing, on a painful migration into my own eyes.… Fastidious contemporaries, democratic visitors—wealth of this city. It stinks… here surviving is now the most painful ordeal of all." Both artists had emigrated to West Berlin from East Germany—Schönebeck in 1955 and Baselitz two years later—and in their work responded to debates among German artists about the relevance of the legacy of German Expressionism for their work. They were also reacting against the climate of political and economic recovery prevailing in West Berlin and the general refusal to confront the country's recent Nazi past and the trauma caused by the division of Germany.

—M. B.

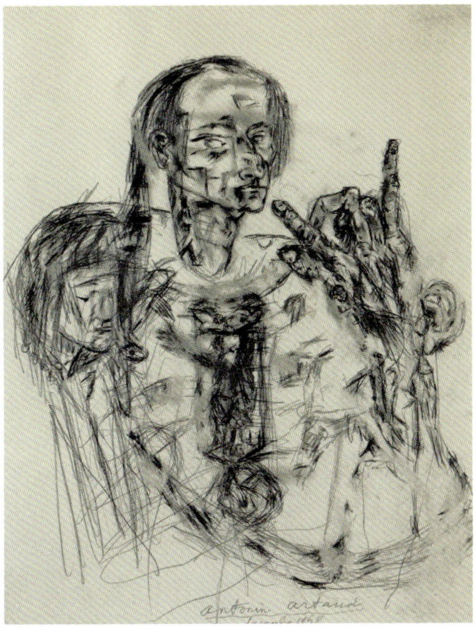

Fig. 10 **ANTONIN ARTAUD**
Self-Portrait, 1947
Graphite on paper, 25 1/2 x 19 5/8" (65 x 50 cm)
Musée national d'art moderne, Centre de création industrielle, Centre Georges Pompidou, Paris. Bequest of Paule Thévenin, 1993

Pop art, like any movement, is an oversimplified label for diverse artists working at the same time and with interwoven but diverse concerns. While certainly commercial art was important, to a number of artists folk art and modern art, tribal and indigenous art, and historical styles relegated to the margins of art history also were absorbed. In short, the 1960s produced an astonishingly vigorous and inventive array of new figurative art in which drawing and collage played a central role.

In Germany, beginning in the 1960s many artists reckoned with the rupture of the Nazi era, attempting to renew a national identity and responding to the emphasis on the materialism of the country's so-called economic miracle—the postwar issues of "meaning and mourning."[34] Sigmar Polke, while influenced by American Pop art, inflected his work with a personal touch, more in keeping with an Expressionist tradition (plate 72). In the magisterial drawing *Spiderman* (1971–74; plate 75), he depicts the American comic book hero but surrounds him with "myriad visual emblems of Western civilization, drawn indifferently from Baroque and Art Deco architecture, 1950s comic-book illustration, or travel brochures."[35] Polke's choice of subject and its setting almost assuredly was not neutral but came from the vantage point of a European artist looking at American culture. As curator Margit Rowell has observed: "Perhaps, for Polke, the character of Spiderman represented far more than just another popular subject. According to the comic-book myth, Spiderman came to understand that 'with great power come great responsibilities.' "[36] In contrast, Georg Baselitz, working in Berlin at a remove from the mainstream of cultural life of Western Europe, developed a new figurative art strongly within the German Expressionist tradition and influenced by modern outsiders, such as Antonin Artaud (fig. 10).[37] Baselitz's Pandemonium manifestos, written in 1961 and 1962, gave voice to his paintings and drawings of decaying and misshapen figures (plates 86 and 87).[38] By the mid-1960s the figures had become more resolute, what he would identify as the "heroes" and "new types" (fig. 11).

In Latin America, a political Pop art emerged in the 1960s. For the Brazilian artist Antonio Dias, his drawings "polluted the innocent fantasy world of comic books with visceral symbols of

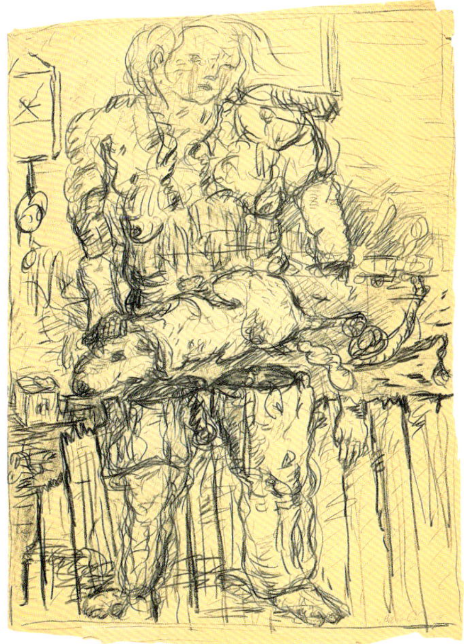

Fig. 11 **GEORG BASELITZ**
Untitled (***Hero***), 1967
Pencil and charcoal on paper, 26 3/16 x 18 3/8" (66.5 x 46.7 cm)
Collection Janie C. Lee

OTRA FIGURACIÓN

In his 1965 text "Anti-Estética" the Argentine artist and theorist Luis Felipe Noé wrote, "What does it mean to assume chaos? It means to become one with the disorder." This assumption of chaos was the goal of four artists—Noé, Ernesto Deira, Rómulo Macció, and Jorge de la Vega—who exhibited jointly as Otra Figuración between 1961 and 1965. The four shared a number of aims: to find a means to evoke the human figure without resorting to mimetic representation, to transcend the abstract-figurative binary, and to employ expressive means while avoiding what they viewed as the decorative tendency that prevailed among Informalist painters.

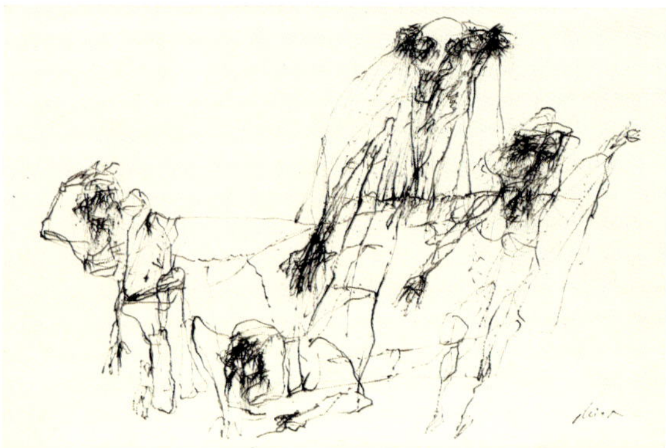

ERNESTO DEIRA
Untitled, 1963
Ink on paper, 12 5/8 x 18 7/8" (32 x 47.9 cm)
The Museum of Modern Art, New York.
Inter-American Fund, 1965

In their joint statement, published on the occasion of their first exhibition at Buenos Aires's Peuser Gallery in 1961, the artists declared: "We are not a movement, not a group, not a school. We are simply painters that in our freedom of expression felt the need to incorporate the freedom of the figure." The figure allowed each artist in his own way to express existential anxieties. In the case of Noé and Deira, these were related to the effects of political repression and violence—since 1955 Argentina had been subject to military coups and regimes—while for de la Vega they were explorations of primal impulses and the world of childhood. Drawing was important for all four artists. In 1962, returning to Buenos Aires after several months in Paris, they held a show titled *Esto* at the Lirolay Gallery, comprising solely works on paper. Their paintings incorporated techniques, including assemblage and collage, that led to the undermining of divisions and hierarchies between media. In their drawings and mixed-media paintings gesture, mark, and expressive line, as well as the incorporation of chance to create drips or stains, were regarded by the artists as a means to take part in what de la Vega called "an organic process" through which "the figures themselves used me as a vehicle for their own emergence." —M. B.

humanity and violence: flesh, genitalia, intestines, bones, guns, bombs, gas masks, flags and skulls, thus transforming the deliberately neutral messages of Pop art with direct references to the crisis of contemporary Brazil" (plates 78 and 79).[39] Jorge de la Vega, from Buenos Aires, established himself in the early 1960s as part of the **Otra Figuración** movement, characterized by expressive, tormented figures (fig. 12).[40] But after spending time in the United States in the mid-1960s, his style dramatically changed, and he began attaching faces taken from television, newspapers, advertisements, and other media "to fluidly deformed bodies which entangled and intermeshed . . . a keen and humorous critique of consumer society" (plates 80 and 81).[41]

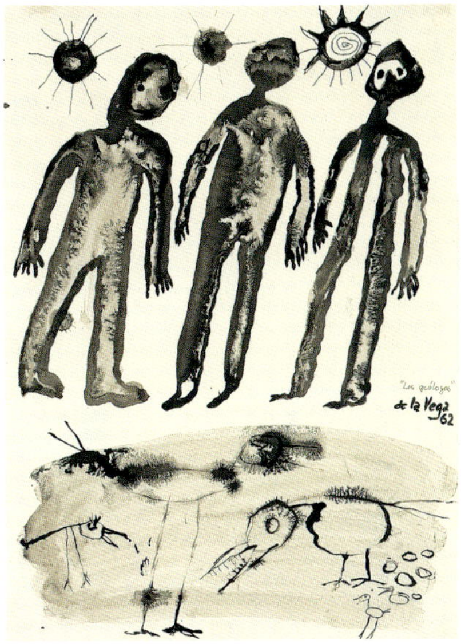

Fig. 12 **JORGE DE LA VEGA**
The Geologists, 1962
Pen and brush with ink and wash on paper, 19 3/4 x 13 7/8" (50.1 x 35.2 cm)
Jack S. Blanton Museum of Art, The University of Texas at Austin. Gift of Barbara Duncan, 1974

Black American artists such as Jacob Lawrence and Romare Bearden, working in a graphic style, depicted the life of the Black American community at odds with the consumer culture at the base of much of Pop art (plates 88 and 89). In the works seen here, figures are not iconic and isolated. Instead, the compositions are dense and animated. They depict teeming neighborhoods of closely tied individuals, the public life of the street the source of identity. Pathos and dignity rather than distance and irony animate the work.

In New York, two of the masters of Abstract Expressionism—Willem de Kooning and Philip Guston—vigorously renewed their art in the 1960s. Guston gave up abstraction in 1966 and through his drawings worked out a new figurative vocabulary and style indebted to cartoonists (George Herriman, Al Capp, Walt Disney), Max Beckmann, and his own art of the 1930s and 1940s depicting the hooded figures of the Ku Klux Klan (fig. 13; plates 82 and 83). The Klan figure has manifold significance, representing the artist "hiding behind a disguise"[42] and as a witness to the social and political turmoil of the period in the United States. While widely criticized at the time for being crude and vulgar, Guston's late work has come to be immensely influential for subsequent generations of artists and recognized for its innovation, for its intensity and honesty, and for what curator Magdalena Dabrowski has described as "a deeply human drama whose uncomfortable truth—disclosed by a mode of drawing bordering on the grotesque—could induce a shock of recognition."[43]

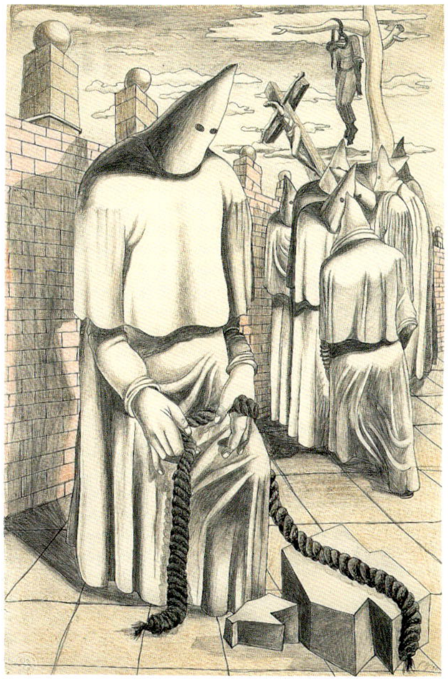

Fig. 13 **PHILIP GUSTON**
Drawing for ***Conspirators***, 1930
Graphite, ink, colored pencil, and crayon on paper, 22 1/2 x 14 1/2" (57.2 x 36.8 cm)
Whitney Museum of American Art, New York. Purchase, with funds from the Hearst Corporation and the Norman and Rosita Winston Foundation, Inc.

NON-COMPOSITION

One of modernism's motivating fantasies is the tabula rasa, the blank slate upon which a novel pictorial universe might be inscribed. Artists from many different eras and locations have been inspired by this idea of starting over from scratch, of being able to leave the history of art behind and strike out to invent a new world, both imagined and real. One of the major strategies artists have used in these attempts to forge new art has been to undermine what they consider to be the essential characteristics of the art of the past. Though perhaps perverse, chief among their targets has been the fundamental idea of the artist as an individual creator. Indeed, many artists have felt that a prerequisite to making truly new art was to destroy the very notion of individual, artistic subjectivity.

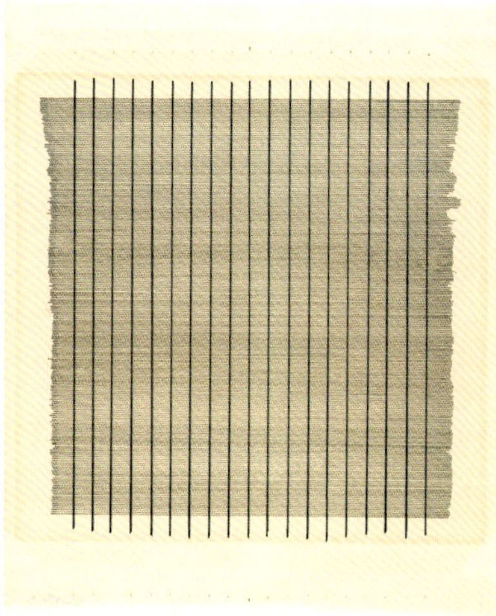

AGNES MARTIN
Organ Note, 1962
Ink on paper, 11 3/4 x 9 3/8" (29.8 x 23.8 cm)
The Museum of Modern Art, New York.
The William S. Paley Collection, 1990

One common way artists try to undermine this subjectivity is to reduce the number of "arbitrary" decisions they must make in creating a new artwork. Rejecting conventions of composition—in which the lines and colors in a work are determined according to (ideologically laden) rules of taste—is one strategy in this cause. As art historian Yve-Alain Bois has detailed in numerous publications, artists from Kazimir Malevich to Ellsworth Kelly to the Minimalists all developed methods of "non-composition" as part of their assault on the traditional values of art and personal artistic subjectivity. These methods are as diverse as these artists are inventive, and include the use of chance, the allover grid, the monochrome, and the readymade. Ironically, of course, in their assault on individual decision-making through the use of non-composition, these artists have fashioned unique and distinctive bodies of work that—far from being anonymous or blank, and sometimes quite distinct from their intention—bear the unmistakable mark of their own sensibilities. —J. K.

De Kooning's *Woman* from 1965 is a monumental work in which the iconic subject of the female form is given fresh, exhilarating life, freed from the ferocity of the 1950s (plate 85). The figure congeals from a range of sharp, heavy outlines, faint, wispy, shadowlike markings, and rubbed smears equivalent to the strokes of a loaded brush. Caught at the moment of disrobing, she is a giantess who, if standing, would tower over the viewer, a cartoonish floozy formidable in her power and fluidly at ease. The drawing captures de Kooning's humor and use of caricature. It also shows him as an artist who unceasingly reinvented his own virtuoso skills as a draftsman.

SYSTEMS, INDEXES, AND ALLEGORIES

Line as both descriptive of an object in the world and as revelation of the personality or being of the artist, no matter how far removed from the styles and technical procedures of past generations, still is within a lineage at the heart of Western art. More radical were the wide-ranging and diverse array of drawings that are notational, diagrammatic, and reductivist—those that give form to ideas. Such drawings, labeled as Minimal and Conceptual art, act "as an abstract means of intellectual pursuit, liberated from the world of representation...opening infinite possibilities of investigation."[44] Historian Joseph Helfenstein observes: "Drawing has long been considered the best medium for transmitting abstract ideas into perceptible form, for translating and synthesizing the complexity of concepts and processes into something immediate and tangible."[45]

The intentions of the artists and the meanings, the significance, the value they give to these works cannot be summarized or reduced to a common ground. Yet much of this work is a setting down on paper of ideas, a first step to consider how form may be given to thought. In some cases drawings are self-contained and autonomous, but often they are studies for how to proceed to make a painting or a sculpture, an installation in a room, or a work in the landscape. Generally, a smallness of scale aligns with the intimacy, the directness of encounter with the artist's mind. Often they are playful, alert, open; subtle, nuanced, delicate. The grid, the square, geometric structure—methods of **non-composition**—are used frequently as a foil for exploratory digression, a counterpoint to the touch of the hand, a check to subjective expression.

The idea of drawing as a reflection of the mind and thought, registered through the autographic mark and gesture of the hand, was explicitly challenged, even poked fun at, by artists in the 1960s. Even as artists proclaimed rupture and revolution, the iconoclastic spirit of early modernism, as analyzed by Jodi Hauptman in *Drawing from the Modern, 1880–1945*, was often consciously reengaged. Piero Manzoni, for example, in his drawing

INDEX In 1951, after lining up sheets of paper so that they covered more than twenty-two feet of a downtown Manhattan street, Robert Rauschenberg directed John Cage to drive his car—a Model A Ford—with inked tires, over them. The result, made not with the artist's hand and far beyond the scale of the sketchbook-size sheet, may, nonetheless, be called a drawing. A simple impression, Rauschenberg's *Tire Print* is also, in semiological terms, an index: a type of sign with a physical relationship to its referent. It was Charles Peirce, the American founder of semiotics, who set out definitions of three basic types of sign. In addition to the "index," Peirce described the "icon," which resembles what it stands for (as in figurative painting), and the "symbol," which bears only an arbitrary link to its referent (as in language). Other examples of an index include a footprint in the sand, a photograph, or a shadow. Devoid of gesture or expression, without the struggle of perception or composition—and in the case of the *Tire Print*, made mechanically—the index can only reflect, and thus poses a challenge to conventional forms of art.

If in traditional drawing, the hand (and the line it makes) stands for skill, authority, and soul, the index, as Rosalind Krauss has demonstrated in her important two-part essay "Notes on the Index," has been a key strategy for artists, a way to contest long-standing methods of art-making. The index, for example, is a challenge to the hand's supposed mastery. In his last painting on canvas, *Tu m'* (1918), Marcel Duchamp combines painted shadows of his readymades with an actual shadow created by a real bottle brush attached to the surface of the canvas. Throwing the artist's originality and expertise even further into question, Duchamp hired a professional sign painter to paint a pointing hand in the center of the canvas. In presenting what Krauss calls "a panorama of the index," Duchamp demonstrates not only that art can be made from shadows but that the artist no longer has to make his own work.

Using the index as a form of borrowing, artists can avoid composition and mediation. Direct borrowing can be seen in the Surrealist frottages of Max Ernst as well as in the gravestone rubbings of Sari Dienes (plate 36). The index can also assert the presence of the author without the traditional skilled mark. In *Diver* (1962–63; plate 43), Jasper Johns's own handprints define the shape of the diving (or surfacing) figure, while in *Thumbprint* (1960; plate 97) Piero Manzoni frames an inked print of his own thumb. —J. H.

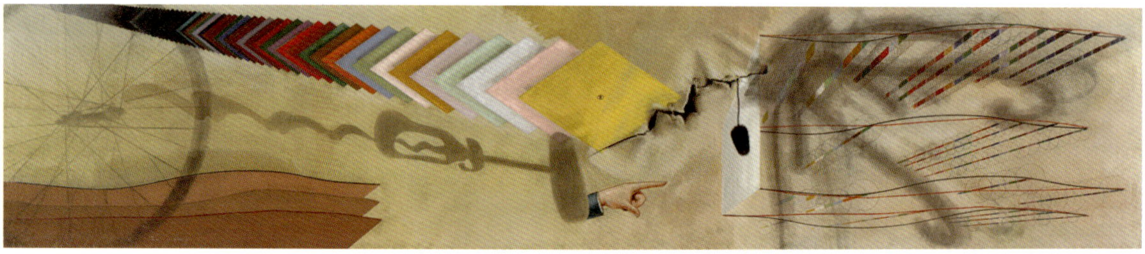

MARCEL DUCHAMP
Tu m', 1918
Oil and pencil on canvas, with bottle brush, three safety pins, and a bolt, 27 1/2" x 10' 2 3/4" (69.9 x 309.9 cm)
Yale University Art Gallery, New Haven, Connecticut. Gift of the Estate of Katherine S. Dreier

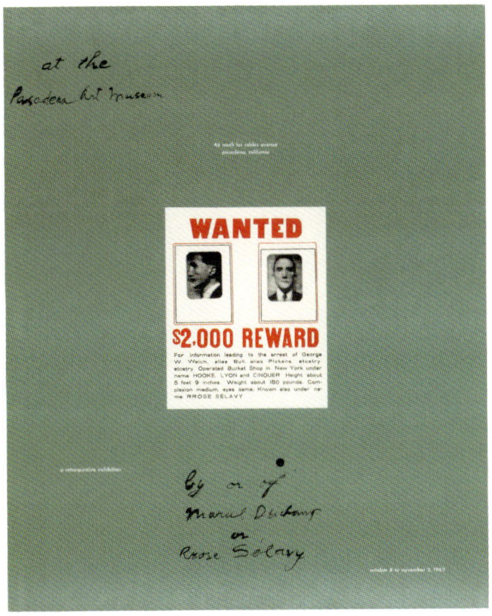

Fig. 14 **MARCEL DUCHAMP**
Wanted $2,000 Reward, A Retrospective Exhibition by or of Marcel Duchamp or Rrose Sélavy, 1963
Offset lithograph, 34 1/2 x 27" (87.6 x 68.5 cm)
The Museum of Modern Art, New York.
Gift of the Pasadena Art Museum, 1963

Thumbprint most efficiently but elegantly inked his thumb and put it to the center of a page (plate 97), creating a cousin to Duchamp's most-wanted poster, the artist as outsider and pseudo-criminal (fig. 14). The fingerprint, unlike an artistic style, cannot be faked, but remains a true index to the artist himself. Carl Andre tapped out the numbers 1 to 9 with his fingers on a typewriter, the contrasting densities of the numbers creating a vibrating, optical grid, analogous to his sculptures of stacked or gridded commercial materials (plate 98).[46] Roy Lichtenstein made a drawing of a thumbprint, perhaps an acknowledgement that his seemingly impersonal style of Pop art indeed had an author (plate 51). The next year Lichtenstein began his series of brushstroke paintings and drawings (plate 52). In these works he mimics the freeform strokes of Abstract Expressionism—and the authentic revelation of the artist supposedly expressed in this loose gesture—but does so with a carefully composed grid of hand-drawn dots imitating the Benday dot system of commercial printing.

While much has been made of the purported impersonality of Minimal and Conceptual art, as comparisons are made across a wide field of these drawings the individuality of each artist becomes increasingly apparent. Choices of materials and papers, compositional structure, spatial organization, and treatment of line are enormously varied. While reticent in relation to the gestural boldness of Abstract Expressionism or the punch of Pop art, inventiveness and the presence of alert intelligence are palpable. In fact, the optical and perceptual character of these drawings is no less important than the ideas contained in them.

Drawings, as noted above, often were the first forays into imagining and planning sculptures, paintings, installations, and environmental works. Four of the artists most closely associated with Minimal art—Carl Andre, Dan Flavin, Donald Judd, and Frank Stella—used drawings to work out structure, proportion, internal division, and spatial relations for sculptures or, in Stella's case, for paintings.[47] For example, Andre's *Blue Lock* (1966; plate 111) registers his idea for a floor sculpture as both a square and a rectangle, with language propelling the viewer to turn the sheet, as the sculpture would pull the viewer around it. As art historian Christine Mehring has written: "The *Lock* sculptures fluctuate between order and disorder. The grid structure 'locks' or fastens all its modules in place.... Whereas the figures in the lower section follow the thicker lines of the paper grid, those in the upper section deviate

SYSTEMS

The artistic process is usually considered to be one of boundless invention, free-form thinking, and individual expression. Yet during the 1960s a number of artists found that working at the opposite end of this spectrum—allowing systematic methods and programmatic procedures to guide their work—yielded even more productive results. By determining the organizational principle in advance, such as a grid, chart, or diagram, these artists freed themselves of decision-making and invention. It can be argued that in many ways the art ended up making itself, with the artist functioning as a conduit for this more cerebral mode of artistic production. Indeed, the concept was just as or even more crucial than the end product, as in the written instructions that Sol LeWitt began to sell for wall drawings that could be realized by anyone.

While artists found success in transforming these systematic methods into object-oriented works—Minimalist sculpture, for example—working their ideas out on paper often proved to be more effective. Turning to graph paper was one solution, with the paper's grid offering a premade schema onto which the artist could map out his or her markings, such as Lawrence Weiner's hatch-like scribblings that record the passing of time (plate 118) or Carl Andre's repetitive vertical and horizontal lines that reiterate the grid (plate 111). The grid also functions as an open field for data entry, for example in Agnes Denes's diagrams that investigate language and communication (plate 134) and Hanne Darboven's numerical tables that offer countless variations and permutations based on her own logic (plate 119). In addition to the use of ready-made graph paper, some artists found that rendering their own grid from scratch offered distinctive possibilities (plates 104, 114, and 122).

Driven by such conceptual and schematic systems (and thus denying description outright), this approach to art inevitably results in a depersonalized mode of abstraction. It also abandons any sense of the improvisatory, since the chosen system guarantees a self-generating internal structure of relational forms and seriality. Yet this is not simply an art of abstraction based on easy repetition. Instead, by investigating these systems through the deployment of lines, letters, numbers, and other graphic elements—an exploration often best suited to working on paper—such works, in which information is not always understandable or easily digested, offer an intellectualized visual language that often turns language itself on its head. —T. P.

from it, creating a tension between the drawn and the printed grid."[48] Flavin's *Untitled (to Barnett Newman) One and Three* (1971; plate 108) records two of four permutations of a sculpture made from fluorescent lighting tubes arranged to form a rectangle to be installed in the corner of a room. The sculptures were made as homages to Barnett Newman, who had died the year before, and Flavin's use of primary colors refers to a series of late paintings by Newman entitled *Who's Afraid of Red Yellow and Blue*. In the case of these two works, the horizontal, four-foot-long tubes of yellow light would face out of the corner while the vertical, eight-foot-long tubes of red and blue would turn inward, bleeding outside of the edge of the lighting fixtures.[49] Frank Stella's study for *Valle de los Caídos* (1966; plate 110) was conceived as the last of his series of Black Paintings, begun in 1958 (fig. 15). Commissioned by New York State in the mid-1960s for the new Albany Mall, the painting was never approved and never made. This series of paintings was nevertheless among the touchstones of what would develop to be Minimal art and was Stella's attempt to force "illusionistic space out of painting at constant intervals by using a regulated pattern."[50]

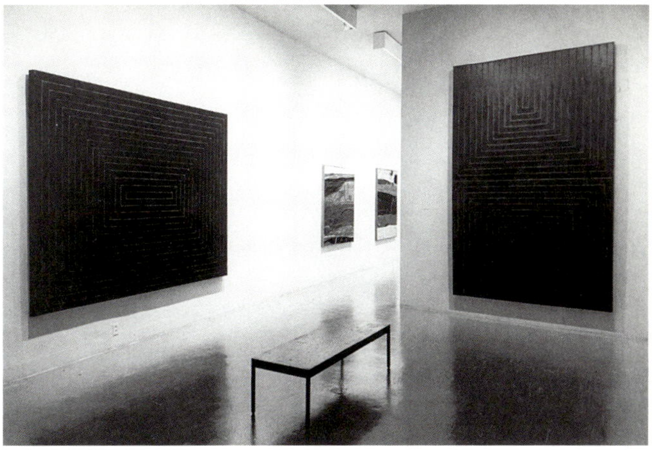

Fig. 15 Installation view from the exhibition ***Sixteen Americans***, The Museum of Modern Art, New York, December 1959–February 1960, showing Frank Stella's Black Paintings

A number of artists working in New York in the mid-1960s quickly developed approaches that would open up the constrained structures of Minimal art. The idea of using systems that would then generate the work of art, removing the artist as much as possible from its authorship, was the most logical and immediate development. Sol LeWitt was among the first artists to begin working with systems, and works on paper have consistently been the seedbed for new developments in LeWitt's work.[51] One of his great innovations was his "wall drawing," an architectural-scale drawing executed directly on a wall, an attempt to dissolve any distinction between a drawing and its support (fig. 16). The first wall drawings and related works on paper were developed from every combination of vertical, horizontal, and diagonal lines, set in four- part grids (plate 122). While LeWitt himself made the drawings on paper, the wall drawings are executed by draftsmen, following a general set of instructions. As

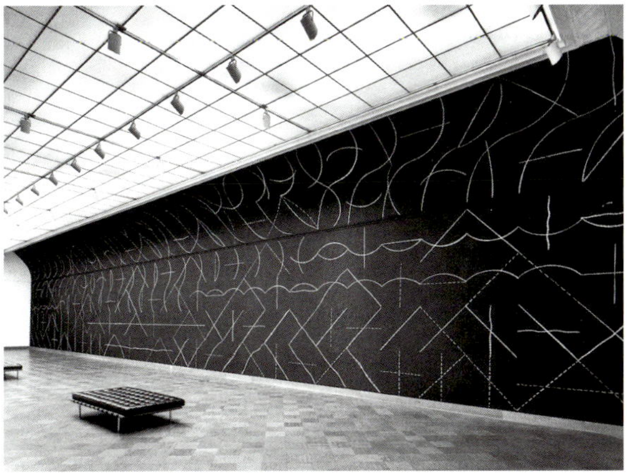

Fig. 16 **SOL LEWITT**
On Black Walls, All Two-Part Combinations of White Arcs from Corners and Sides, and White Straight, Not-Straight, and Broken Lines, 1975
White chalk on black wall, dimensions variable
The Museum of Modern Art, New York. Fractional gift of an anonymous donor, 1978

LANGUAGE Humans are linguistic beings. The use of language allows us to objectify things through representations, going beyond purely expressive and communicative functions that we share with other animals. In his studies of the epistemology of knowledge, philosopher Karl Popper argues that what is unique to mankind is the use of language for argument, the power to organize signs that express opinions, explanations, and theories about the world that surrounds us. Language thus allows us to communicate our rationality and emotion, making them possible subjects of discussion and analysis. By language we generically mean the entire arsenal of signs that allows us to represent the world or ourselves, including figurative or abstract images, symbols or icons. But the arrangement of these signs is endlessly changeable. Indeed, the structure of language itself recalls a chessboard, where the altering of a single term implies an entire change in sense.

Ferdinand de Saussure, the founder of modern linguistics, observed that nothing within language allows one to anticipate how speakers will put signs into play. There is thus between the faculty of language and the act of discourse a gap that cannot be bridged or accounted for by a theory. Acts of language—discourses—are absolutely individual, unpredictable, and accidental. This is particularly significant when we extend the notion of language into the field of visual arts. Not only does this gap provide a consistent explanation of modern art as an autonomous language, but it also sheds light on some contemporary artistic practices, such as Conceptual art. Driven by the concept of tautology—the overlapping or repeating of an idea or a form—Conceptual artists made language a fundamental subject of their work. The presence of language in works by artists such as Mel Bochner underlines the notion that there is no autonomous visual understanding—that all meaning is ultimately intertwined with our link to language. As one can see in Bochner's *Mental Exercise: Estimating a Centered Vertical* from 1972, drawing delves into the space in which language and image become equivalent fields of possible meaning. —L. E. P. O.

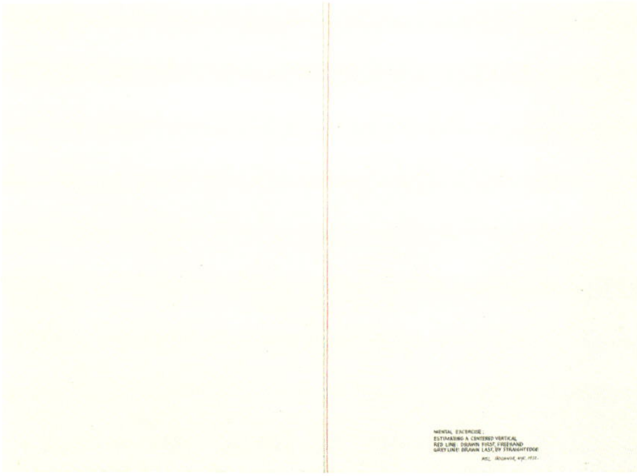

MEL BOCHNER
Mental Exercise: Estimating a Centered Vertical, 1972
Pencil, colored pencil, and ink on paper, 22 3/8 x 30" (56.8 x 76.2 cm)
The Museum of Modern Art, New York. Acquired with matching funds from Mr. and Mrs. Eugene Victor Thaw and the National Endowment for the Arts, 1973

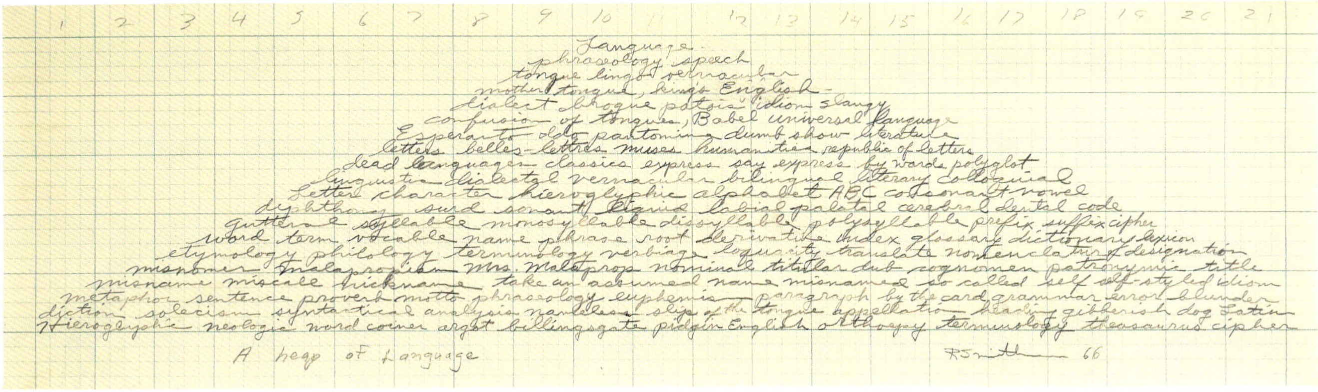

Fig. 17 **ROBERT SMITHSON**
A Heap of Language, 1966
Pencil on paper, 6 ½ x 22" (16.5 x 55.9 cm)
The Over Holland Collection

evident in his works on paper, which are exquisitely rendered, he "is not indifferent…to the visual quality of the work as it emerges, and in that sense his (wall) drawings, hand-executed by individuals, have to do with sensuous touch—but not his."[52] An elegant beauty has never been absent from LeWitt's work, even when at its most conceptual and reductive.

Though LeWitt initially was associated with Minimal art, he became one of the leaders of Conceptual art, and his written statements "Paragraphs on Conceptual Art" in 1967 and "Sentences on Conceptual Art" in 1969 became de facto manifestos for the movement.[53] Conceptual art is a broad and porous umbrella for many disparate artists and tendencies that continued to evolve and change within a relatively short period of time. Language, however, is certainly at the core of Conceptual art, with artists testing and playing with the elasticity of words as sign, index, notation, autograph, and calligraphy, and even as a material and as image (fig. 17). Mel Bochner, also among the pioneers of Conceptual art, used language to articulate potential relationships within a raw physical space, to prod the mind and imagination to transform this tabula rasa into an arena of human action (plate 125).

Other counterpoints to Minimal art also developed in the mid-1960s. Bridget Riley's paintings took the notion of non-illusionism to the outer edge of optical play, worked out carefully in drawings of filigreed, undulating linear webs (plate 117). Richard Tuttle was making lithe and playful sculptures that hovered against the plane of the wall, as seen in *First Green Octagon*, a cloth work in which the contour dissolves the distinction between line and form, as well as the related drawing (plate 120). Bruce Nauman's study for *Storage Capsule for the Right Rear Quarter of My Body* (1966; plate 112), a sculpture that was never realized, appears in his preparatory drawing as a geometric but anthropomorphic floating sentinel, catching a wash of light in an indeterminate space. Robert Smithson was among the pioneering artists who began to make works integrated into the landscape, counterposing the geometries of culture and the mind with the bodily presence and sensuality of nature (plates 126 and 127). From the care and precision with which these works are rendered, with their formal

PROCESS In the late 1960s and early 1970s a number of artists working predominantly in sculpture and installation art, including Lynda Benglis, Eva Hesse, Robert Morris, and Richard Serra, explored the ways in which a work of art literally comes into being. The term "process art" came to encompass the intrinsically physical materialization of these artists' active and even performative methods, the result being works whose amorphous, indeterminate, and often mucky appearance contrasted with the pristine, manufactured look of contemporary Minimalist sculpture.

Although the notion of process is now commonly associated with sculpture and installation art from this time—works often understood as tangible manifestations of an artist's bodily actions—the approach carried over to drawing with fruitful results. Functioning as the physical records of an artist's more intimate gestures, these drawings reveal the process of their unfolding, for example the repetitive, indexical traces of Jasper Johns (plate 43), the beautifully wrought circles of Eva Hesse (plate 113), the systematic, analytic diagrams of Agnes Denes (plate 134), the hesitant, haunting scrawls of William Anastasi (plate 130), and the seemingly simple yet cerebral forms of Dorothea Rockburne (plate 131).

Unlike Edward Ruscha's drawings (plate 55) or Ellsworth Kelly's collages (plate 33), which do not expose the individual steps taken to make them, in these process-oriented drawings the method of their formation appears before our very eyes. Yet they do not only lay bare the materialization of their creation. According to art historian Pamela Lee, they also reveal the actual duration of their making, an interpretation best exemplified by Robert Morris's series of Blind Time drawings, in which the artist, with eyes closed during prescribed amounts of time, marked sheets of paper over and over with bare hands covered in dry graphite. Through the physical process of creation, this mode of drawing unveils the temporal, lived experience of the artist, thus offering a continued, active engagement with the viewer. —T. P.

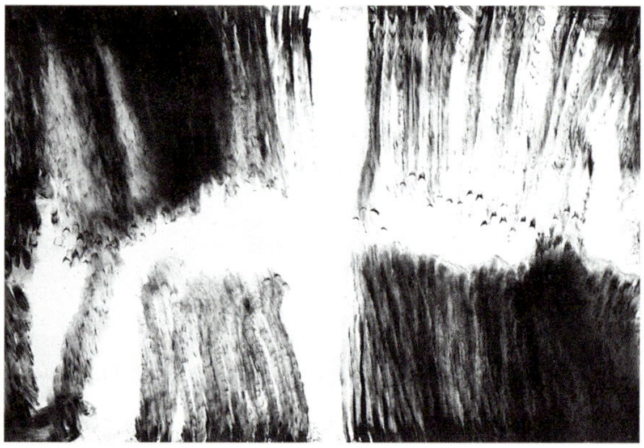

ROBERT MORRIS
Blind Time XIII, 1973
Graphite on paper, 35 1/8 x 46 1/8" (89.2 x 117.2 cm)
The Museum of Modern Art, New York. Acquired with matching funds from The Lily Auchincloss Foundation, Inc. and the National Endowment for the Arts, 1974

beauty and, in fact, composition, it would be difficult to classify them as simply working drawings but rather they are precisely finished works.

Agnes Martin, a painter, and Eva Hesse, a sculptor, both made numerous drawings that were independent of their other work. The drawings offer particular insight into the character and spirit of their art. From 1960 to 1966 Martin made small drawings on paper, close to a square in shape, with geometric forms composed of parallel or gridded lines almost filling the sheet (plates 103 and 104). The lines are delicate and hand-drawn, with the slightest variations and irregularities, setting up undulating visual fields. Though the works are resolutely abstract, the titles often reference nature. Martin, however, "sought not a representation of nature but a visual correlative for the feeling of exultation that nature elicits."[54] In a letter sent to the collector who had acquired *Wood I* (and now attached to the back of the drawing), Martin wrote: "All great artwork attempts to represent our joy in moments of clarity of mind and vision.... Please study your response to art very carefully (and to everything else) as it is the road to self knowledge and the truth about life."[55] Hesse's drawings from the mid-1960s are generally of similar small scale, but are slightly vertical rectangles with a gridded field of hand-drawn circles set within the perimeter. Rather than nature or landscape, Hesse obliquely references the body. The concentric circles of some drawings may recall breasts, and the modulations of surface and irregularities of shape reflect the pressure and movement of the hand (plates 113 and 114). Hesse's sculptures extend the physicality of Pollock's paintings into three-dimensions—with Pollock's skeins becoming skins, surrogates to a shimmering, living presence in the world—but it is her drawings that serve as windows into the presence and being of the artist (fig. 18).

In the bold drawings of Brice Marden and Richard Serra, the intense materiality of Abstract Expressionism is melded with the rigorous geometric structure and analytical underpinnings of Minimal art. Marden is identified as a painter and Serra as a sculptor, but for both artists drawing is fundamental within their work. For both, drawings are as much a physical as a visual encounter for the viewer, in which the process of making the work is palpable. In his drawings from the 1960s and 1970s, Marden builds up sensuous surfaces of graphite and/or charcoal, often mixed into beeswax, densely overworked, shimmering

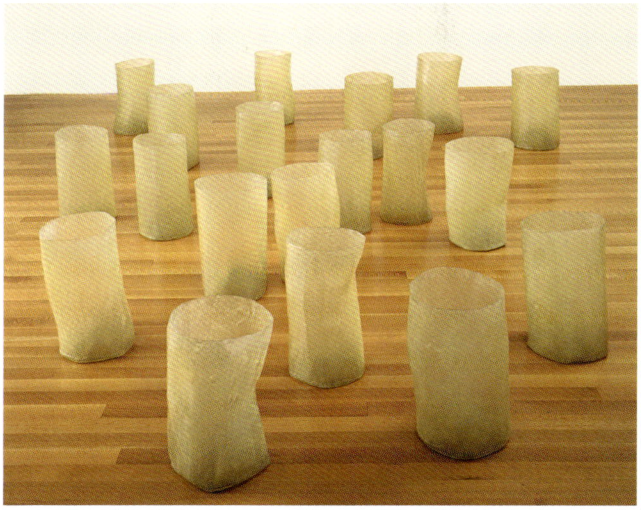

Fig. 18 **EVA HESSE**
Repetition Nineteen III, 1968
Fiberglass and polyester resin, nineteen units,
each 19 to 20 1/4" (48 to 51 cm) x 11 to 12 3/4" (27.8 to 32.2 cm)
The Museum of Modern Art, New York. Gift of Charles and Anita Blatt, 1969

NEO-CONCRETE

Starting in the late 1950s, a group of poets, critics, and visual artists—among them the poet and critic Ferreira Gullar, critic Mário Pedrosa, and artists Hércules Barsotti, Aluisio Carvão, Amilcar de Castro, Lygia Clark, Lygia Pape, and Franz Weissmann, all working in Rio de Janeiro—formed what they called the Grupo Neoconcreto, launching the movement and its eponymous 1959 exhibition at the Museu de Arte Moderna in the Brazilian capital. In his "Manifesto Neoconcreto" of that same year, Gullar stated that "Neo-Concrete art…denies the validity of scientific and positivist attitudes in art and raises the question of expression." The artists who took part in the group's activities saw their work as being in opposition to what they regarded as the rigid and formulaic rationalism that characterized Concrete art in the rest of the country (particularly in São Paulo).

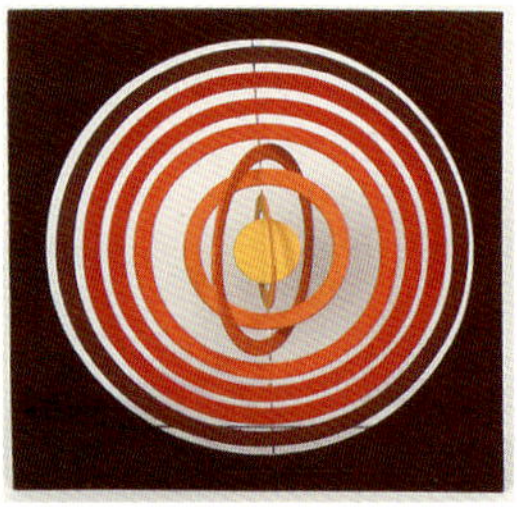

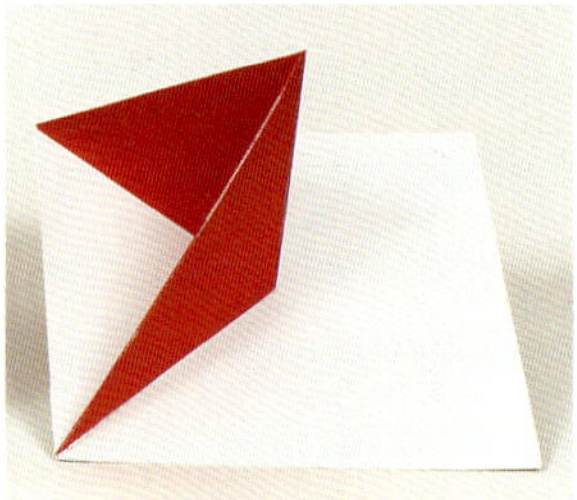

LYGIA PAPE
Book of Creation, 1959–60
Gouache on cardboard, two of eighteen components, each 12 x 12" (30.5 x 30.5 cm)
The Museum of Modern Art, New York. Fractional and promised gift of Patricia Phelps de Cisneros, 2001

The theoretical position of the Neo-Concrete group was informed by the philosopher Maurice Merleau-Ponty's book *Phénomenologie de la perception* (1945). As Paulo Herkenhoff has argued, for the Neo-Concretists "perception is conditioned by corporeal existence, which is, in turn, converted into an existential act." In writing about the work of his friend and collaborator Pape, Hélio Oiticica described this mode of perception as "the search for the direct sensorial consciousness for the act of seeing, or feeling by touch—intellect defying itself." Poetry and visual art were often intertwined in the work of the Neo-Concretists, as in Lygia Pape's *Book of Creation* of 1959–60, a book-poem comprising eighteen gouache-on-paper components. Each part of this book is an abstract sculpture that may be manipulated by the viewer, who is thus transformed into a participant who completes the artwork. Pape's version of the creation story creates parallels between the organic development of the earth and man's creativity—itself inextricably related to nature. This focus on the organic and stress on individual subjectivity is also fundamental for understanding works like Lygia Clark's *Animals (Bichos)* of 1960–63, a series of metal sculptures made up of several hinged sections. As with Pape's work, the way in which the work is placed can be endlessly transformed. By moving the constituent parts, the viewer's perception of the work incorporates not just seeing but all the senses—drawing attention to the fact that the form of a work comes into being through its relation with an individual's subjectivity. —M. B.

and flickering, with the traces of the hand palpable (plate 132). A rectangular format is set off against the edge of the paper, and internally organized by a grid, "to break the gray area down to make it tighter and have the surface be more taut."[56] De Kooning and Johns loom as large influences, their intense marks and gestures and rich surfaces transmuted into even denser, stilled presence. Marden insistently sketches in what he calls "workbooks," and his drawings are generally worked on over a long period of time. In contrast to so many drawings of the period, which are records of process, for Marden a drawing is a complete, finished work of art: "It wasn't just a study or something on the way toward something else, and so I've always had that in mind about drawing. A drawing is a complete experience in itself."[57]

Richard Serra's sculptures and drawings are closely interlinked, independent but parallel practices. His large-scale sculptures of lead or steel plates are echoed in his immense drawings built up from black acrylic oil stick, in some cases overdrawn with charcoal (plate 133). The forces of gravity and inertia are suspended in a taut balance. For Serra himself the drawings are "a physical extension of one's own body and gesture" and the actions of the hand and arm, their movement, their pressure are visible and felt.[58] With his drawings, Serra took Pollock's break from art as depictive and extended it into an arena of action.

Drawing in the 1960s and 1970s thrived as much in Latin America and Europe as in the United States. In Latin America, the extraordinary surge of drawing across the continent was diverse—figurative and abstract, expressionistic and geometric, finished and notational.[59] Drawing did not require large or specialized studio space or expensive materials; it was portable and accessible; it was viewed as democratic with a potential for engagement and participation. Drawing as an ethical and moral, philosophical and existential activity united this array of activity.

While figurative art in Latin America from this period has been more broadly recognized in the United States recently, some of the most inventive and important artists worked with abstraction, in many respects parallel to but independent from developments in the United States. Brazilian artist Hélio Oiticica, working in Rio de Janeiro, made scores of drawings but only for a brief period at the beginning of his career. These works were still within the **Neo-Concrete** movement of geometric abstraction but pointed toward his mature work in which space would be

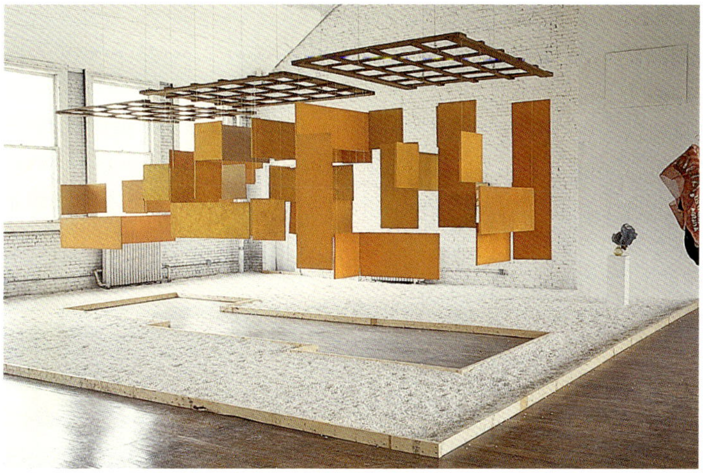

Fig. 19 **HÉLIO OITICICA**
Large Nucleus, 1960
Oil on wood and stones. Installation view from the exhibition *Brazil Projects*, P.S.1 Contemporary Art Center, Long Island City, New York, 1988

opened up and the audience enticed to directly engage, walk through, and participate with his art (fig. 19).[60] He called the drawings *metasquemas*, an invented word for which no precise translation exists but which Oiticica described variously as "obsessive dissection of space" and "space without time: cracks in the mute plane."[61] Each form is subtly distinct, almost imperceptibly escaping touch, a precisely fractured, animated field. The Venezuelan artist who took the name Gego (shortened from Gertrud Goldschmidt) fluidly moved between making sculpture, drawing, and prints. By the late 1960s she had developed a distinct structural system based on repetitive modules and the triangle, which she called *reticuláreas*, or "reticulations," combining the root "reticula" with "area," the grid plus a real area, becoming an organic space (plate 91). In both her sculptures and her drawings, the rational grid is broken, warping and shifting between two and three dimensions, the logical structure subjected to the malleable character of life (fig. 20). León Ferrari, a pioneer of Conceptual art in Argentina, made a series of drawings between 1962 and 1964 that move between the calligraphic and the gestural (fig. 21; plate 94). Their fine, curling lines evoke body hair as well as the hand, erotic and neutral, physical and abstract. The line, the word, the body are fused. About his work, Ferrari has said, "I draw silent handwritten words, which tell things, with lines that recall voices. And I write drawings that recite memories that words cannot say."[62] Mira Schendel, a Brazilian artist working in São Paolo, made diverse works throughout her career, including many hybrids of drawing and sculpture. During one intense period in 1964 she made between two and three thousand drawings, scratching and marking onto glass, which then was pressed onto Japanese tissue paper, fusing her line and gesture into the surface (plates 92 and 93). Language and space become one, semiotic and pictographic. In one drawing the letters "ARA" appear, the Latin word for altar, and in another the word "vermilho," Portuguese for "red," is scratched into the red ground like graffiti onto a wall. Both evoke drawing as a meeting point between artist and public, as a place for the exchange of meaning, for the creation of community.

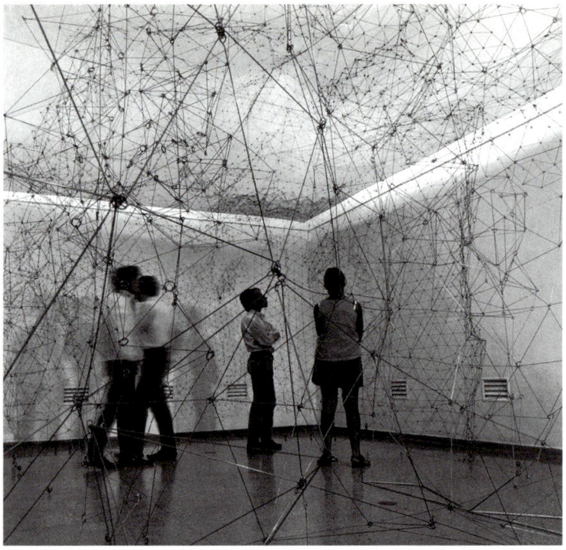

Fig. 20 **GEGO**
Reticulárea (ambientación), 1969
Wire, dimensions variable
Fundación Galería de Arte Nacional, Caracas.
Installation view, Museo de Bellas Artes de Caracas, 1969

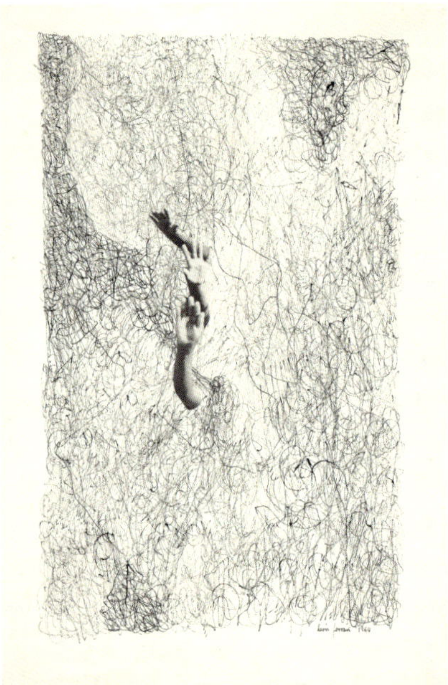

Fig. 21 **LEÓN FERRARI**
Untitled, 1964
Cut-and-pasted printed paper and ink on paper, 19 x 12 1/4" (48.3 x 31.1 cm)
The Museum of Modern Art, New York.
Purchase, 2003

The idea of drawing as a carrier of poetic and political meaning, as a kind of allegory to open insight into contemporary life, found its most profound expression in the work of two of the most significant artists in Europe in the 1970s—Marcel Broodthaers and Joseph Beuys. Broodthaers, a Belgian, began as a poet and only in the later part of his life turned to art, but often with language paired with image. For him, as for his compatriot and predecessor René Magritte, words and images ricochet off one another, setting up possibilities of meaning for either that before may have been latent or nonexistent (plate 145). Counterposed, they become sparks for fantasies, imaginings of places and journeys beyond the quotidian. But Broodthaers was interested in the collective possibilities of meaning rather than private musings. His work invokes books, films, and museums—the world of culture—repositories for shared human experience.

Joseph Beuys, a German artist already discussed for his early work, by the 1970s had shifted from drawing as personal and intimate to a tool of his teaching and political activity. He believed the artist was an agent for creative social change, whose imaginative intelligence could inspire personal and social transformation. Often he lectured, making diagrammatic drawings on blackboards as tools of his teaching. In the drawing *Untitled (Sun State)* (1974; plate 147), made during a lecture at the Art Institute of Chicago in 1974, many of Beuys's key iconic symbols are present: the stag, representing masculine power but also, through his antlers, renewal; the heart "an organic 'battery' connected to primal nature."[63] Beuys, summarizing the significance of this drawing, has stated that it represents freedom: "It unites the cosmic and the terrestrial as it maps an ideal state in which the social order is conceived of as a living, evolving organism, intimately linked to the natural order, in an ideally balanced ecological cycle. The sun creates energy, which is circulated through the labyrinthine system... energetic matter of creation is alchemically converted and circulates through the looping line, it takes form in a threefold system of culture—art, science, and religion—and goes toward the ideal state in which the key democratic questions govern...."[64] About the character and quality of art, Beuys has stated: "The expanded concept of art is not a theory but a way of proceeding which says that the inner eye is very much more crucial than the external images that develop anyway. The precondition for good outward pictures, which can also be hung in museums, is that the inner image, the thought-form, the structure of thought, imagination, and feeling, has the quality required of a corresponding picture."[65]

IMAGINATION AFFIRMED

Drawing gives physical presence to the thoughts and imaginings of humans in the most direct and intimate way. Through drawings artists may discover forms and meanings that had been unknown. We, in turn, may find that we must reconsider the definitions and descriptions of art, its meaning and value, and even how we understand the world and our place in it. As John Elderfield has written: "At its best, drawing goes through objects with the directness of words, and recalls from the cave of memory shapes and lines and colors that confirm our experience of the world and that reveal worlds the like of which we had thought—until they were made comprehensible to us—we had never known."[66]

Drawing traversed a thirty-year course from 1945 to 1975 that could not have been imagined before it happened. No amount of reasoning or argument could have foreseen how artists would return to and renew this most fundamental of art forms or the range of that invention. The history of drawing itself has been altered: the traditions of Western drawing yet again broken and reinvented; the ruptures and revolutions of modernism in the first half of the century sustained and invigorated.

Drawing is the most accessible of art forms, at its most basic the product of no more than a pen or pencil taken to a sheet of paper. Any material that may make a mark or leave a trace can be used. Any support, from manifold varieties of paper to the wall of a room, may sustain the act of drawing. Drawings may also be fragile and evanescent; their plight is to disappear. While we certainly may admire skill, we also have come to admire the singular touch of the human hand, the presence of human intelligence distilled. Drawing, even during this era of enormous change in art, continued to confirm the resilience of imagination.

NOTES

1 The very notion of an avant-garde or advanced art has become problematic at this stage in history. Texts grappling with this issue include Peter Bürger, *Theory of the Avant-Garde*, trans. Michael Shaw (Minneapolis: University of Minnesota Press, 1984); Benjamin Buchloh, "The Primary Colors for the Second Time: A Paradigm Repetition of the Neo-Avant-Garde," *October* 37 (summer 1986): 41–52; and Hal Foster, "What's Neo about the Neo-Avant-Garde?," *October* 70 (fall 1994): 5–32. For excellent discussions regarding values and interpretations, see Leo Steinberg, "Contemporary Art and the Plight of Its Public" and "Other Criteria," in *Other Criteria* (New York: Oxford University Press, 1972), 3–16 and 55–91.

2 In relation particularly to art from the mid-1940s forward, the arguments of Clement Greenberg played a decisive role, especially in the United States, but have now been subjected to intense reconsideration and refutation. See Rosalind E. Krauss, *The Optical Unconscious* (Cambridge, Mass.: The MIT Press, 1994); and Thierry de Duve, *Clement Greenberg Between the Lines: A Previously Unpublished Debate with Clement Greenberg*, trans. Brian Holmes (Paris: Édition Dis Voirs, 1996).

3 Recent scholarship has documented and examined the global reach and diversity of these movements. On Latin American Pop art, see Jacqueline Barnitz, "New Figuration, Pop, and Assemblage in the 1960s and 1970s," in Waldo Rassmussen, ed., *Latin American Artists in the Twentieth Century* (New York: The Museum of Modern Art, 1992), 122–34; and Anna Longoni and Mariano Mestman, "After Pop, We Dematerialize: Oscar Masotta, Happenings, and Media Art at the Beginnings of Conceptualism," in Inés Katzenstein, ed., *Listen, Here, Now! Argentine Art of the 1960s: Writings of the Avant-Garde* (New York: The Museum of Modern Art, 2004), 156–72; on Minimalism, see Lynn Zelevansky, *Beyond Geometry: Experiments in Form, 1940s–70s* (Cambridge, Mass.: The MIT Press, 2004); on Conceptual art, see László Beke et al., *Global Conceptualism: Points of Origin, 1950s–1980s* (New York: Queens Museum of Art, 1999).

4 In particular on Arte Povera, see Richard Flood and Francis Morris, *Zero to Infinity: Arte Povera, 1962–1972* (Minneapolis: Walker Art Center, 2001); on Neo-Concretism, see Mari Carmen Ramírez and Héctor Ol, *Inverted Utopias: Avant-Garde Art in Latin America* (New Haven, Conn.: Yale University Press; Houston: Museum of Fine Arts, Houston, 2004); on Gutai, see Alexandra Munroe, *Japanese Art after 1945: Scream Against the Sky* (New York: Harry N. Abrams, 1994).

5 As Jodi Hauptman has noted: "…it is in drawing's intimate laboratory—in the erasing and smudging, tearing and pasting—that we can see most clearly…the ways in which artists negotiate opposing terms, ideals, and beliefs." Hauptman, "Drawing from the Modern: Imagination without Strings," in *Drawing from the Modern, 1880–1945* (New York: The Museum of Modern Art, 2004), 52.

6 Thomas B. Hess, *Willem de Kooning Drawings* (Greenwich, Conn.: New York Graphic Society, 1972), 36.

7 Bernice Rose, *Jackson Pollock, Drawing into Painting* (New York: The Museum of Modern Art, 1980), 8.

8 Hess, *Willem de Kooning Drawings*, 13–14.

9 Judd, quoted in Rose, *Jackson Pollock*, 9.

10 For discussion of the role of figuration in Pollock's late work, see Jordan Kantor, "Jackson Pollock's Late Paintings, 1951–1955" (PhD diss., Harvard University, 2003). Throughout his career, de Kooning would move through periods alternating between figuration and abstraction; see Thomas Hess, *Willem de Kooning: Works 1921–1967* (New York: The Museum of Modern Art, 1968); and Gary Garrels, *Willem de Kooning. The Late Paintings, the 1980s* (San Francisco: San Francisco Museum of Modern Art; Minneapolis: Walker Art Center, 1995).

11 Richard Schiff, "de Kooning Controlling de Kooning," in Cornelia H. Butler and Paul Schimmel, *Willem de Kooning: Tracing the Figure* (Los Angeles: Museum of Contemporary Art, 2002), 163. For a discussion of these issues in subsequent American art, see Michael Fried, *Three American Painters: Kenneth Noland, Jules Olitski, Frank Stella* (Cambridge, Mass.: Fogg Art Museum, 1965).

12 Rose, *Jackson Pollock*, 13.

13 Pollock, quoted in ibid., 21.

14 Newman, quoted in Brenda Richardson, *Barnett Newman: The Complete Drawings, 1944–1969* (Baltimore: The Baltimore Museum of Art, 1979), 18.

15 Richardson, *Barnett Newman*, 20.

16 Ibid., 26.

17 Dore Ashton, *A Critical Study of Philip Guston* (New York: Viking, 1976), 97.

18 Jack Flam, "The Modern Drawing," in Flam et al., *New York Collects: Drawings and Watercolors, 1900–1950* (New York: The Pierpont Morgan Library, 1999), 21.

19 Schiff, "de Kooning Controlling de Kooning," 155.

20 Bernice Rose and Ann Temkin, *Thinking Is Form: The Drawings of Joseph Beuys* (Philadelphia: Philadelphia Museum of Art; New York: The Museum of Modern Art, 1993), 27.

21 Bernice Rose, *Drawing Now* (New York: The Museum of Modern Art, 1976), 26.

22 Rose and Temkin, *Thinking Is Form*, 79.

23 Michaux, interview with John Ashbery, in Catherine de Zegher and Raymond Bellour, *Untitled Passages by Henri Michaux* (New York: The Drawing Center, 2000), 165.

24 Roland Barthes, *Cy Twombly: Paintings and Drawings, 1954–1977* (New York: Whitney Museum of American Art, 1979), 22.

25 See Robert Storr, *Modern Art despite Modernism* (New York: The Museum of Modern Art, 2000).

26 David Rosand, *Drawing Acts: Studies in Graphic Expression and Representation* (Cambridge: Cambridge University Press, 2002), 13.

27 See Mary Harris, *Remembering Black Mountain College* (Asheville, N.C.: The Black Mountain College Museum and Arts Center, 1996); and Vincent Katz, ed., *Black Mountain College: Experiment in Art* (Cambridge, Mass., and London: The MIT Press, 2002).

28 See Walter Hopps, *Robert Rauschenberg, the Early 1950s* (Houston: Menil Collection and Houston Fine Art Press, 1991).

29 For an extended discussion of this series, see Rose, *Drawing Now*, 24–29.

30 Hess, *Willem de Kooning Drawings*, 21.

31 Nan Rosenthal and Ruth E. Fine, *The Drawings of Jasper Johns* (Washington, D.C.: The National Gallery of Art, 1990), 19.

32 Ellsworth Kelly, "Notes from 1969," in *Ellsworth Kelly: Paintings and Sculptures, 1963–1979* (Amsterdam: Stedelijk Museum, 1979), 32.

33 Adam Gopnik, "Advertising," in Kirk Varnedoe and Adam Gopnik, *High & Low* (New York: The Museum of Modern Art, 1990), 361.

34 Ann Temkin, "Joseph Beuys: An Introduction to His Life and Work," in *Thinking Is Form*, 12. See also Dorothea Dietrich-Boorsch, *German Drawings of the 60s* (New Haven, Conn.: Yale University Art Gallery, 1982); and Eric L. Santner, *Stranded Objects: Mourning, Memory, and Film in Postwar Germany* (Ithaca, N.Y.: Cornell University Press, 1990).

35 Margit Rowell, ed., *Sigmar Polke: Works on Paper, 1963–1974* (New York: The Museum of Modern Art, 1999), 20.

36 Ibid., 22.

37 See Margit Rowell, *Antonin Artaud: Works on Paper* (New York: The Museum of Modern Art, 1996).

38 The two Pandemonium manifestos are published in English in *Georg Baselitz: Paintings, 1960–83*, ed. Nicholas Serota and Mark Francis, trans. David Britt (London: Whitechapel Art Gallery, 1983), 23–29.

39 Edith A. Gibson, "Re-Aligning Vision: Alternative Currents in South American Drawing," in Mari Carmen Ramírez, ed., *Re-Aligning Vision: Alternative Currents in South American Drawing* (Austin: Archer M. Huntington Art Gallery, The University of Texas at Austin, 1997), 56.

40 See Guillermo Whitelow, *Otra Figuración: veinte anos despues* (Buenos Aires: Fundación San Telmo, 1981).

41 John Wineland, "Jorge de la Vega," in *Re-Aligning Vision*, 208. On de la Vega, see also Marcelo Pacheco, *Jorge de la Vega: A Contemporary Artist* (Buenos Aires: Editorial el Ateneo, 2003).

42 Magdalena Dabrowski, *The Drawings of Philip Guston* (New York: The Museum of Modern Art, 1988), 32.

43 Ibid., 45.

44 Mari Carmen Ramírez, "Un-Drawing Boundaries," in *Re-Aligning Vision*, 21.

45 Josef Helfenstein and Jonathan Fineberg, eds., *Drawings of Choice from a New York Collection* (Champaign: Kranner Art Museum, University of Illinois at Urbana-Champaign; Little Rock: Arkansas Arts Center, 2002), 13.

46 Andre considers such a work more a poem than a drawing, but there is a long history of blurred lines between poetry and drawing in the twentieth century. On Concrete poetry, see Mary Ellen Solt, ed., *Concrete Poetry: A World View* (Bloomington: Indiana University Press, 1968).

47 For a recent comprehensive overview of Minimal art, see Ann Goldstein, *A Minimal Future? Art As Object 1958–1968* (Los Angeles: Museum of Contemporary Art; Cambridge, Mass.: The MIT Press, 2004).

48 Christine Mehring, "Carl Andre," in Pamela Lee and Christine Mehring, *Drawing Is Another Kind of Language: Recent American Drawings from a New York Private Collection* (Cambridge, Mass.: Harvard University Art Museums, 1997), 28.

49 See Helfenstein and Fineberg, eds., *Drawings of Choice*, 46–47.

50 Stella, quoted in Mehring, "Frank Stella," in *Another Kind of Language*, 204.

51 Gary Garrels, "Sol LeWitt: An Introduction," in Garrels, ed., *Sol LeWitt: A Retrospective* (New Haven, Conn.: Yale University Press, 2000), 22–35. See also Sol LeWitt, "Paragraphs on Conceptual Art," *Artforum* 5, no. 10 (June 1967): 79–83, reprinted in Garrels, ed., *Sol LeWitt*, 369–71.

52 Rose, *Drawing Now*, 76.

53 For a comprehensive overview of Conceptual art, see Ann Goldstein and Anne Rorimer, *Reconsidering the Object of Art, 1965–1975* (Los Angeles: Museum of Contemporary Art; Cambridge, Mass.: The MIT Press, 1995); for an overview of Conceptual art in Great Britain, see Clive Phillpot, *Live in Your Head: Concept and Experiment in Britain, 1965–75* (London: Whitechapel Art Gallery, 2000).

54 Eun Young Jung, "Agnes Martin," in *Drawings of Choice*, 106.

55 Ibid.

56 Brice Marden, interview with Janie C. Lee, in *Brice Marden Drawings* (New York: Whitney Museum of American Art, 1998), 13.

57 Ibid., 21.

58 Rose, *Drawing Now*, 87.

59 Gibson, "Re-Aligning Vision," 44–71.

60 See Guy Brett et al., *Hélio Oiticica* (Rio de Janeiro: Centro de Arte Hélio Oiticica, 1997).

61 Ibid., 27. See also Luciano Figueiredo, ed., *Hélio Oiticica: cor, imagem, poética*, trans. Renato Rezende (Rio de Janeiro: Centro de Arte Hélio Oiticica, 2003).

62 Ferrari, quoted in John Wineland, "Léon Ferrari," in *Re-Aligning Vision*, 146. For more about Ferrari and the context in which he was working, see also Katzenstein, ed., *Listen, Here, Now!*

63 Rose, "Joseph Beuys and the Language of Drawing," in *Thinking Is Form*, 91.

64 Ibid., 110.

65 Beuys, quoted in Wilfried Wiegand et al., *Joseph Beuys: In Memoriam Joseph Beuys. Obituaries, Essays, Speeches*, trans. Timothy Nevill (Bonn: Inter Nationes, 1986), 34.

66 John Elderfield, *The Modern Drawing: One Hundred Works on Paper from The Museum of Modern Art*, (New York: The Museum of Modern Art, 1983), 212.

PLATES

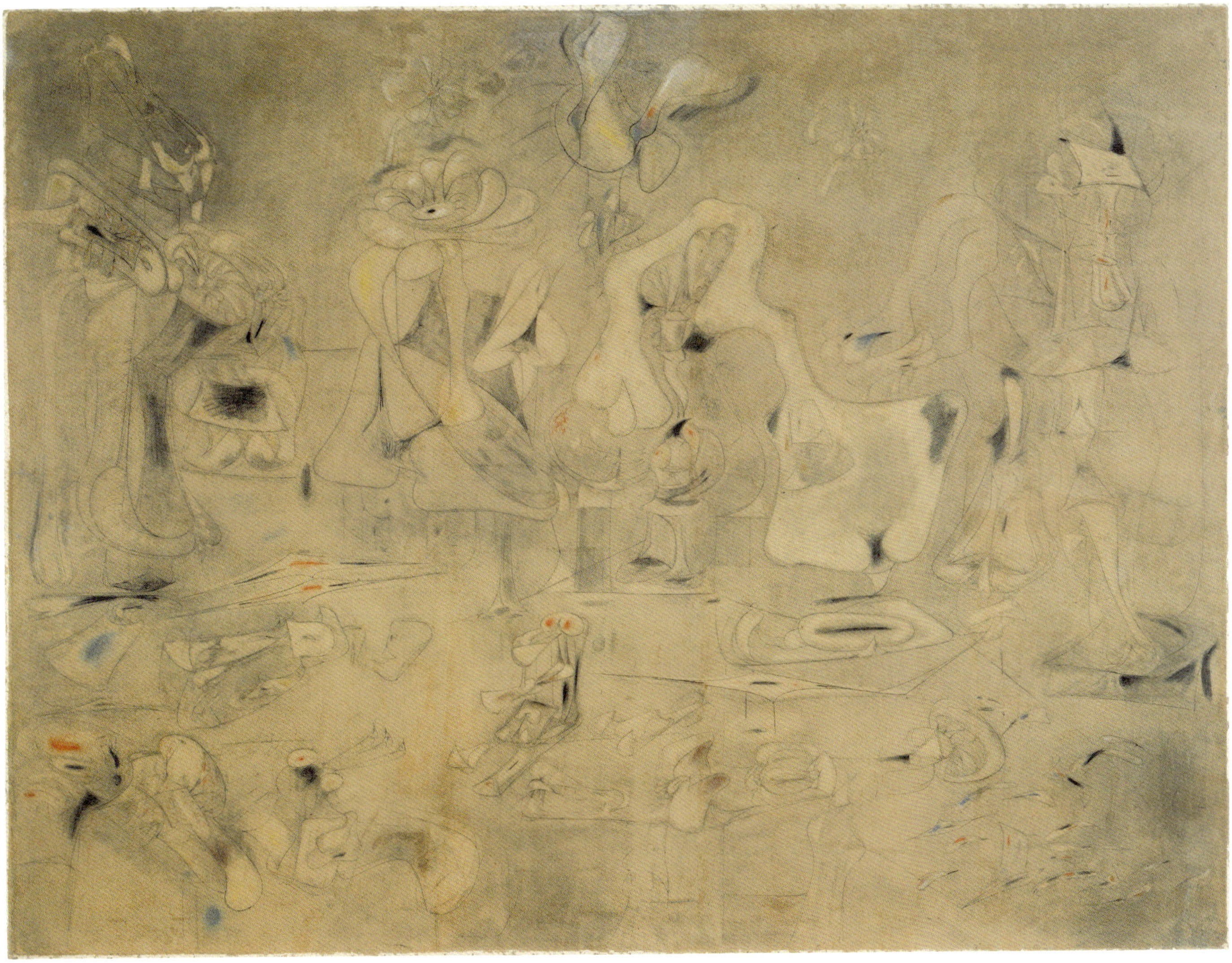

1 **ARSHILE GORKY**

Summation, (1947)

Pencil, pastel, charcoal, and gouache on paper mounted on composition board, 6' 7 5⁄8" x 8' 5 3⁄4" (202.1 x 258.2 cm)

Nina and Gordon Bunshaft Fund, 1969

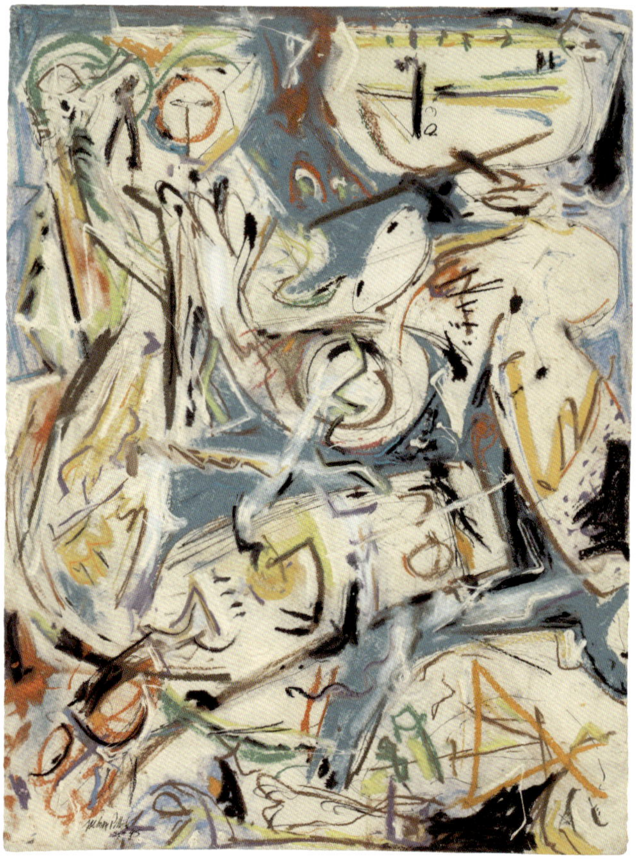

2 **JACKSON POLLOCK**
Untitled, 1945
Pastel, gouache, and ink on paper, 30 5/8 x 22 3/8" (77.7 x 56.9 cm)
Blanchette Hooker Rockefeller Fund, 1958

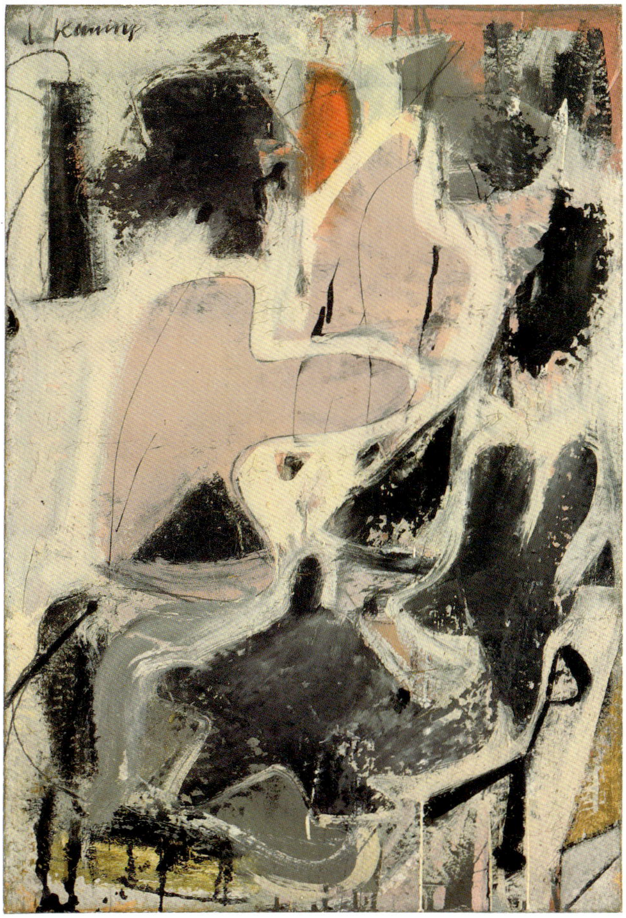

3 **WILLEM DE KOONING**

Valentine. (1947)

Oil and enamel on paper on board, 36 3/8 x 24 1/4" (92.2 x 61.5 cm)

Gift of Mr. and Mrs. Gifford Phillips, 1969

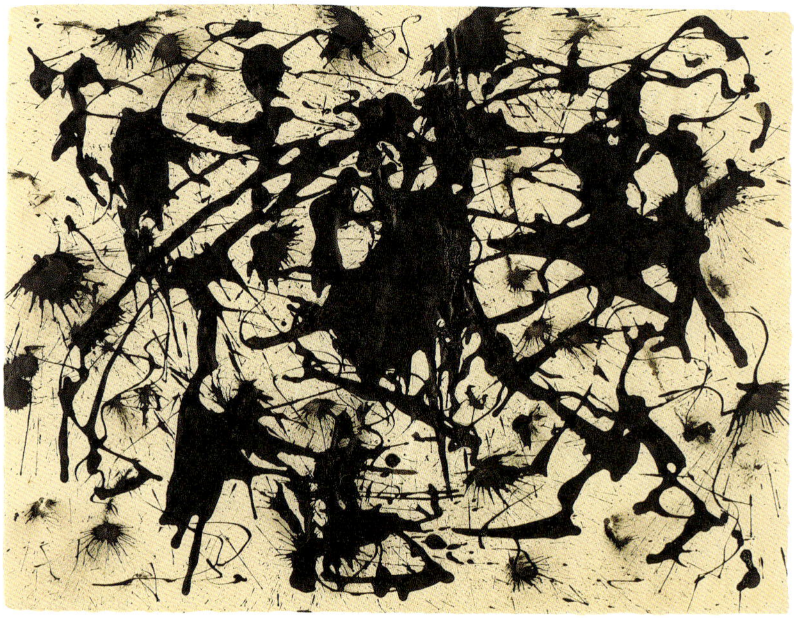

4 **JACKSON POLLOCK**
Untitled, (c. 1950)
Ink on paper, 17 1/2 x 22 1/4" (44.5 x 56.6 cm)
Gift of Jo Carole and Ronald S. Lauder in honor of Eliza Parkinson Cobb, 1982

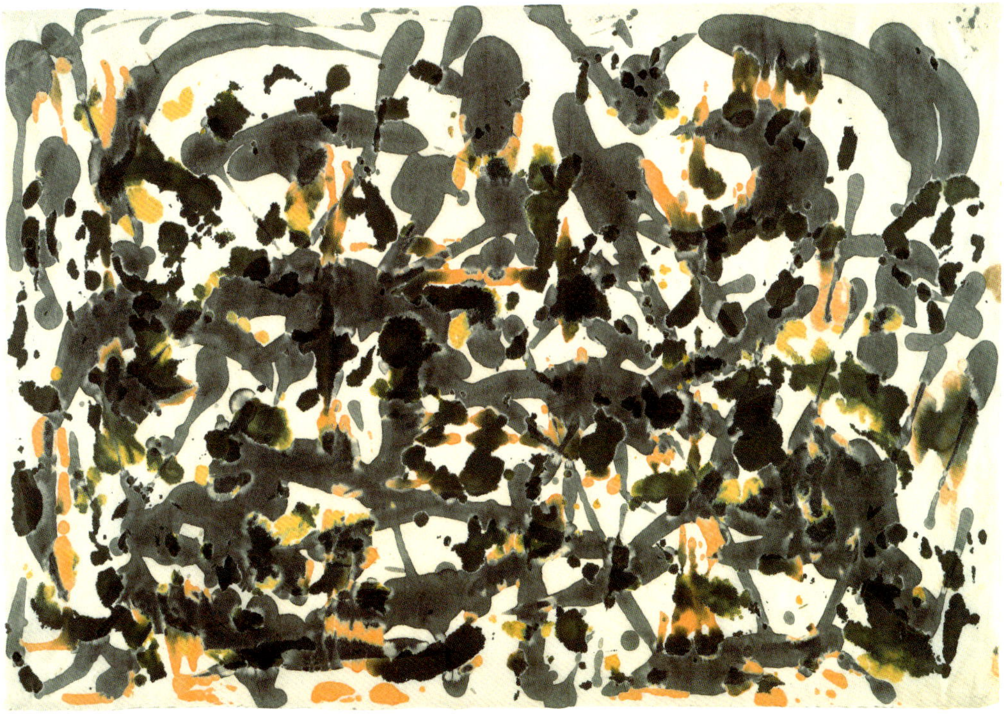

5 **JACKSON POLLOCK**

Untitled, (c. 1951)

Black and colored ink on Japanese paper, 24 3/8 x 34 3/8" (62.1 x 87.3 cm)

The Joan and Lester Avnet Collection, 1978

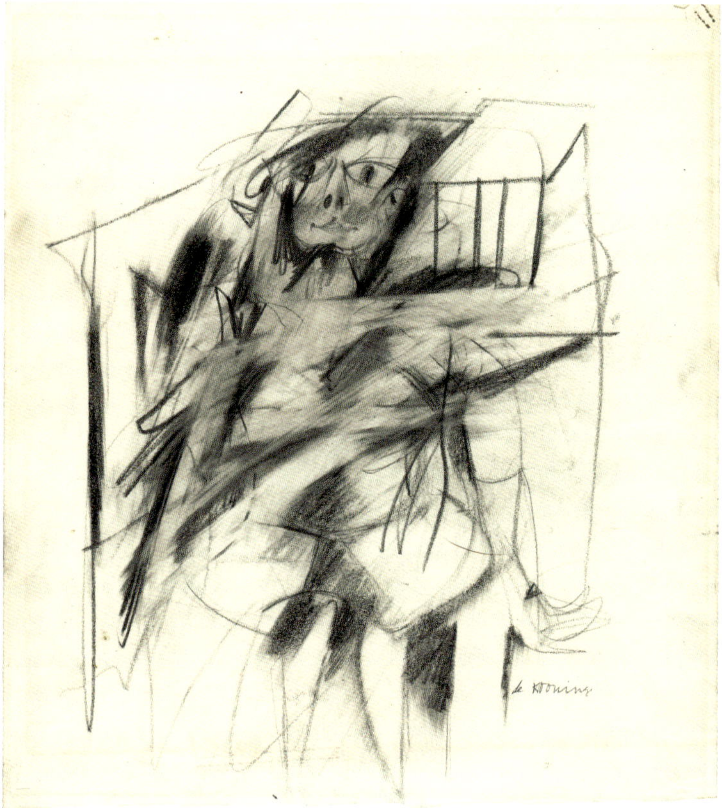

6 **WILLEM DE KOONING**
Seated Woman. (1953–54)
Pencil on paper, 14 x 12" (35.6 x 30.5 cm)
Estate of Stella Waitzkin given in loving memory of Bill Waitzkin and promised gift of an anonymous donor in celebration of The Museum of Modern Art's 75th anniversary, 2004

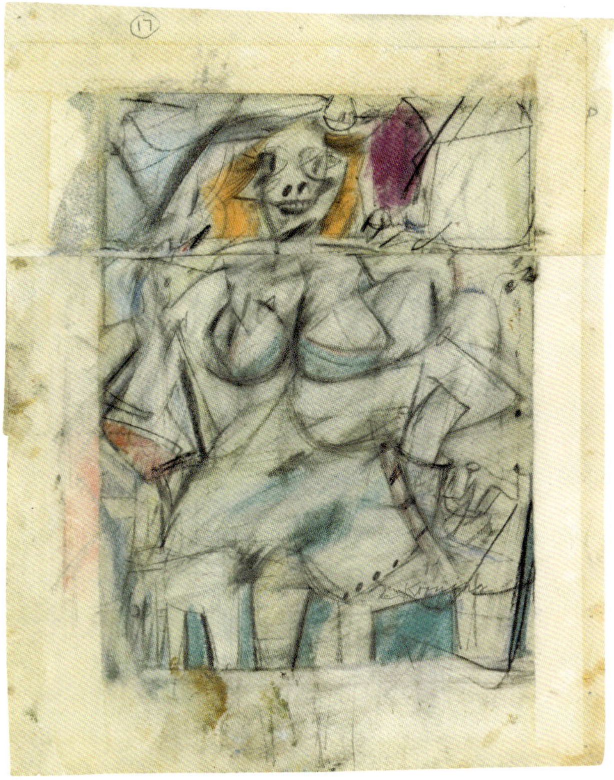

7 **WILLEM DE KOONING**
Seated Woman. (1952)
Pencil, pastel, and oil on two sheets of paper,
12 1/8 x 9 1/2" (30.8 x 24.2 cm)
The Lauder Foundation Fund, 1975

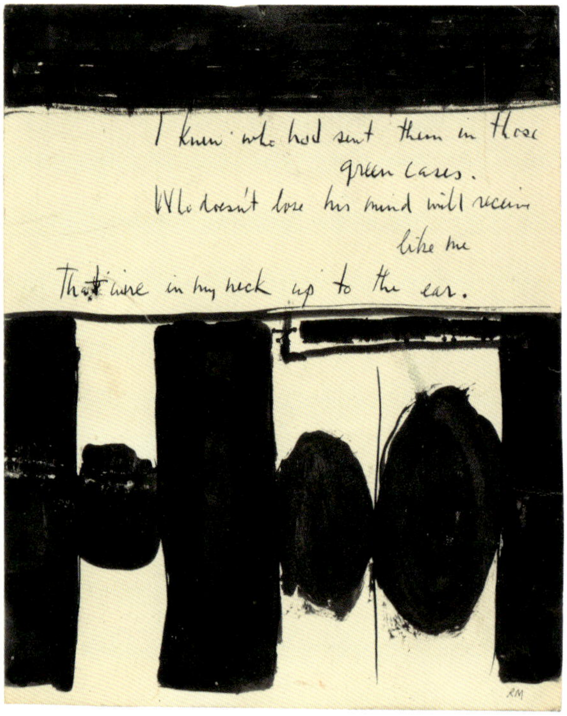

8 **ROBERT MOTHERWELL**
Elegy to the Spanish Republic No. 1, (1948)
Ink on paper, 10 3/4 x 8 1/2" (27.3 x 21.8 cm)
Gift of the artist, 1987

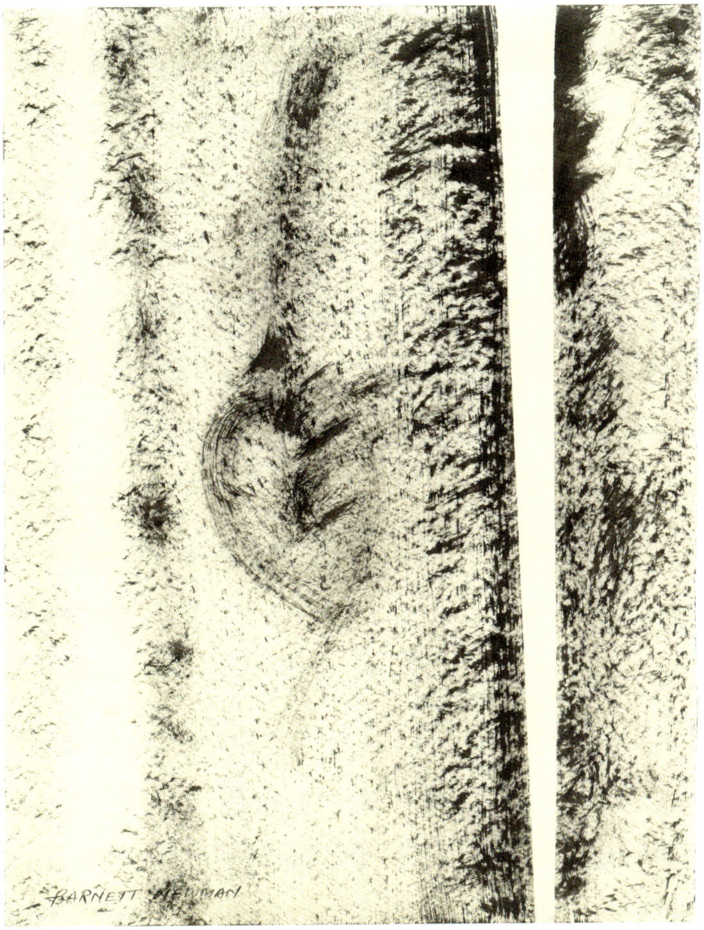

9 **BARNETT NEWMAN**
Untitled. (1946)
Ink on paper, 24 x 18" (61 x 45.8 cm)
Gift of the Committee on Drawings in honor of Richard E. Oldenburg, 1994

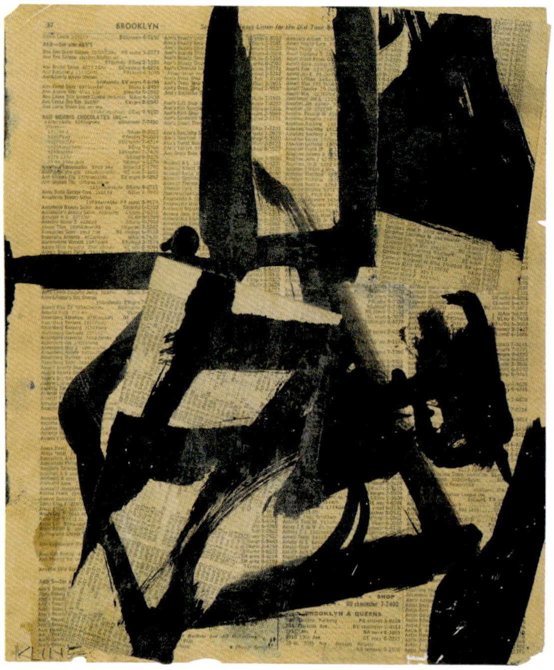

10 **FRANZ KLINE**
Untitled II. (c. 1952)
Ink and oil on cut-and-pasted telephone book pages
on paper on board, 11 x 9" (28.1 x 23 cm)
Purchase, 1983

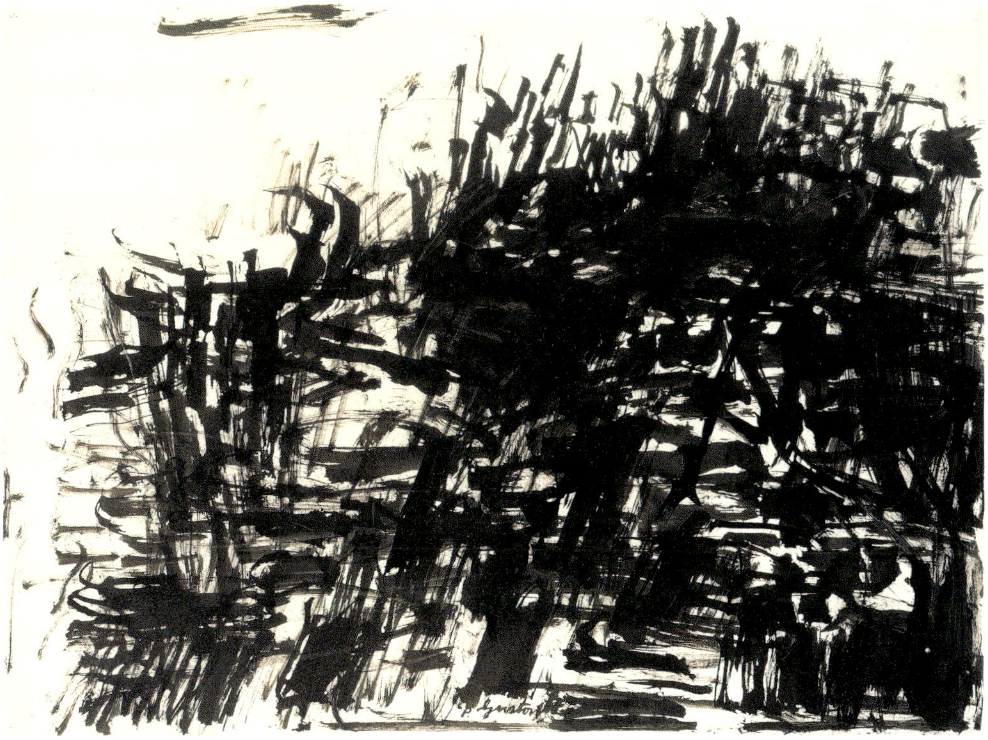

11 **PHILIP GUSTON**
Drawing, 1953
Ink on paper, 17 ¾ x 23 ¾" (45.1 x 60.3 cm)
Promised gift of an anonymous donor in celebration of
The Museum of Modern Art's 75th anniversary, 2004

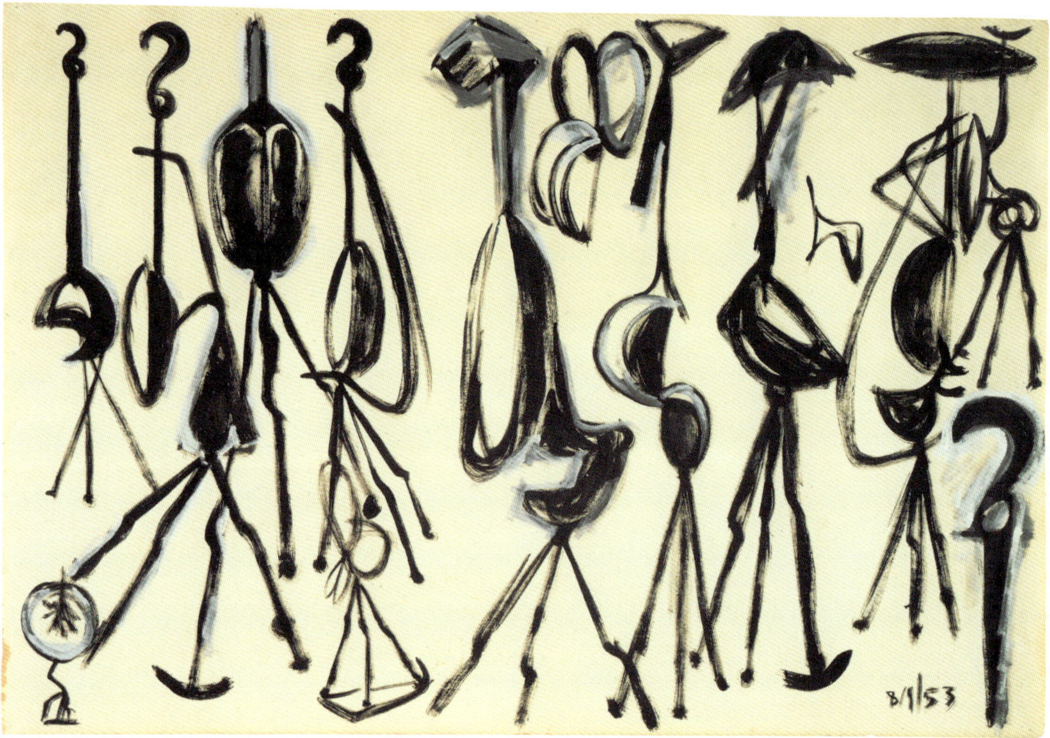

12 **DAVID SMITH**
Untitled (Tank Totems), 1953
Ink and gouache on paper, 29 ¾ x 42 ⅜" (75.6 x 107.6 cm)
Gift of Alexis Gregory, 1976

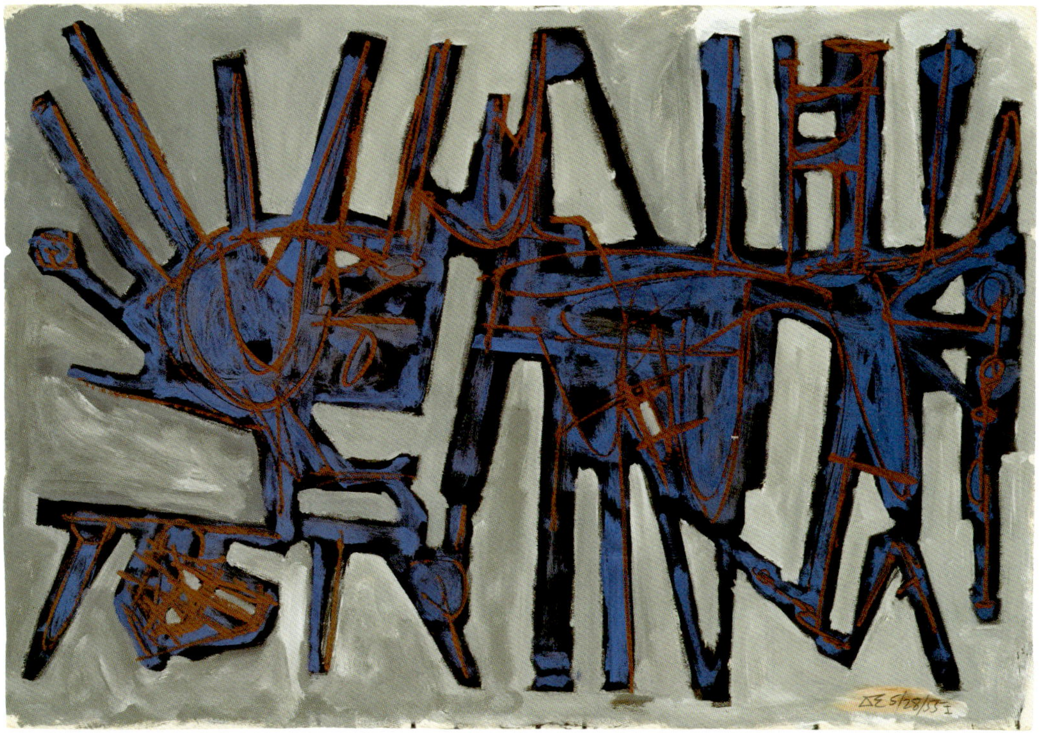

13 **DAVID SMITH**
Untitled 5/28/55, 1955
Oil crayon on paper, 29 ¾ x 42 ⅜" (75.6 x 107.6 cm)
Gift of Barbara G. Pine in memory of Morris Goldman, 1989

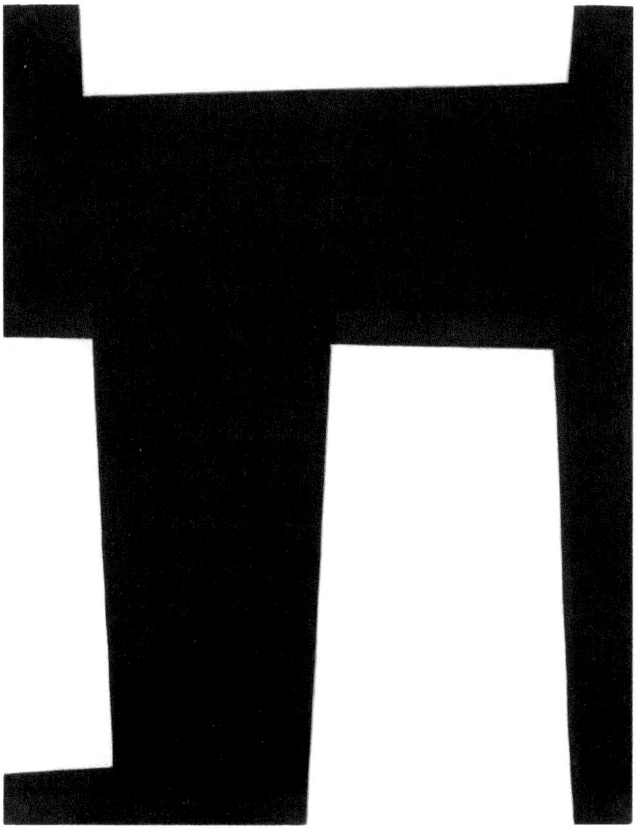

14 **MYRON STOUT**
Untitled, (1950)
Charcoal and pastel on paper, 25 x 19" (63.4 x 48.2 cm)
The Riklis Collection of McCrory Corporation, 1983

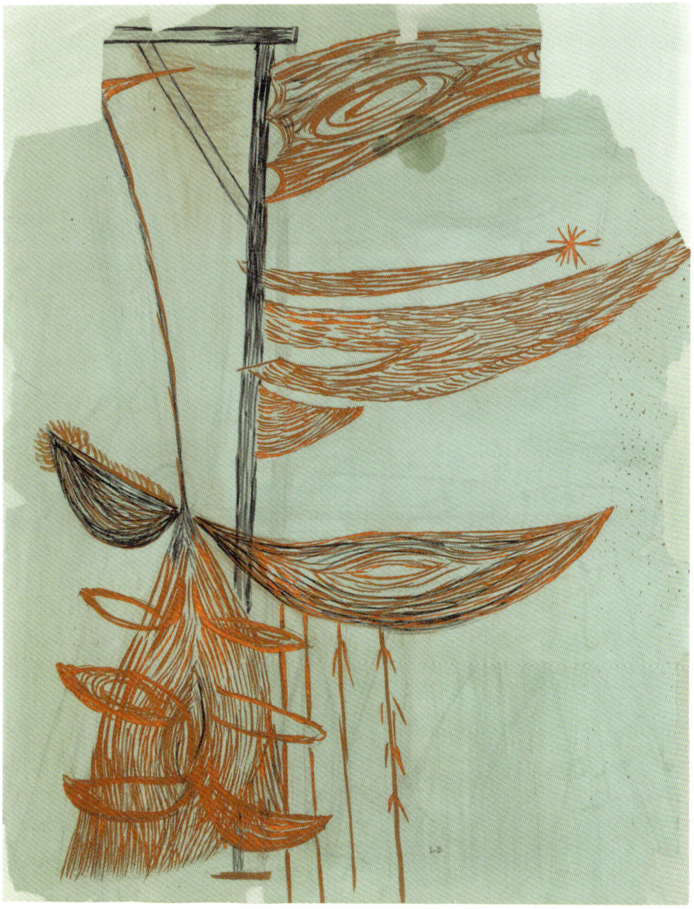

15 **LOUISE BOURGEOIS**
Untitled, (1950)
Gouache, pencil, and colored pencil on blue-green paper,
28 x 21 ⅜" (71.1 x 54.3 cm)
Purchase through the Vincent d'Aquila and Harry Soviak Bequest Fund, 1995

16 **TONY SMITH**
Untitled, (1953–55)
Charcoal on brown paper, 31 1/2 x 39 1/8" (80 x 99.4 cm)
Purchased with funds given by Sarah-Ann and Werner H. Kramarsky, 1996

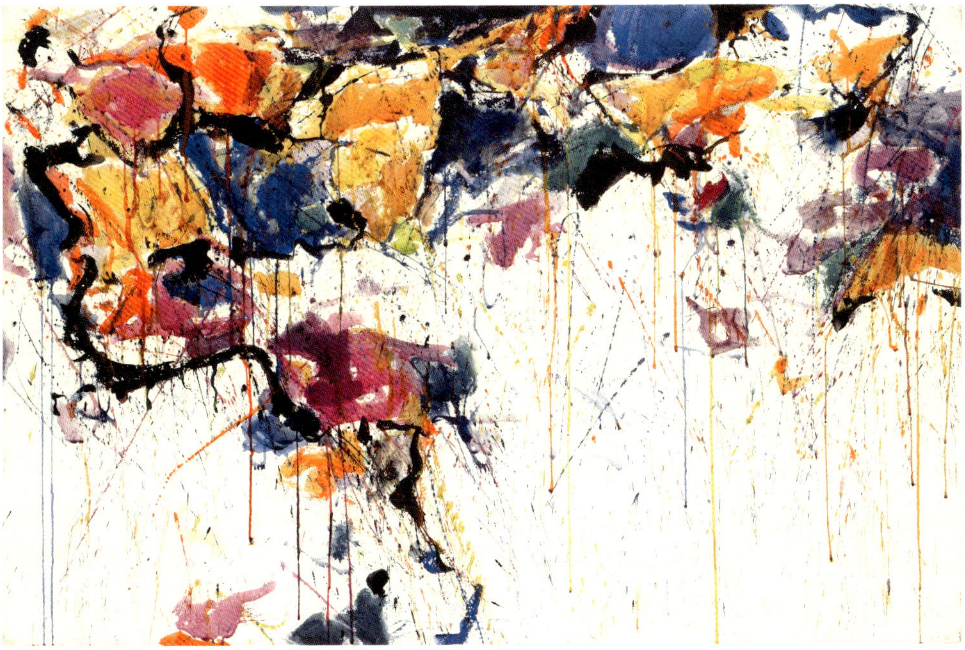

17 **SAM FRANCIS**
Untitled, (1958)
Watercolor on paper, 27 x 40 1/8" (68.6 x 101.9 cm)
Gift of Udo M. Reinach Estate, 1960

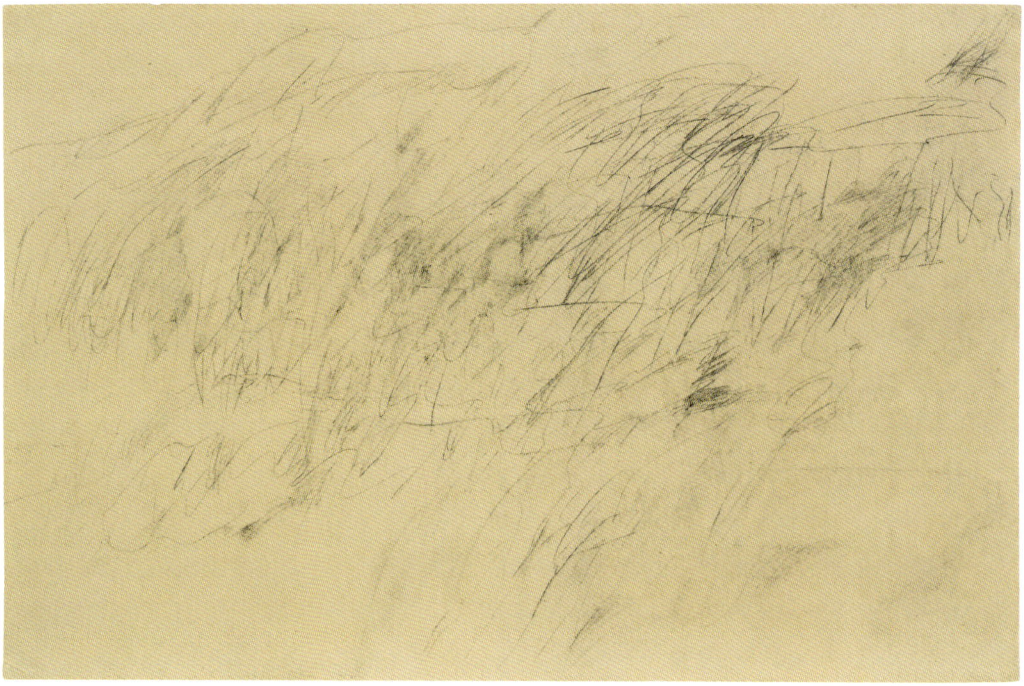

18 **CY TWOMBLY**
Untitled, (1955)
Pencil on paper, 24 3/8 x 36 1/8" (62 x 91.7 cm)
Gift of Jo Carole and Ronald S. Lauder, 1992

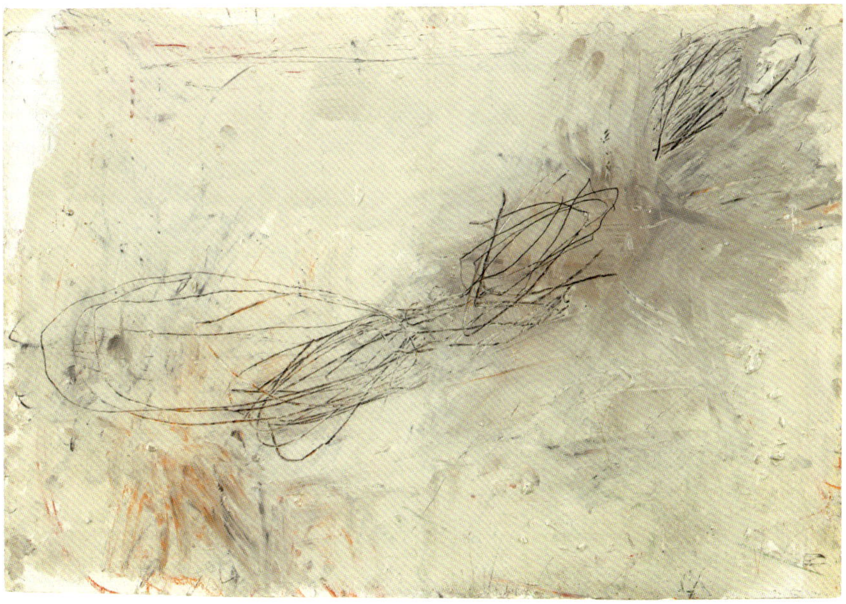

19 **CY TWOMBLY**
Untitled, 1957
Oil, pencil, and crayon on gessoed board on
paper-faced canvas, 19 5/8 x 27 5/8" (49.8 x 70.2 cm)
Gift of Carol O. Selle, the Denise and Andrew Saul Fund,
and Abby Aldrich Rockefeller (by exchange), 1984

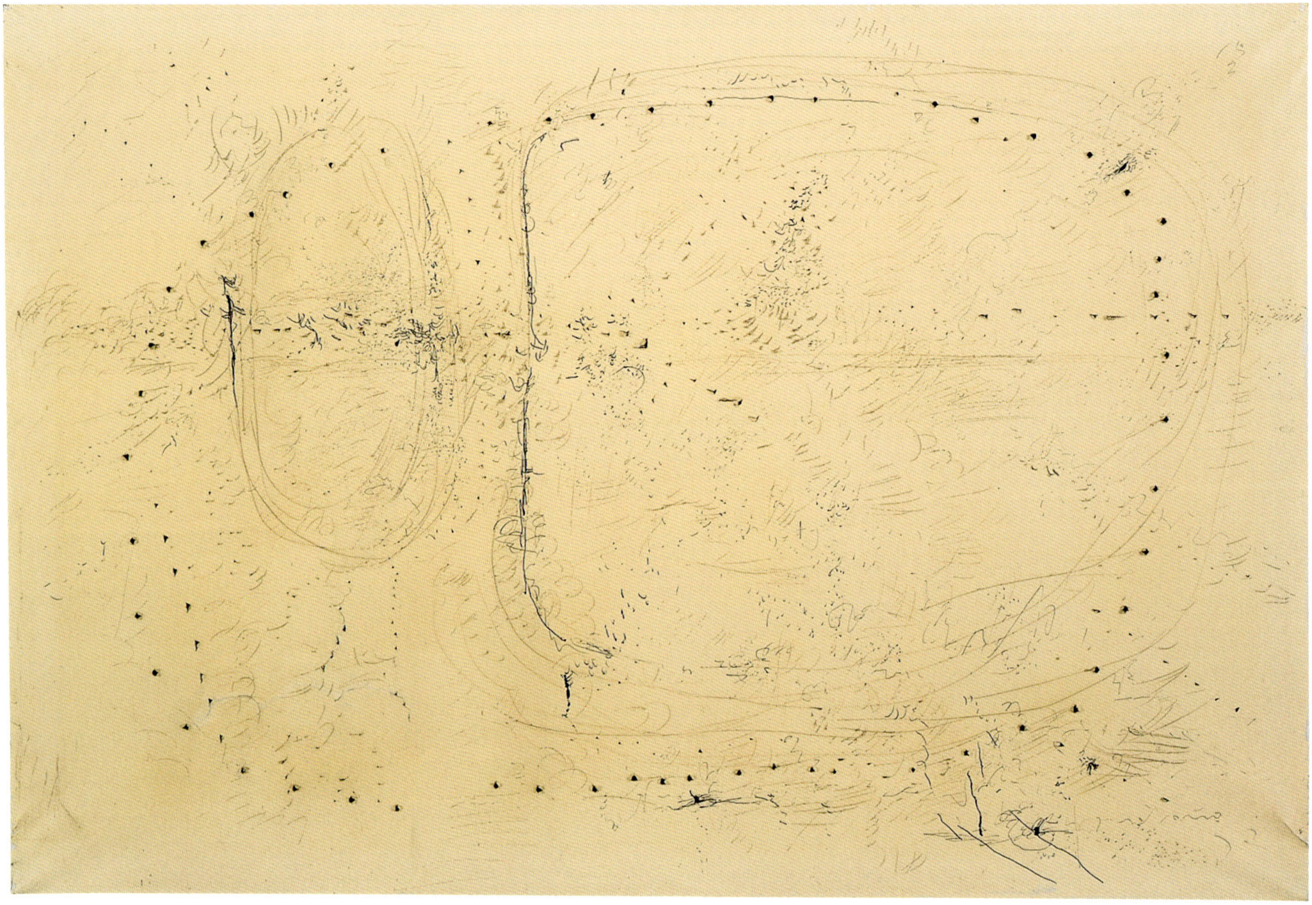

20 **LUCIO FONTANA**
Spatial Concept (Concetto spaziale), 1957
Ink and pencil on paper on canvas, with punctures and scrapes, 55" x 7' 6 7/8" (139.7 x 200.4 cm)
Gift of Morton G. Neumann, 1976

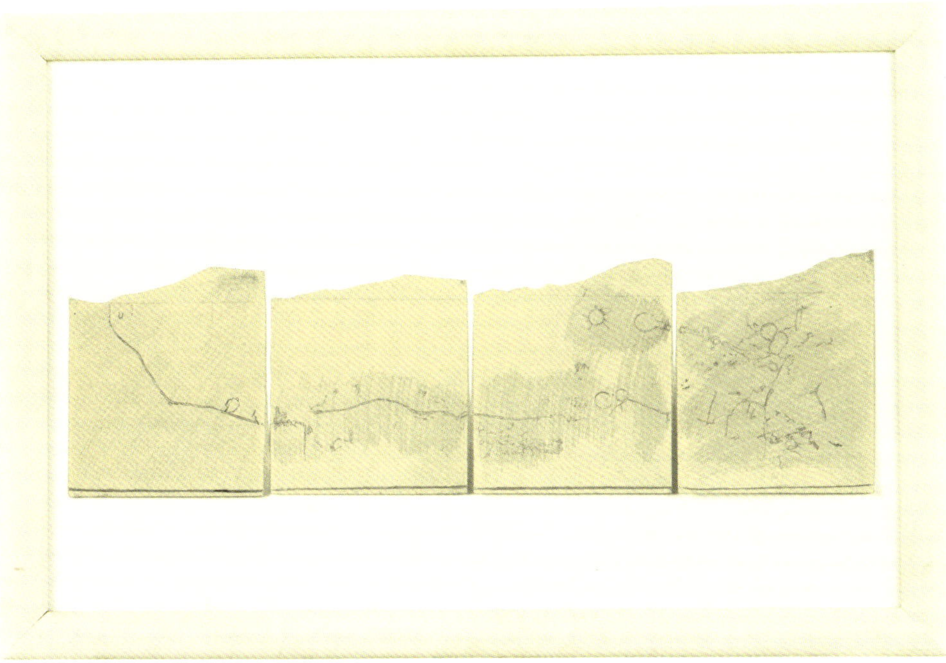

21 **JOSEPH BEUYS**
Untitled, (1947) and (1970s)
Pencil on four sheets of paper on painted wood panel,
with frame, 31 1/2 x 45 1/2" (80 x 115.5 cm)
Gift of Agnes Gund, and Jo Carole and Ronald S. Lauder, 1990

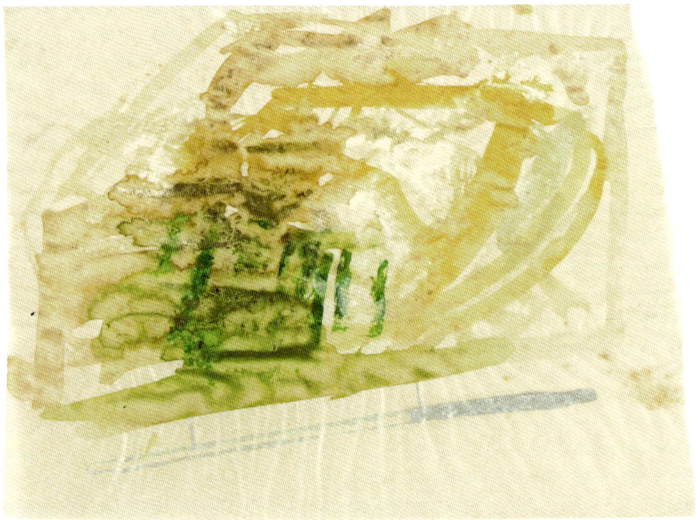

22 **JOSEPH BEUYS**
Untitled (Skull on Ur-Sled), 1957
Watercolor, dirt, and metallic paint on tracing paper,
9⅝ x 12⅞" (24.5 x 32.8 cm)
Gift of Barbara G. Pine and purchase, 1985

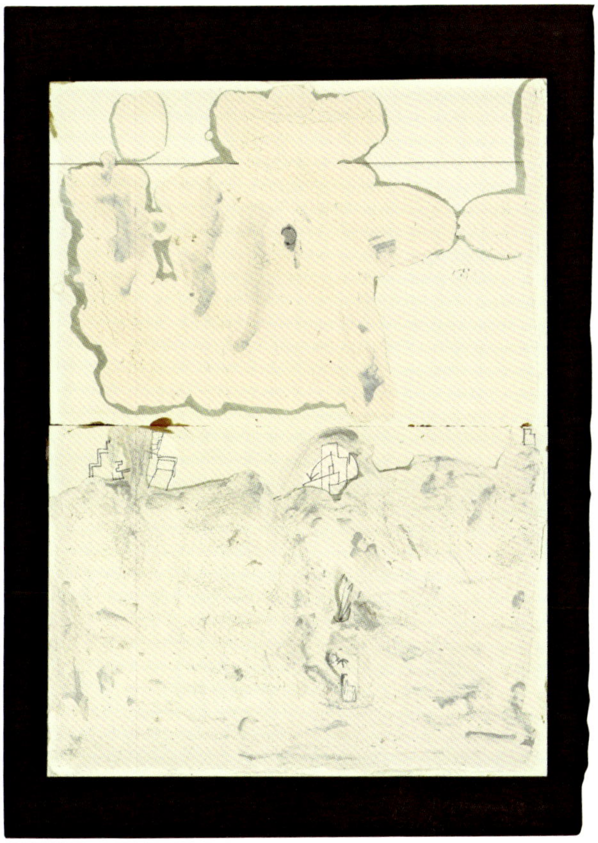

23 **JOSEPH BEUYS**

Dynamis 3, Dynamis, 1960

Oil, pencil, and ink on two sheets of paper on black paper,

16 3/8 x 11 5/8" (41.5 x 29.5 cm)

Purchase, 1983

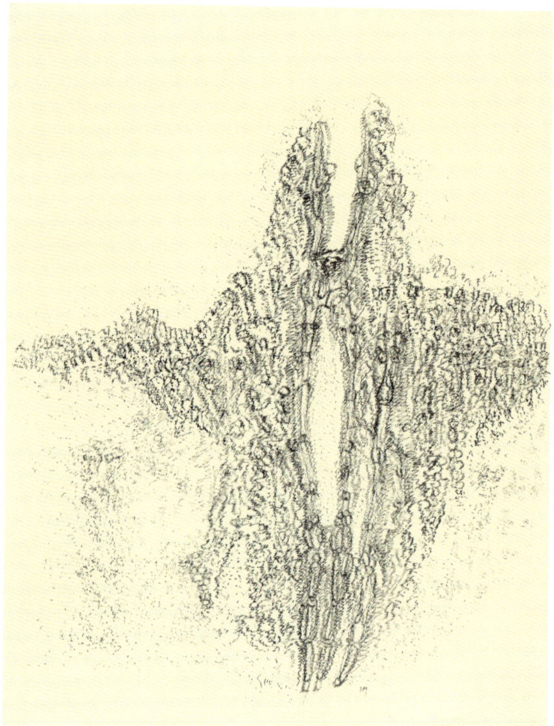

24 **HENRI MICHAUX**
Mescaline Drawing (Mescaline dessin). (1960)
Ink on paper, 12 5/8 x 9 1/2" (32 x 23.9 cm)
Gift of Philip Johnson, 1969

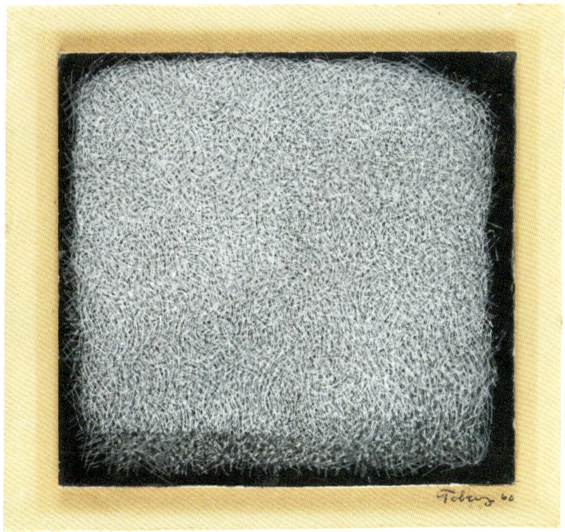

25 **MARK TOBEY**
Space Wall, 1960
Gouache on board mounted on board,
5 1/2 x 5 3/4" (14 x 14.5 cm)
Gift of Mrs. Henry Ives Cobb, 1985

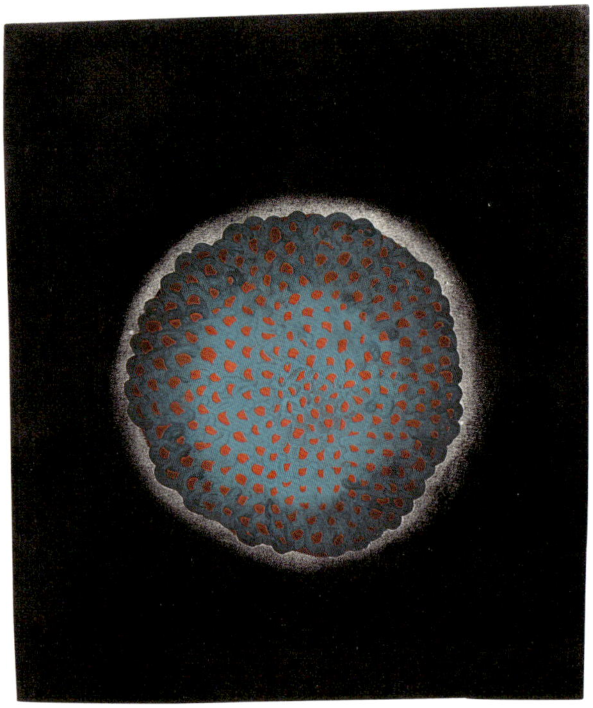

26 **YAYOI KUSAMA**
Flower, 1953 and (1963)
Ink, gouache, and pastel on paper, 15 ¾ x 13 ¼" (40.1 x 33.8 cm)
Purchased with funds given by Sheldon H. Solow, 1996

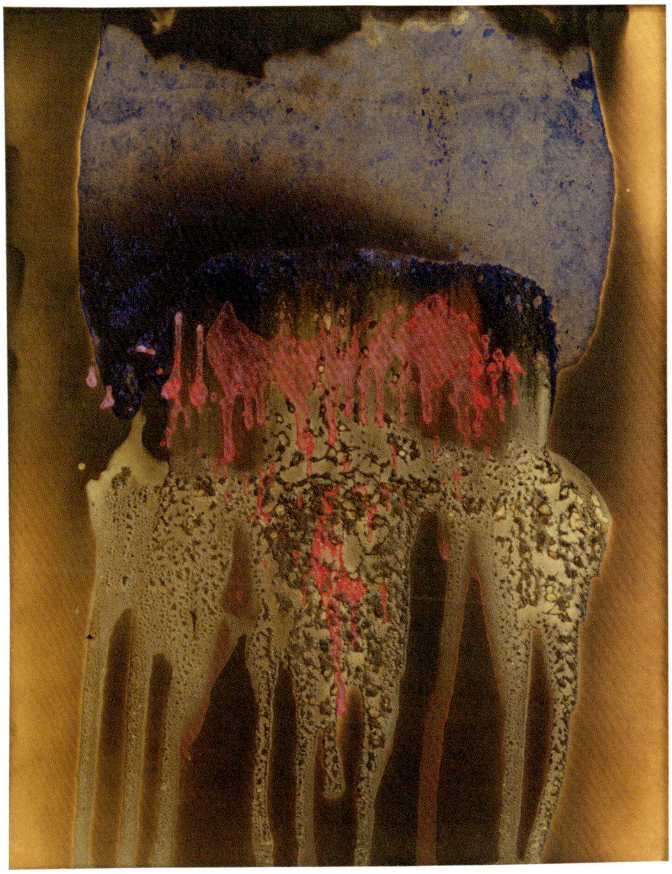

27 **YVES KLEIN**
Untitled (fire-color painting). (1962)
Dry pigment in synthetic resin with gold paint on asbestos-coated paper on board, partially charred, 24 ½ x 19" (62.1 x 48.3 cm)
Gift of the Scaler Foundation and purchase, 1984

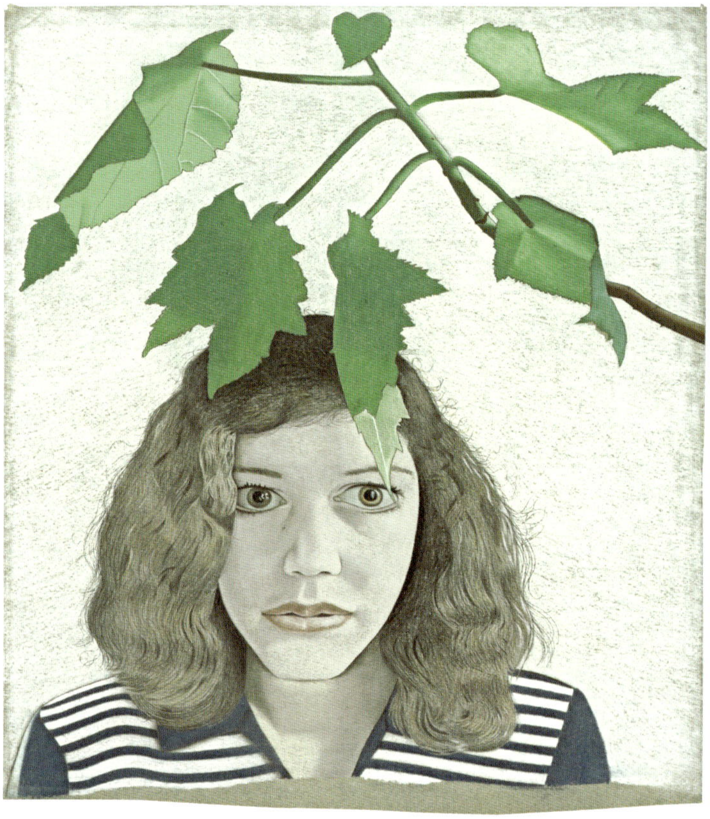

28 **LUCIAN FREUD**
Girl with Leaves. (1948)
Pastel on gray paper, 18 7/8 x 16 1/2" (47.9 x 41.9 cm)
Purchase, 1948

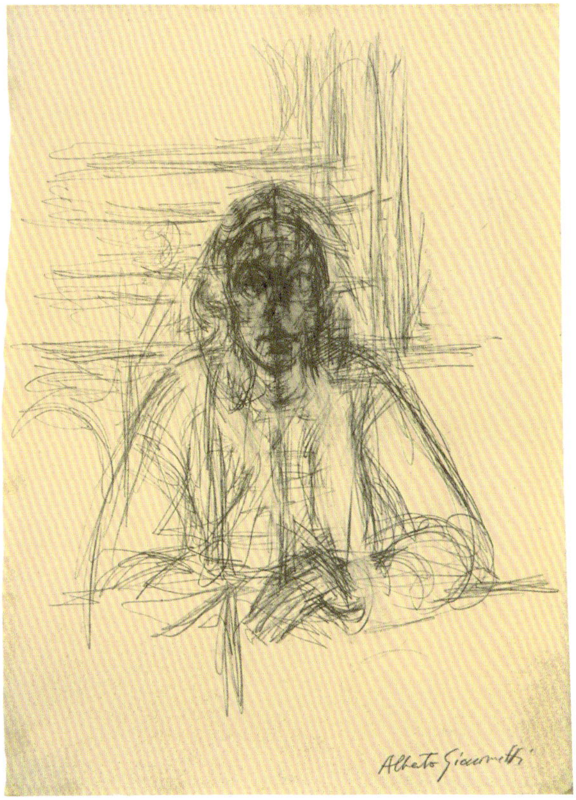

29 **ALBERTO GIACOMETTI**
Annette, (1954)
Pencil on paper, 16 5/8 x 11 3/4" (42 x 29.8 cm)
The Sidney and Harriet Janis Collection, 1967

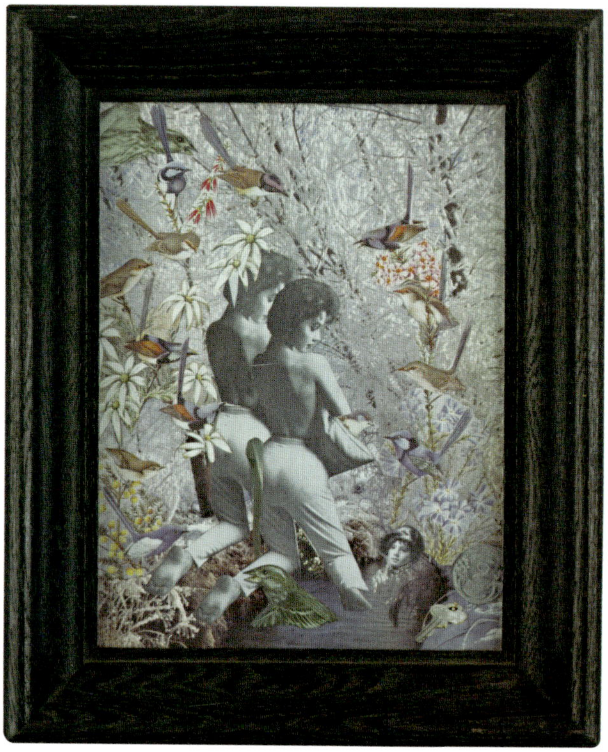

30 **JOSEPH CORNELL**
Allegory of Innocence. (1956)
Cut-and-pasted printed paper on paper mounted on board
in wood frame with antique glass, 15 1/4 x 12 1/4 x 2 1/4" (38.5 x 31 x 5.8 cm)
Purchase, 1980

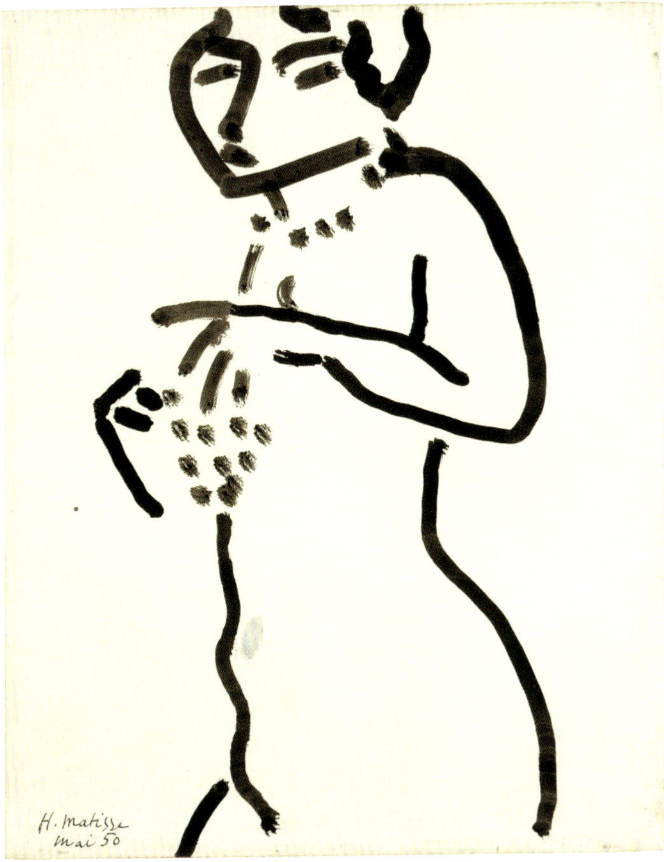

31 **HENRI MATISSE**
The Necklace (Le collier), May 1950
Ink on paper, $20\frac{7}{8} \times 16\frac{1}{8}$" (52.8 x 40.7 cm)
The Joan and Lester Avnet Collection, 1978

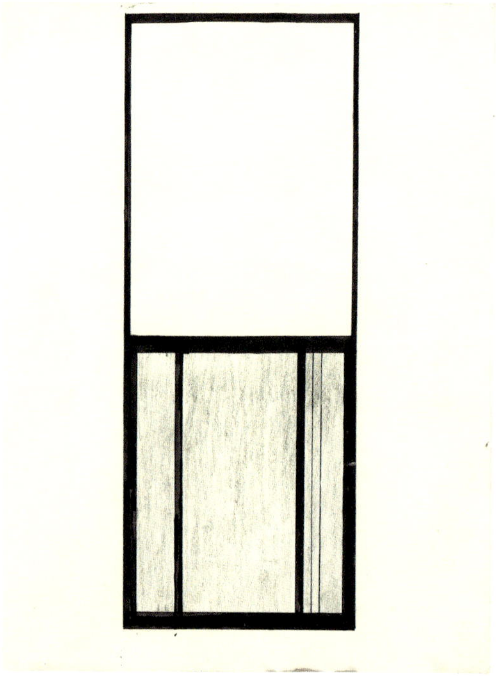

32 **ELLSWORTH KELLY**
Study for *Window, Museum of Modern Art, Paris*. (1949)
Ink and pencil on paper, 16 ½ x 12" (41.9 x 30.8 cm)
Gift of Sarah-Ann and Werner H. Kramarsky, 1997

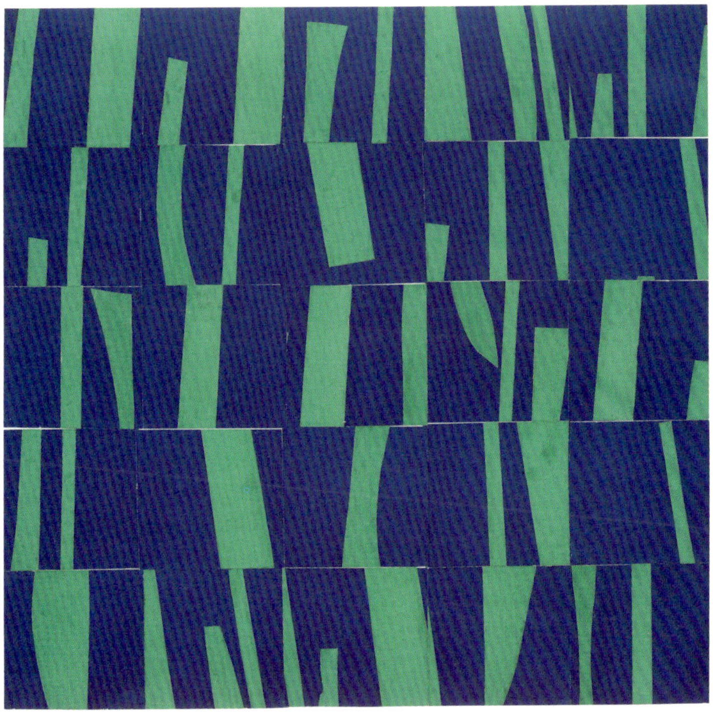

33 **ELLSWORTH KELLY**
Study for *Meschers*, (1951)
Cut-and-pasted printed paper, 19 ½ x 19 ½" (49.5 x 49.5 cm)
Gift of the artist, 1997

34 **ELLSWORTH KELLY**
Study for *Black Ripe*, (1954)
Ink and pencil on paper, 20 x 19 1/4" (52.4 x 48.9 cm)
Purchased with funds given by Mr. and Mrs. Edmond J. Safra
in honor of Mr. and Mrs. Henry R. Kravis, 1998

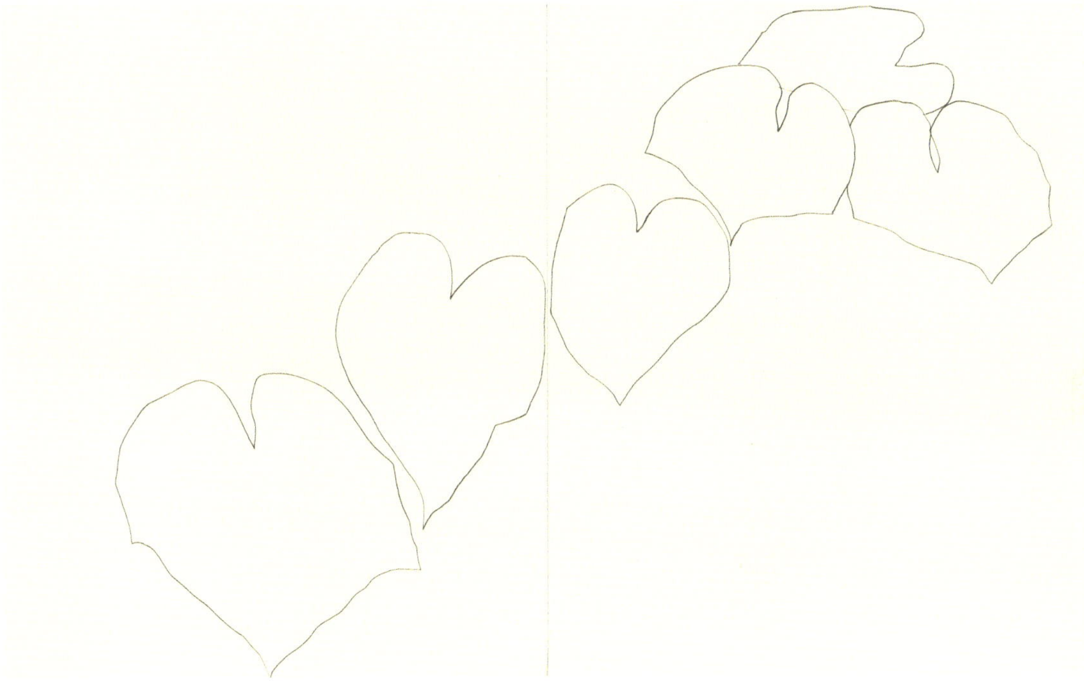

35 **ELLSWORTH KELLY**
Wild Grape, (1960)
Pencil on two sheets of paper, 28 1/2 x 45" (72.4 x 114.3 cm)
Gift of Kathy and Richard S. Fuld, Jr. in honor of
Ellsworth Kelly's 80th birthday, 2003

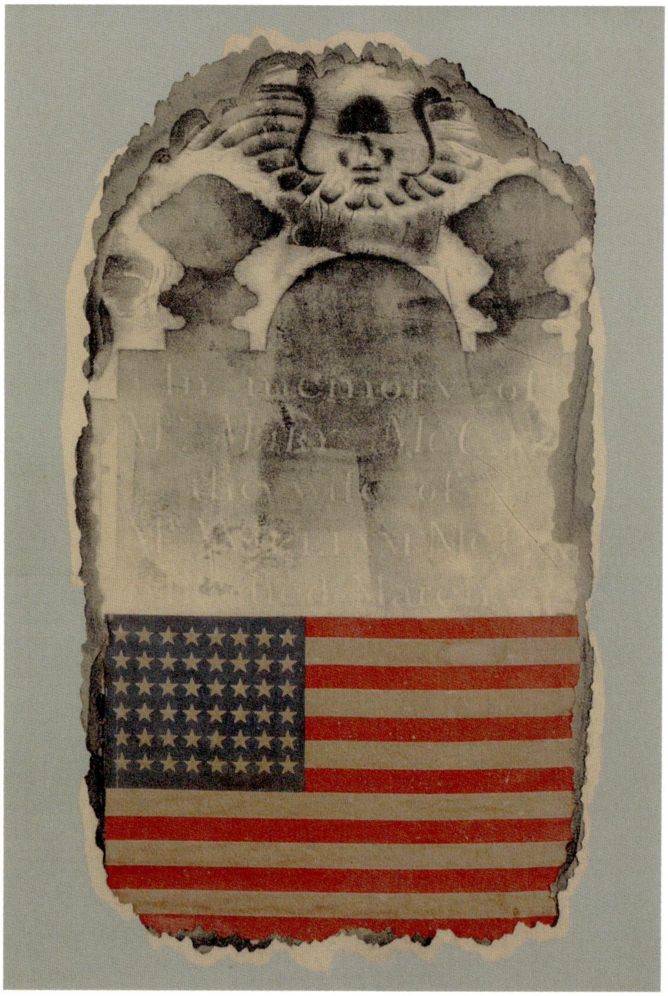

36 **SARI DIENES**
Tomb. (1950)
Crayon on paper, painted textile, torn paper with ink, and torn board, 36 x 24" (91.4 x 61 cm)
Gift of the Sari Dienes Foundation, Inc., 1999

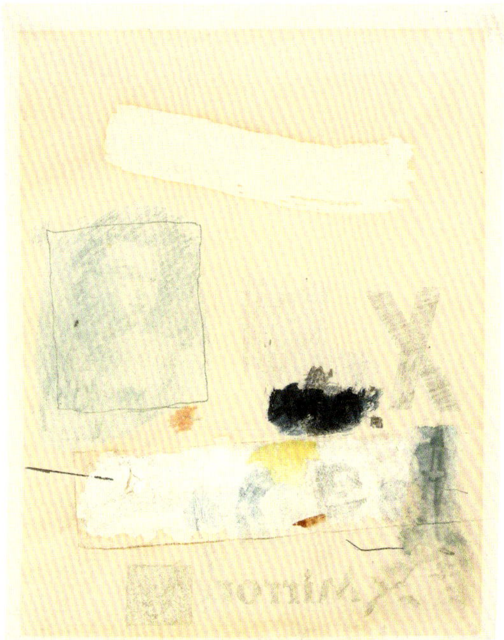

37 **ROBERT RAUSCHENBERG**
Untitled (Mirror). (1952)
Oil, solvent transfer, watercolor, crayon, pencil, and cut-and-pasted paper on paper, 10 ½ x 8 ½" (26.7 x 21.6 cm)
Fractional and promised gift of Sarah-Ann and Werner H. Kramarsky, 2004

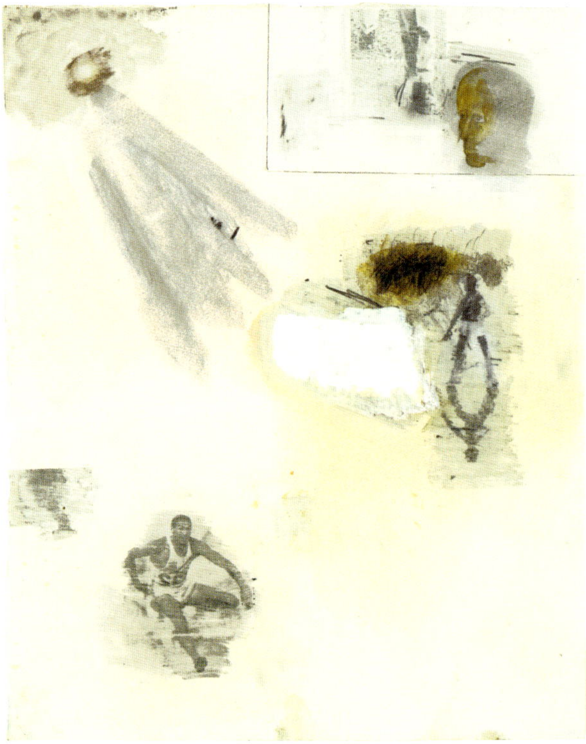

38 **ROBERT RAUSCHENBERG**
Canto XV: Circle Seven, Round 3, The Violent Against Nature
from the series Thirty-Four Illustrations for Dante's Inferno. (1959–60)
Transfer drawing, gouache, watercolor, and pencil on paper,
14 1/2 x 11 1/2" (36.8 x 29.2 cm)
Given anonymously, 1963

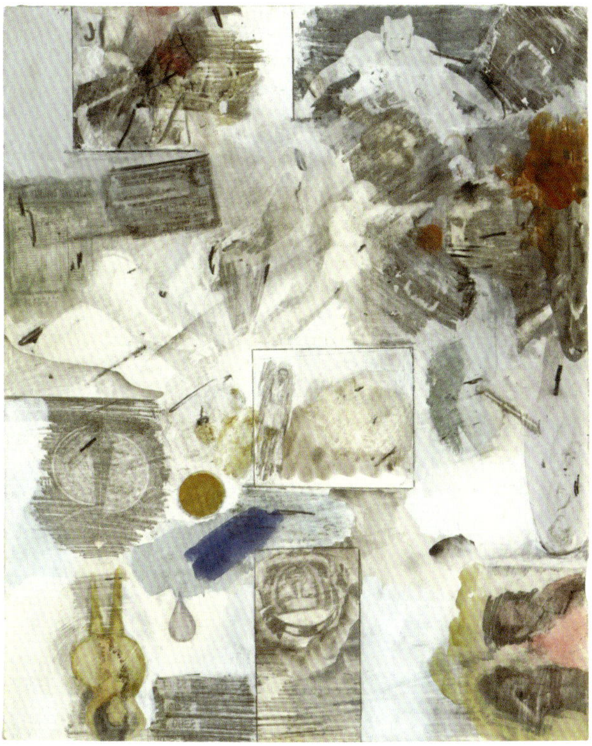

39 **ROBERT RAUSCHENBERG**
Canto XXX: Circle Eight, Bolgia 10, The Falsifiers: The Evil Impersonators, Counterfeiters, and False Witnesses from the series Thirty-Four Illustrations for Dante's Inferno. (1959–60)
Transfer drawing, watercolor, gouache, and pencil on paper,
14 1/2 x 11 1/2" (36.8 x 29.3 cm)
Given anonymously, 1963

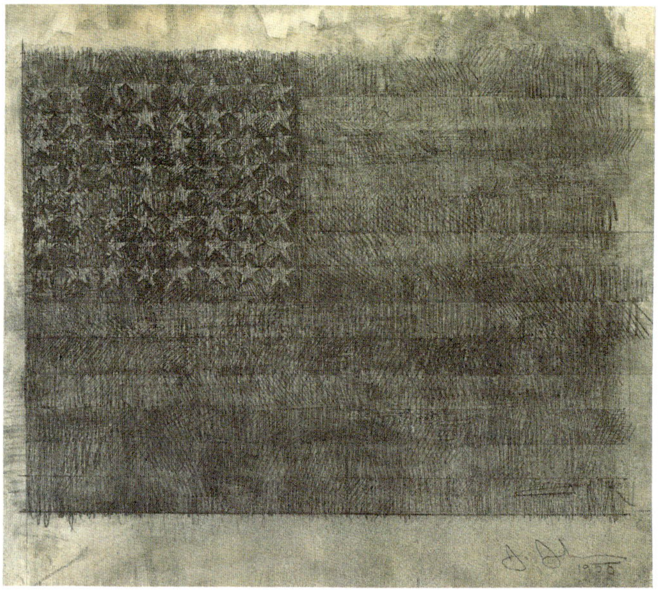

40 **JASPER JOHNS**

Flag. 1955

Graphite and graphite wash on prepared paper,

8 1/2 x 10 1/8" (21.6 x 25.7 cm)

Gift of Edgar Kaufmann, Jr. (by exchange) and purchase, 2004

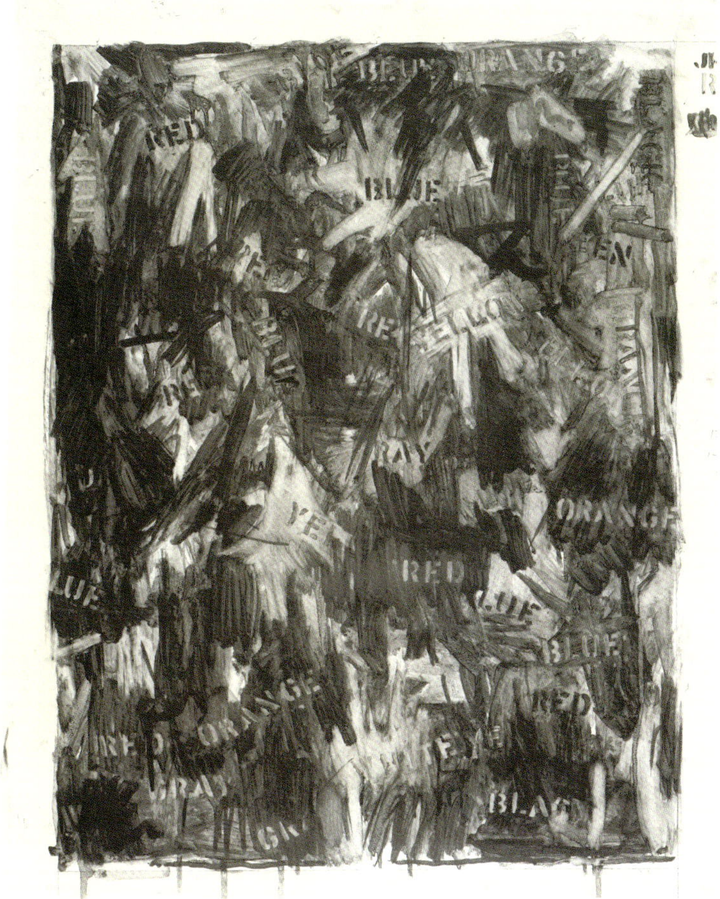

41 **JASPER JOHNS**
Jubilee. (1960)
Graphite wash on paper, 31 ⅛ x 25" (79 x 63.5 cm)
The Joan and Lester Avnet Collection, 1978

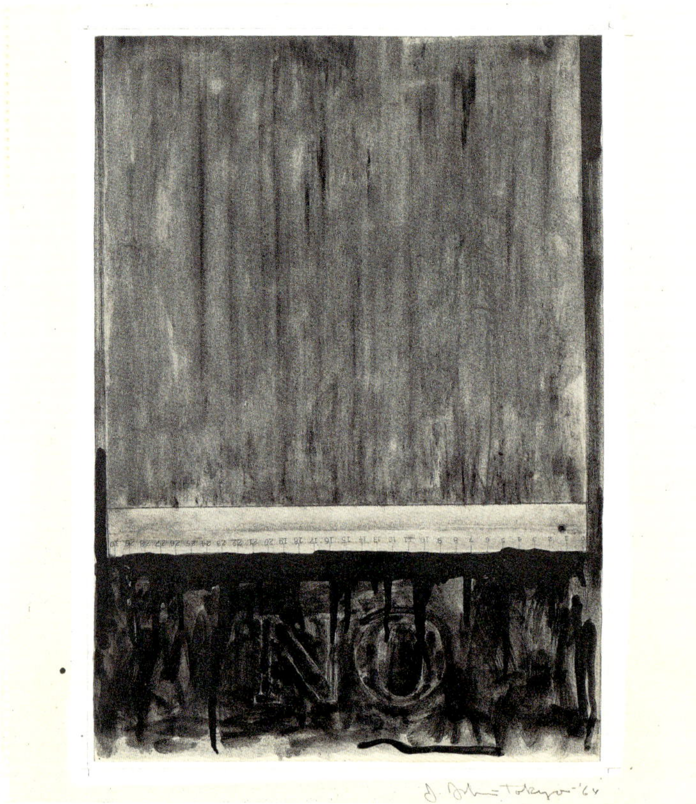

42 **JASPER JOHNS**

No. 1964

Graphite, charcoal, and tempera on paper,

$20\frac{1}{4} \times 17\frac{1}{2}$" (51.4 x 44.5 cm)

Fractional and promised gift of

Sarah-Ann and Werner H. Kramarsky, 2004

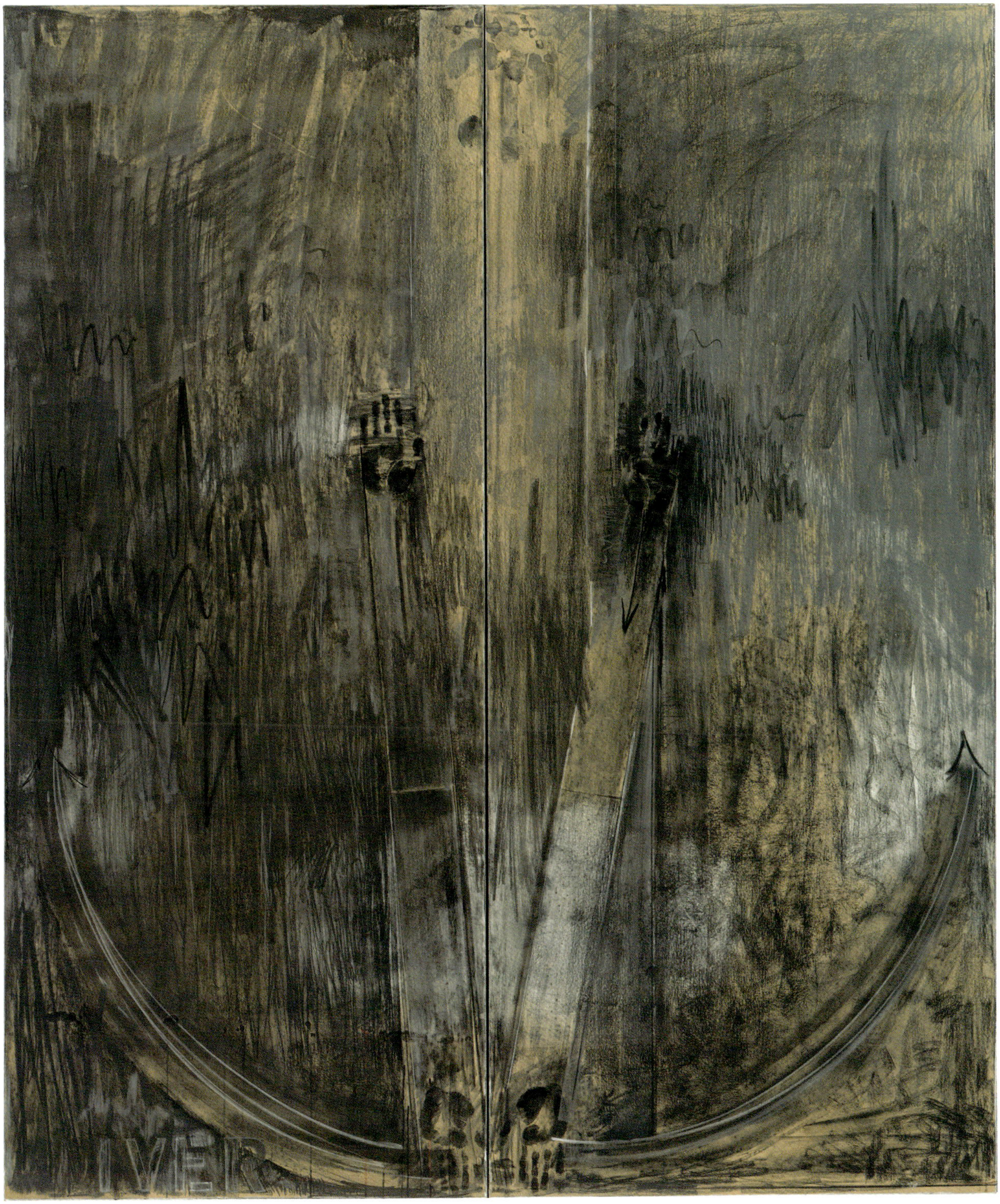

43 **JASPER JOHNS**

Diver, 1962–63

Charcoal, pastel, and watercolor on paper mounted on canvas, two panels, 7' 2 1/2" x 71 3/4" (219.7 x 182.2 cm)
Partial gift of Kate Ganz and Tony Ganz in memory of their parents, Victor and Sally Ganz, and in memory of Kirk Varnedoe; Mrs. John Hay Whitney Bequest Fund; gift of Edgar Kaufmann, Jr. (by exchange); and purchase. Acquired by the Trustees of The Museum of Modern Art in memory of Kirk Varnedoe, 2003

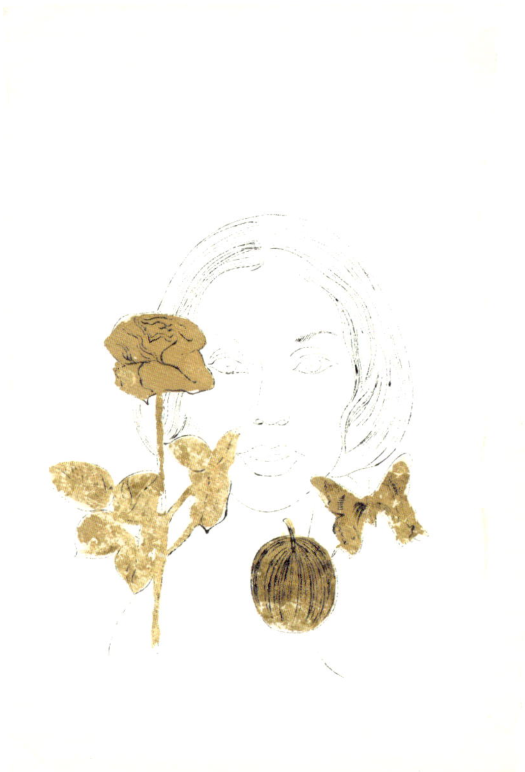

44 **ANDY WARHOL**
Unknown Female. (c. 1957)
Gold leaf and ink on paper, 23 1/8 x 15 1/2" (58.7 x 39.4 cm)
Gift of Sarah-Ann and Werner H. Kramarsky, 1998

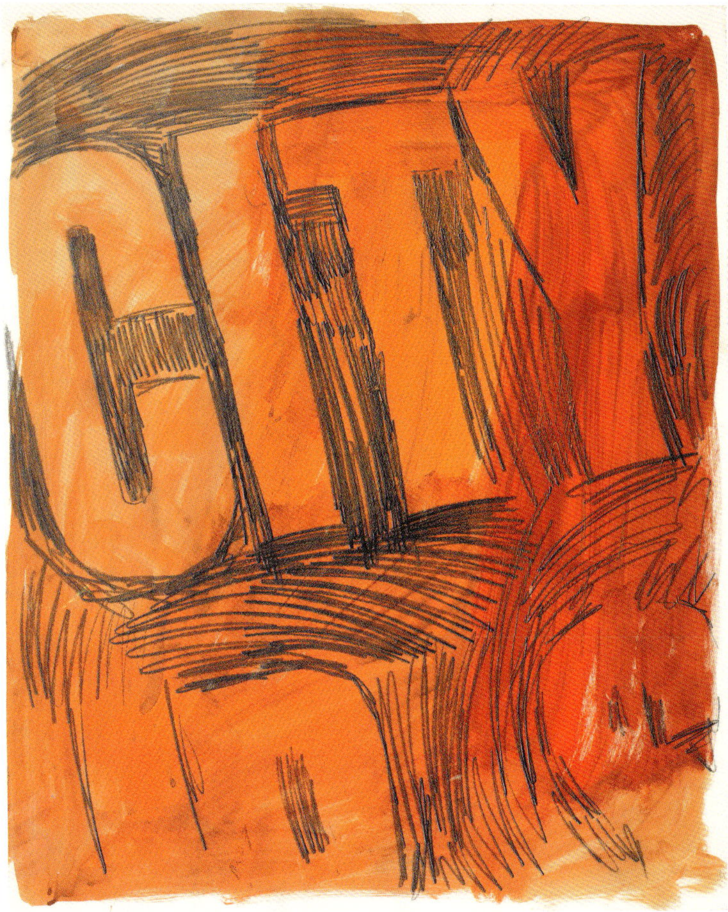

45 **ANDY WARHOL**

Untitled (City Text), (c. 1962)

Pencil and gouache on paper, 29 x 23" (73.7 x 58 cm)

Purchased with funds given by The Edward John Noble Foundation and Purchase Fund, 1999

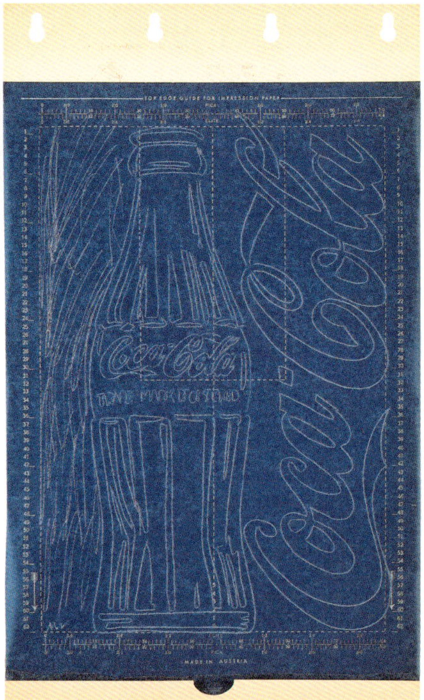

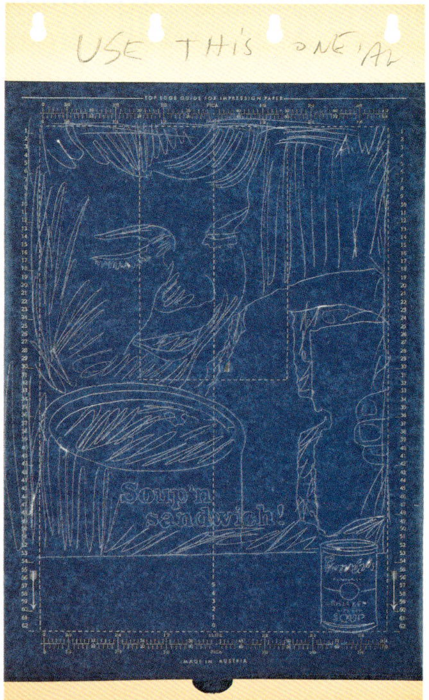

46 **ANDY WARHOL**
Coca-Cola, (1962)
Mimeograph stencil,
14 x 9" (35.6 x 22.9 cm)
Purchase, 2004

47 **ANDY WARHOL**
Soup n' sandwich!, (1962)
Mimeograph stencil,
14 x 9" (35.6 x 22.9 cm)
Purchase, 2004

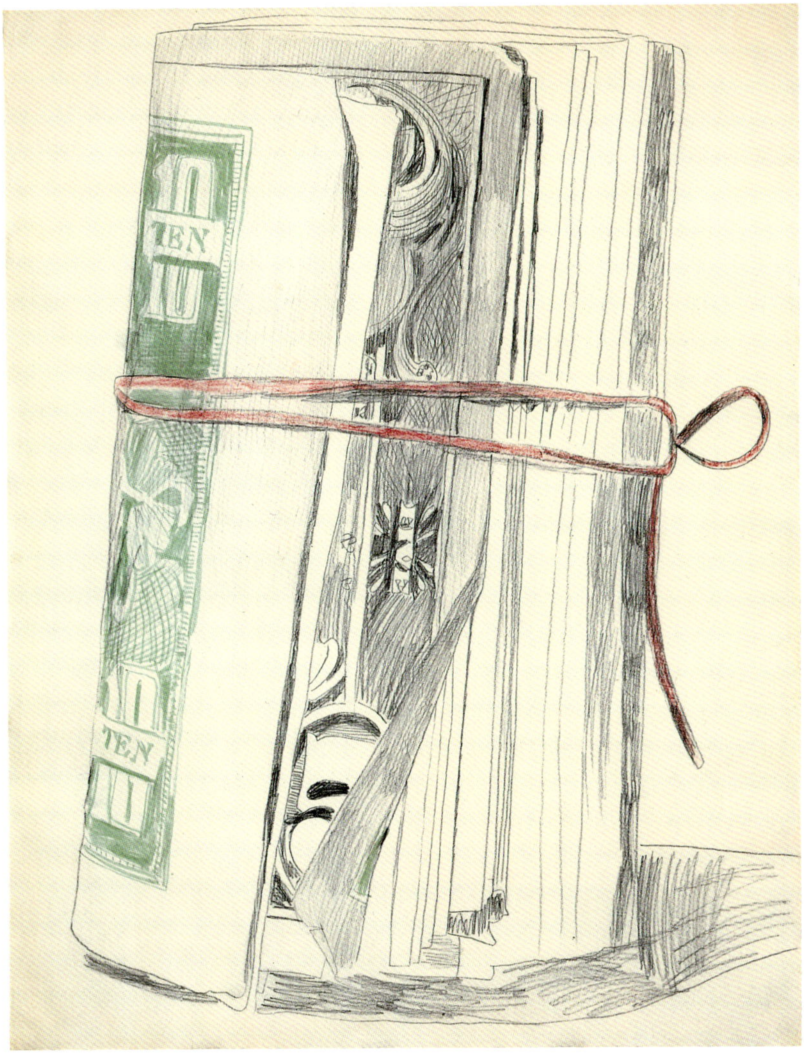

48 **ANDY WARHOL**
Roll of Bills, (1962)
Pencil, crayon, and felt-tip pen on paper,
40 x 30" (101.6 x 76.2 cm)
Purchase, 1984

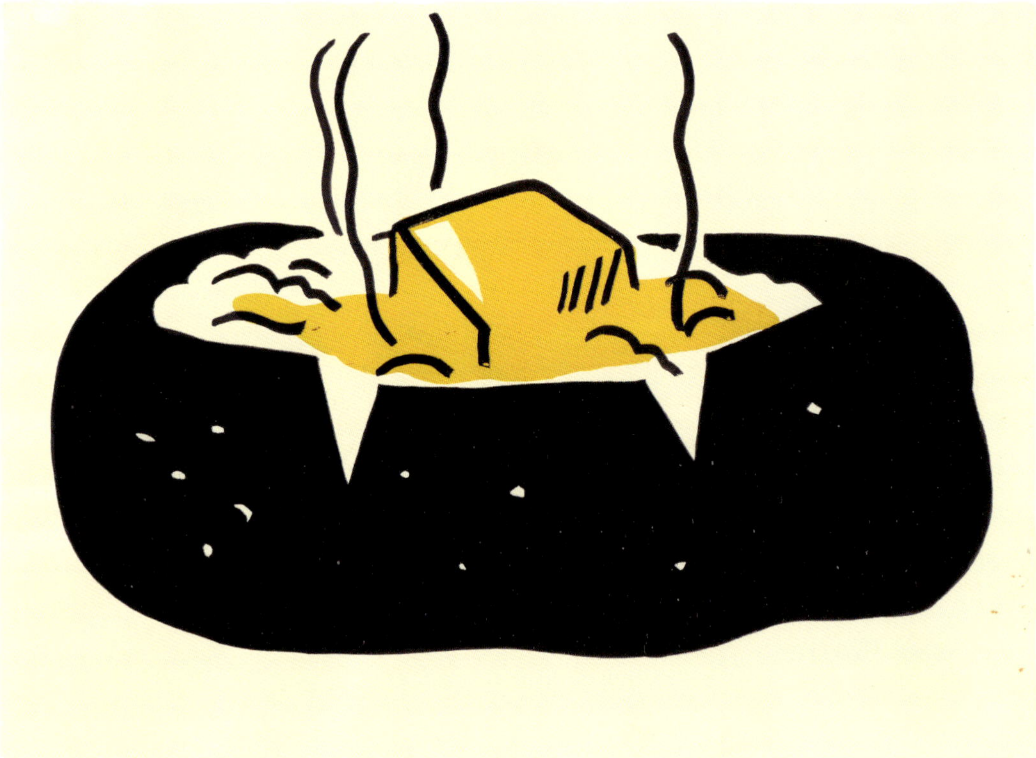

49 **ROY LICHTENSTEIN**
Baked Potato, (1962)
Ink and synthetic polymer paint on paper,
22 1/4 x 30 1/8" (56.6 x 76.5 cm)
Gift of Abby Aldrich Rockefeller (by exchange), 1984

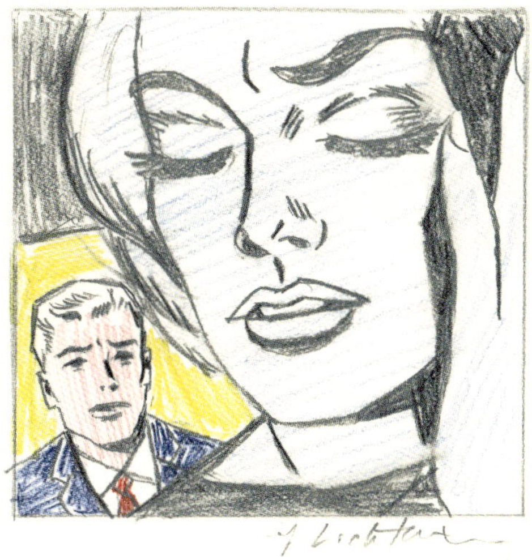

50 **ROY LICHTENSTEIN**
Study for *Tension*, (1964)
Pencil and colored pencil on paper, 5 ¾ x 5 ¾" (14.6 x 14.6 cm)
Purchased with funds provided by the Frances Keech Fund and the
Vincent D'Aquila and Harry Soviak Drawings Bequest Fund, 2004

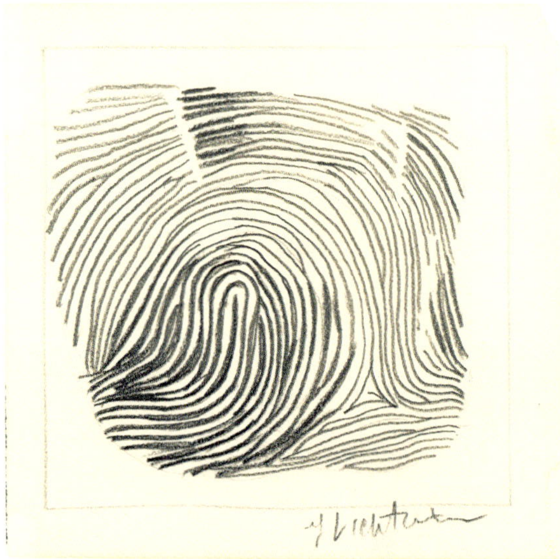

51 **ROY LICHTENSTEIN**
Thumbprint, (1964)
Pencil on paper, 5 ¾ x 5 ¾" (14.6 x 14.6 cm)
Fractional and promised gift of Jan Cowles and Charles Cowles
to honor the memory of Roy Lichtenstein, 1974

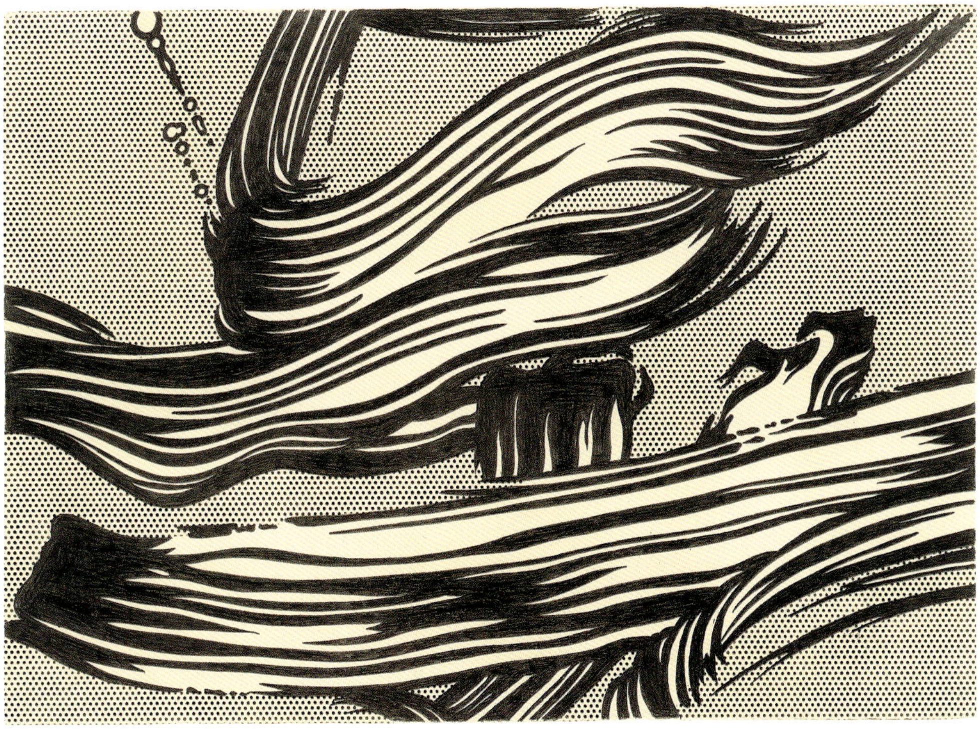

52 **ROY LICHTENSTEIN**

Brushstrokes, 1966–68

Pencil and tusche pochoir on paper, 22 1/8 x 29 7/8" (56.5 x 75.5 cm)

Gift of Leo Castelli in memory of Toiny Castelli, 1987

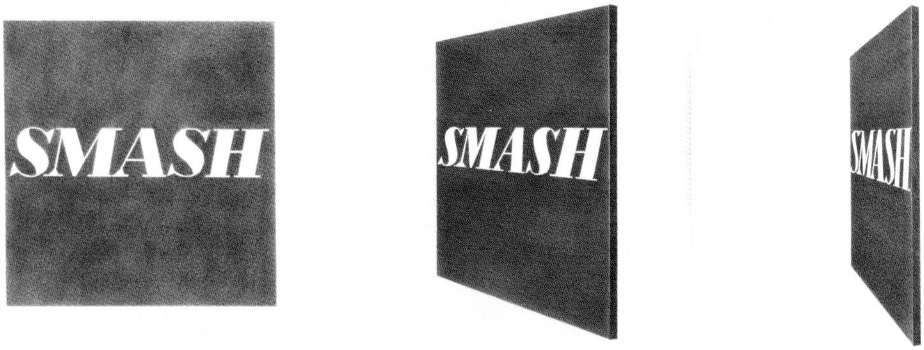

53 **EDWARD RUSCHA**
Smash, 1964
Powdered graphite on three sheets of paper,
overall 11 ¾ x 31 ½" (29.8 x 80 cm)
Purchased with funds given by Agnes Gund, Mr. and Mrs. James R. Hedges IV,
Jo Carole and Ronald S. Lauder, and the General Drawings Fund, 2000

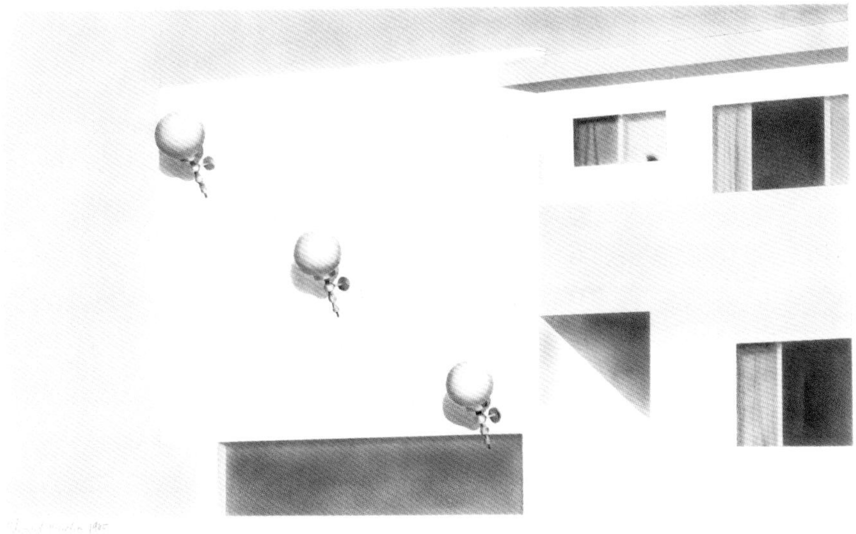

54 **EDWARD RUSCHA**

Normandie, 1965

Powdered graphite and pencil on paper, 14 ⅛ x 22 ½" (36 x 57.2 cm)

Purchased with funds given by Agnes Gund, Mr. and Mrs. James R. Hedges IV, Jo Carole and Ronald S. Lauder, and the General Drawings Fund, 2000

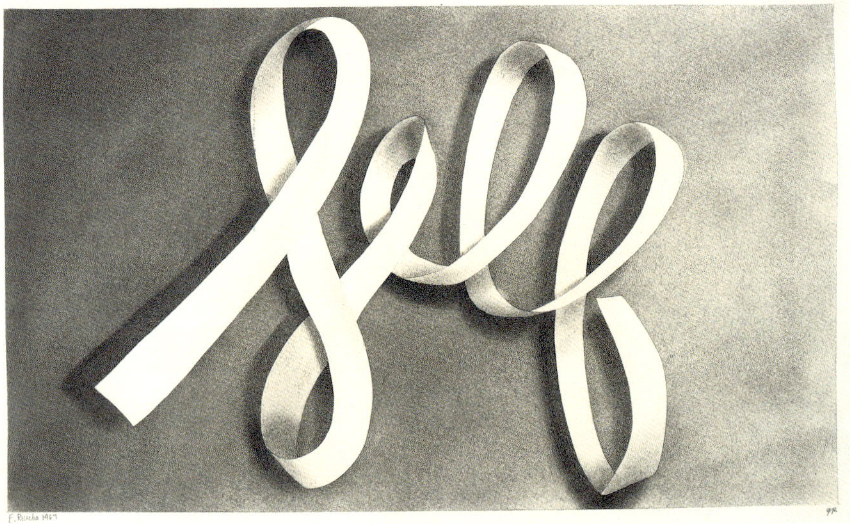

55 **EDWARD RUSCHA**
Self, 1967
Pastel and gunpowder on paper, 14 ½ x 22 ½" (36.8 x 57.2 cm)
Fractional and promised gift of Sarah-Ann and Werner H. Kramarsky, 2004

56 **EDWARD RUSCHA**

Blood Strip, 1973

Gunpowder and blood on paper, 11 1/2 x 29" (29.2 x 73.7 cm)

Purchased with funds given by Agnes Gund, Mr. and Mrs. James R. Hedges IV, Jo Carole and Ronald S. Lauder, and the General Drawings Fund, 2000

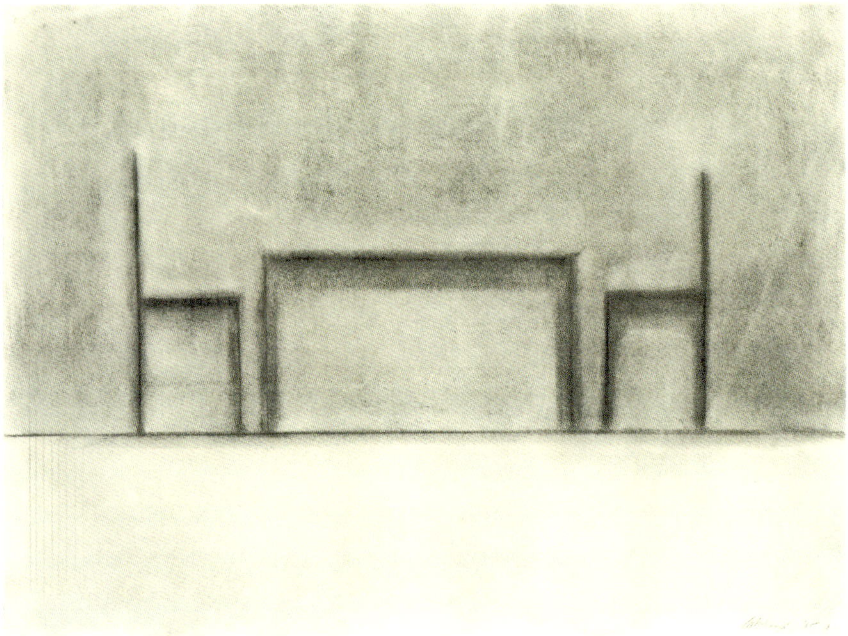

57 **RICHARD ARTSCHWAGER**
Table and Two Chairs, 1965
Charcoal on paper, 19 x 25" (48.3 x 63.6 cm)
Gift of Paul Bianchini, 1969

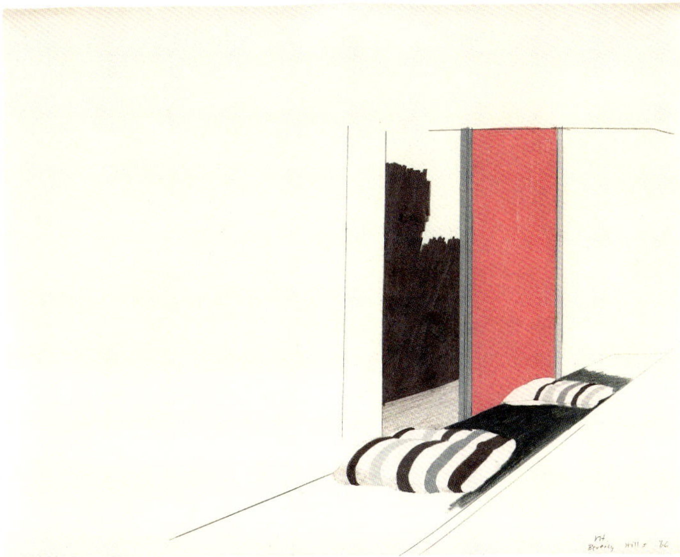

58 **DAVID HOCKNEY**
Beverly Hills Interior. 1966
Colored pencil on paper, 13 ⅜ x 20 ⅛" (34 x 51.1 cm)
Promised gift of Joel Wachs, and purchase, 2004

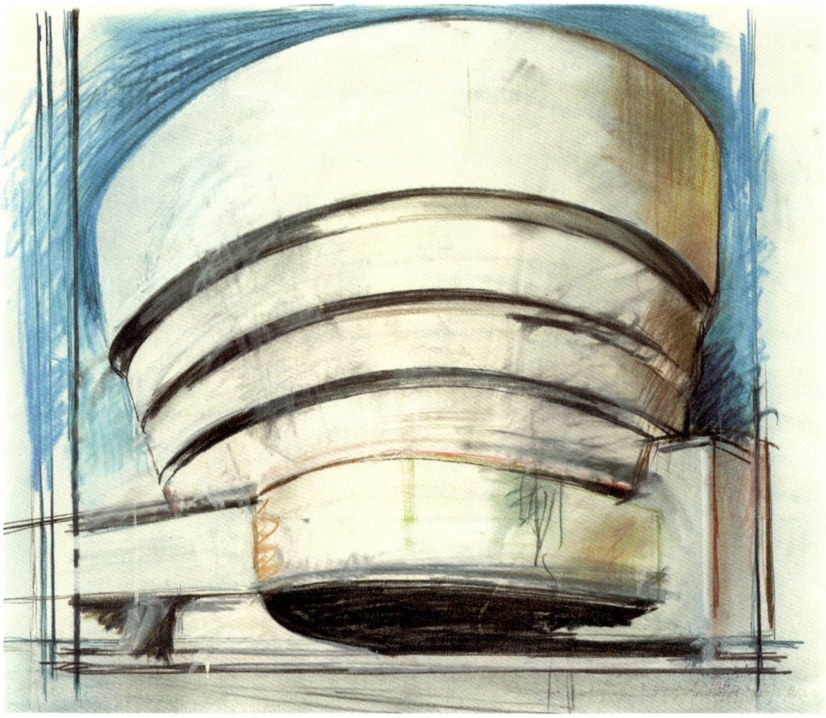

59 **RICHARD HAMILTON**
The Solomon R. Guggenheim – Architect's visual, 1965
Crayon, pastel, synthetic polymer paint, and ink on paper,
20 x 23" (50.7 x 58.4 cm)
Gift of Charles B. Benenson, 1967

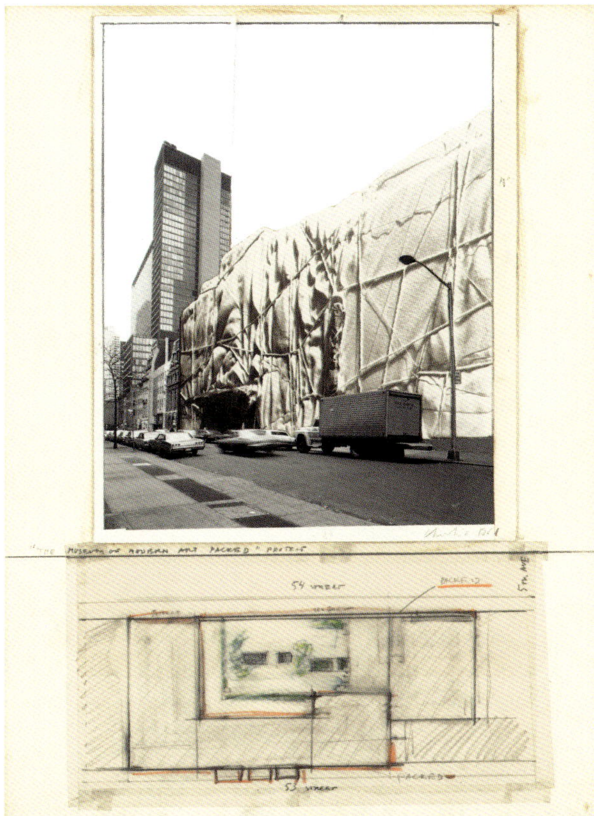

60 **CHRISTO** and **JEANNE-CLAUDE**
"The Museum of Modern Art Packed Project", 1968
Cut-and-pasted gelatin silver prints (by Ferdinand Boesch) with oil on board, pencil, colored pencil, cut and pasted tracing paper, and pressure-sensitive tape on board, $21\frac{3}{4} \times 15\frac{1}{2}$" (55.2 x 39.5 cm)
Gift of D. and J. de Menil, 1968

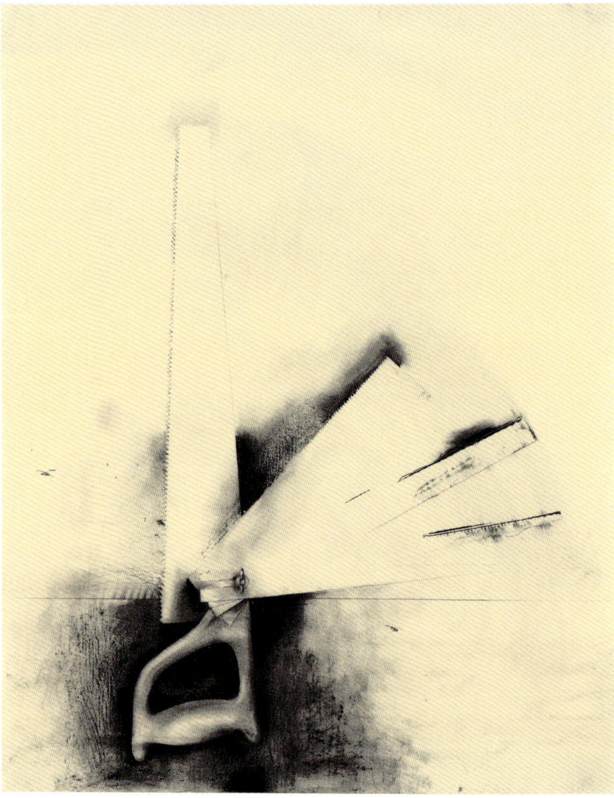

61 **JIM DINE**
Untitled (Five-bladed Saw) from Untitled Tool Series, 1973
Graphite, charcoal, and crayon on paper, 25 5/8 x 19 3/4" (65.1 x 50.2 cm)
Gift of the Robert Lehman Foundation, Inc., 1976

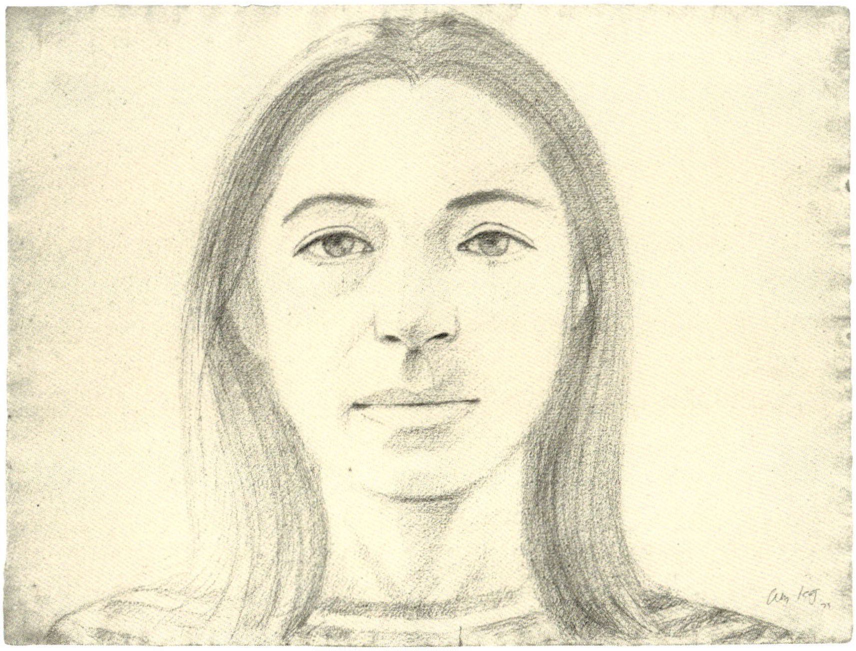

62 **ALEX KATZ**

Ada, 1973

Pencil on paper, 19 ¾ x 26" (50.3 x 66.2 cm)

Gift of Edgar B. Howard, 1980

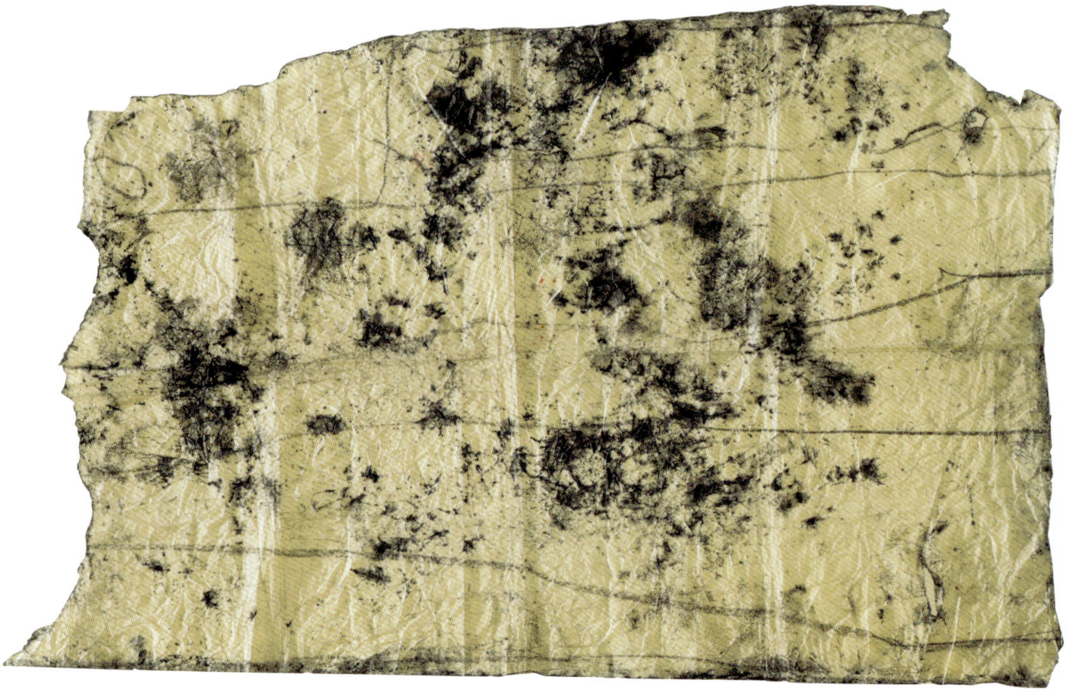

63 **CLAES OLDENBURG**
Flag to Fold in the Pocket. (1960)
Ink and crayon on butcher paper, 29 ½ x 47" (74.9 x 119.4 cm) (irreg.)
Purchase, 1983

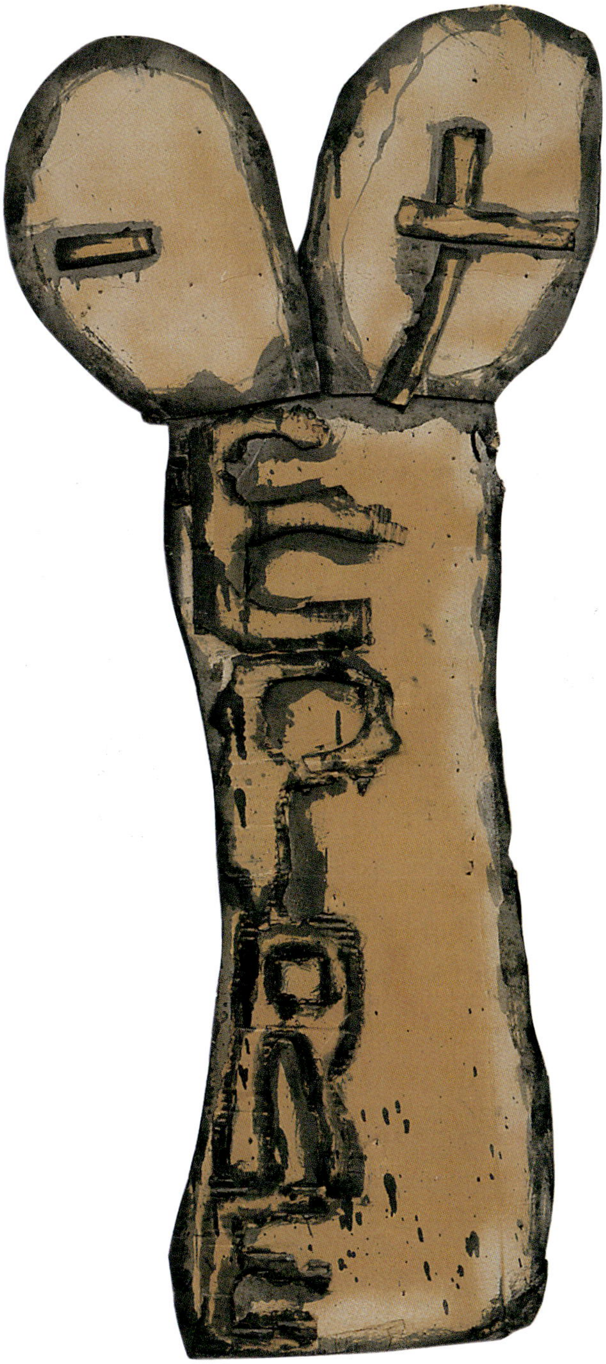

64 **CLAES OLDENBURG**
Empire Sign – With M and I Deleted, (1960)
Casein on cut-and-pasted corrugated cardboard,
54 ¾ x 23 7/8" (139.1 x 60.7 cm) (irreg.)
Gift of Agnes Gund, 1987

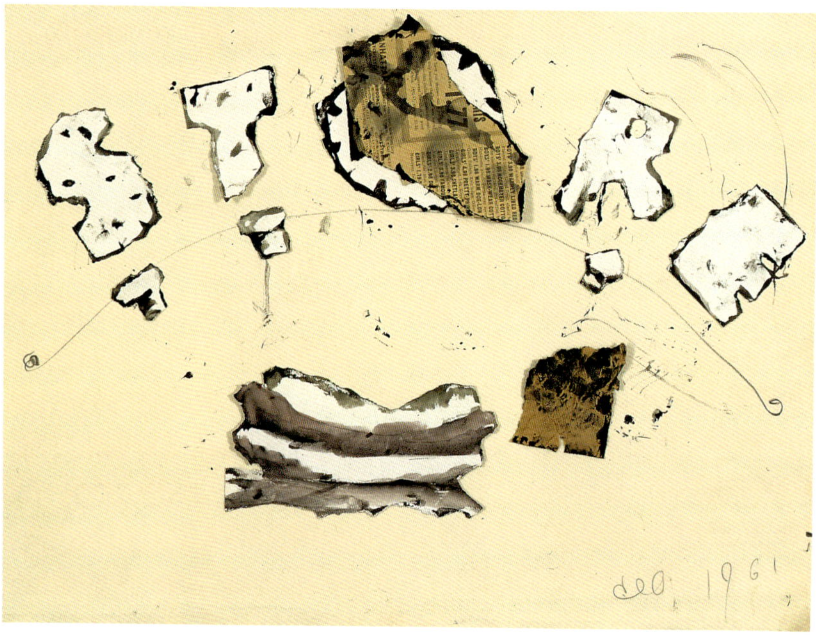

65 **CLAES OLDENBURG**
Store Poster, Torn Out Letters Newspaper Pie Cup Cakes and Hot Dog, 1961
Cut-and-pasted paper and printed paper, watercolor, and
crayon on paper, 20 x 26" (50.8 x 66.1 cm)
Purchased with funds given by Mr. and Mrs. Henry R. Kravis, 1996

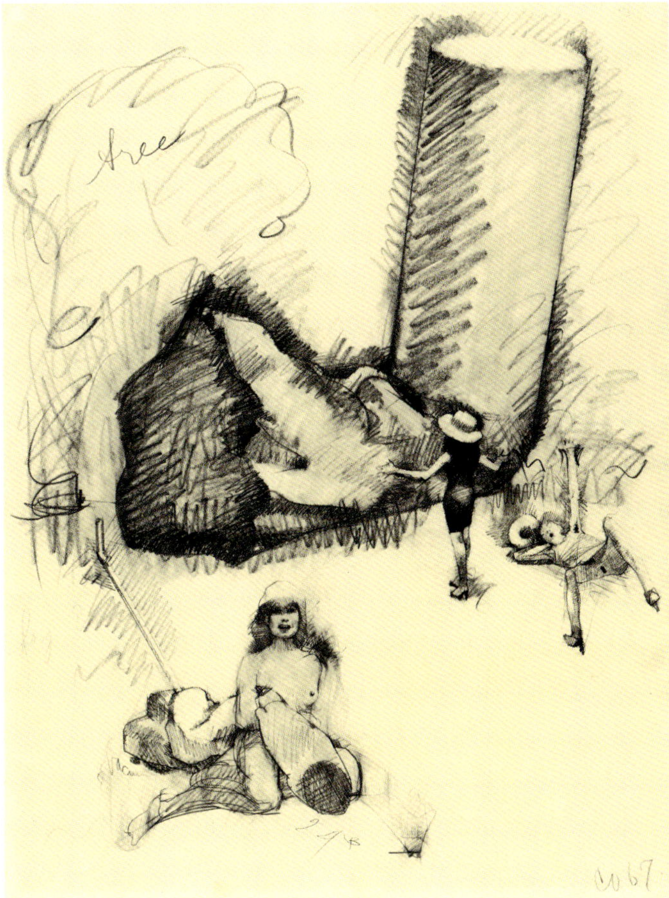

66 **CLAES OLDENBURG**

Colossal Fagend, Dream State, 1967

Pencil on paper, 30 x 22" (76.1 x 56.1 cm)

Gift of Lily Auchincloss, Charles B. Benenson, Jo Carole and Ronald S. Lauder, and purchase, 1988

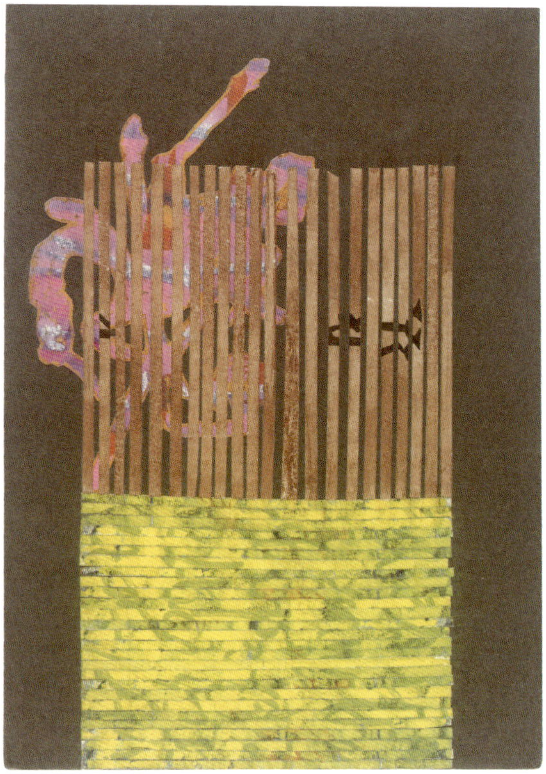

67 **RAY JOHNSON**
Caged. (1959)
Cut-and-pasted painted paper on brown-paper-surfaced board mounted on painted board, 17 ¾ x 13 ½" (45 x 34.2 cm)
Larry Aldrich Foundation Fund, 1965

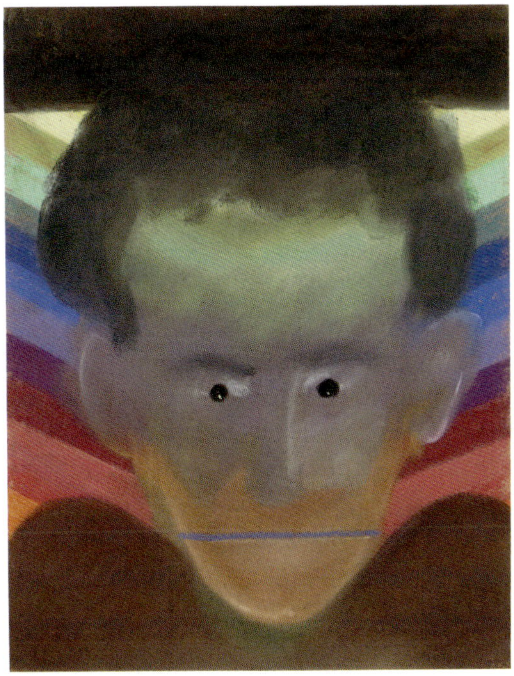

68 **LUCAS SAMARAS**
Untitled, 1961
Pastel on red paper, 12 x 8 ⅞" (30.5 x 22.8 cm)
D. S. and R. H. Gottesman Foundation Fund, 1966

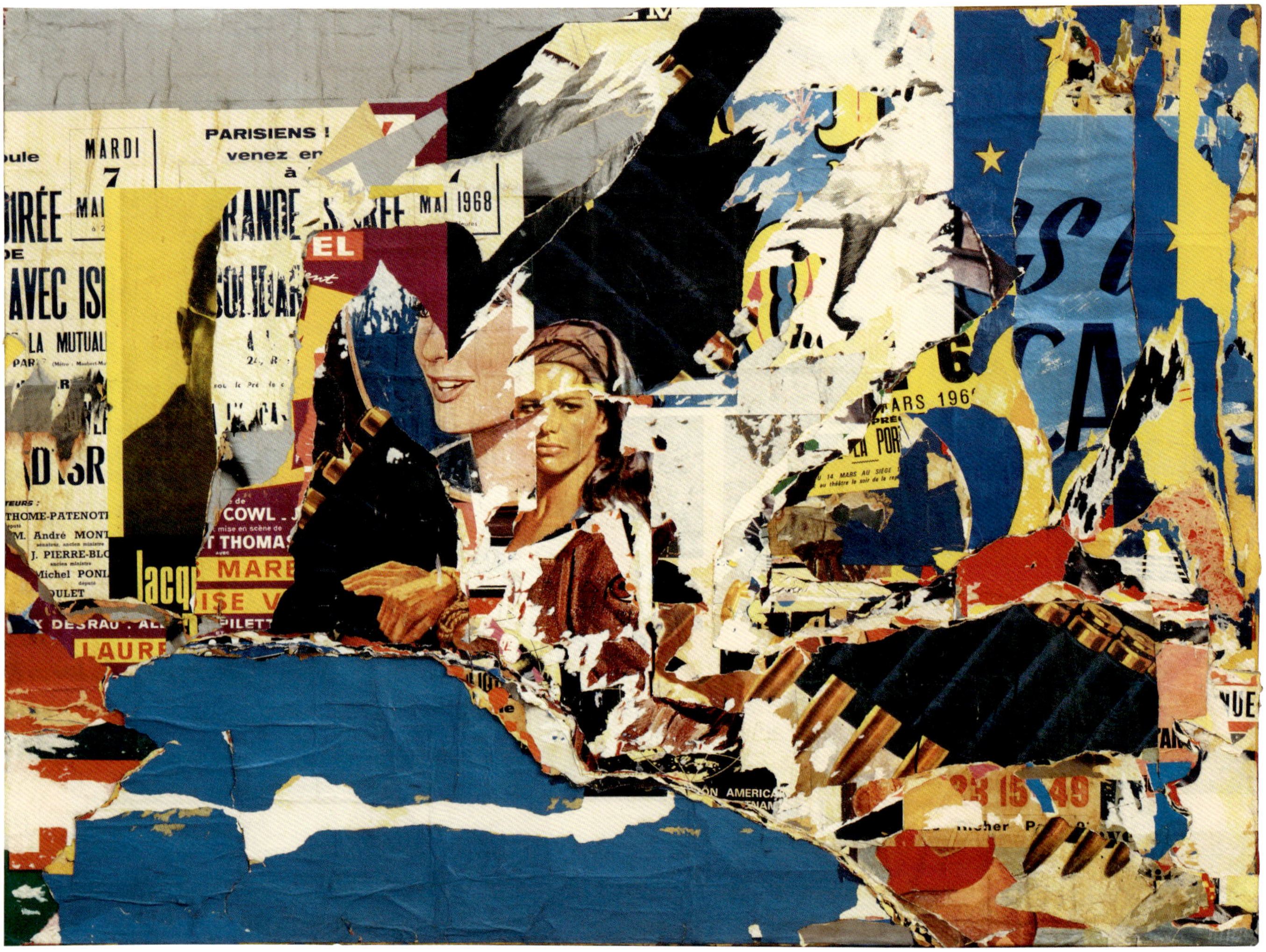

69 **JACQUES DE LA VILLEGLÉ**
122 rue du temple, 1968
Torn-and-pasted printed paper on canvas,
62 5/8" x 6' 10 3/4" (159.2 x 210.3 cm)
Gift of Joachim Aberbach (by exchange), 1988

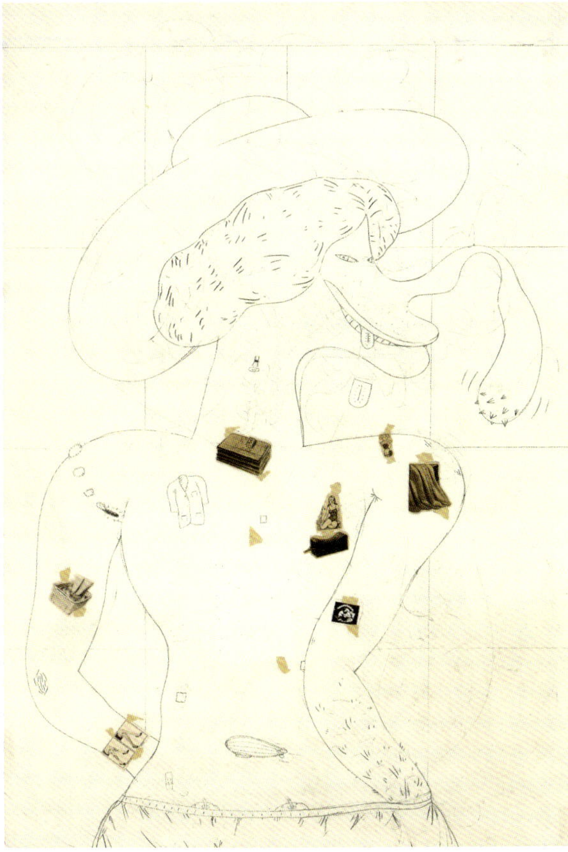

70 **JIM NUTT**
Rosie Comon, (1968)
Pencil, cut-and-pasted printed paper, pressure-sensitive tape,
and gouache on paper, 38 x 25" (96.5 x 63.5 cm)
Purchased with funds provided by Jo Carole and Ronald S. Lauder, 2001

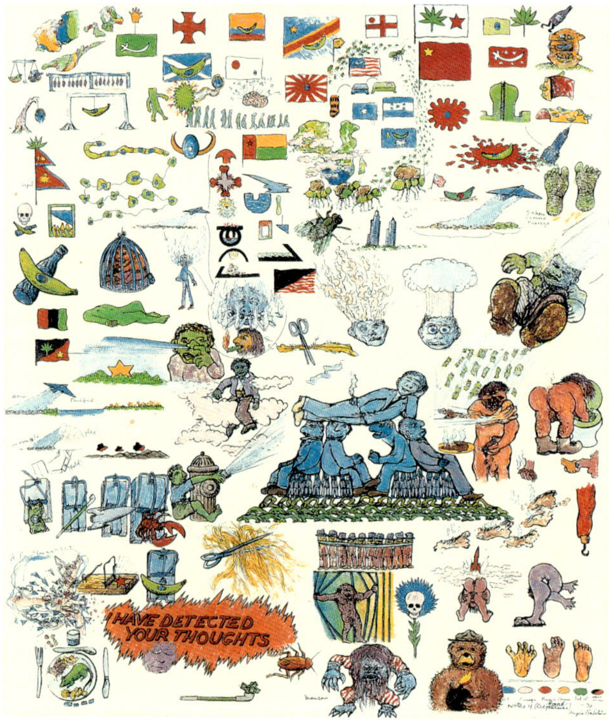

71 **ÖYVIND FAHLSTRÖM**

Notes 4 (C. I. A. Brand Bananas). 1970

Synthetic polymer paint and ink on paper,

16 ⅝ x 14" (42.2 x 35.3 cm)

Mrs. Bertram Smith Fund, 1971

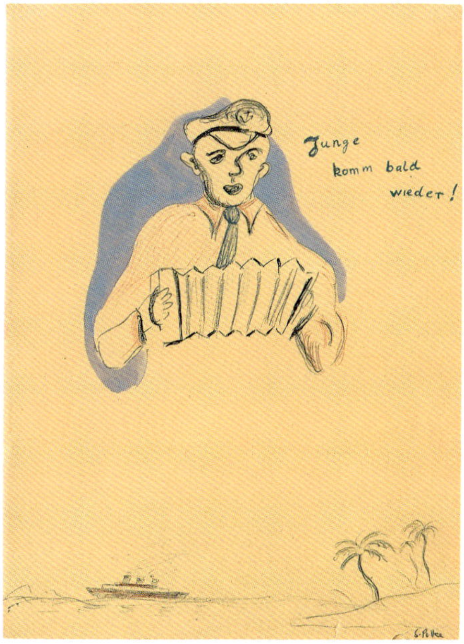

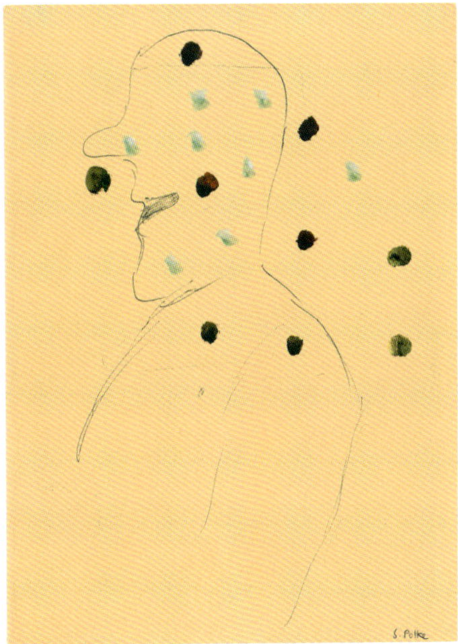

72 **SIGMAR POLKE**
Young Man Come Back Soon (Junge komm bald wieder). (1963)
Ballpoint pen and watercolor on brown paper,
11 3/4 x 8 1/2" (29.8 x 21 cm)
Gift by exchange: Heinz Berggruen and Klaus Perls in memory of Frank Perls, Glickstein Foundation, and Mrs. Alfred P. Shaw, 1997

73 **SIGMAR POLKE**
Untitled (Head with Dots). (1963)
Ballpoint pen, oil, and gouache on brown paper,
11 5/8 x 8 1/2" (29.6 x 21 cm)
By exchange from the Joan and Lester Avnet Collection and John S. Newberry Collection, 1997

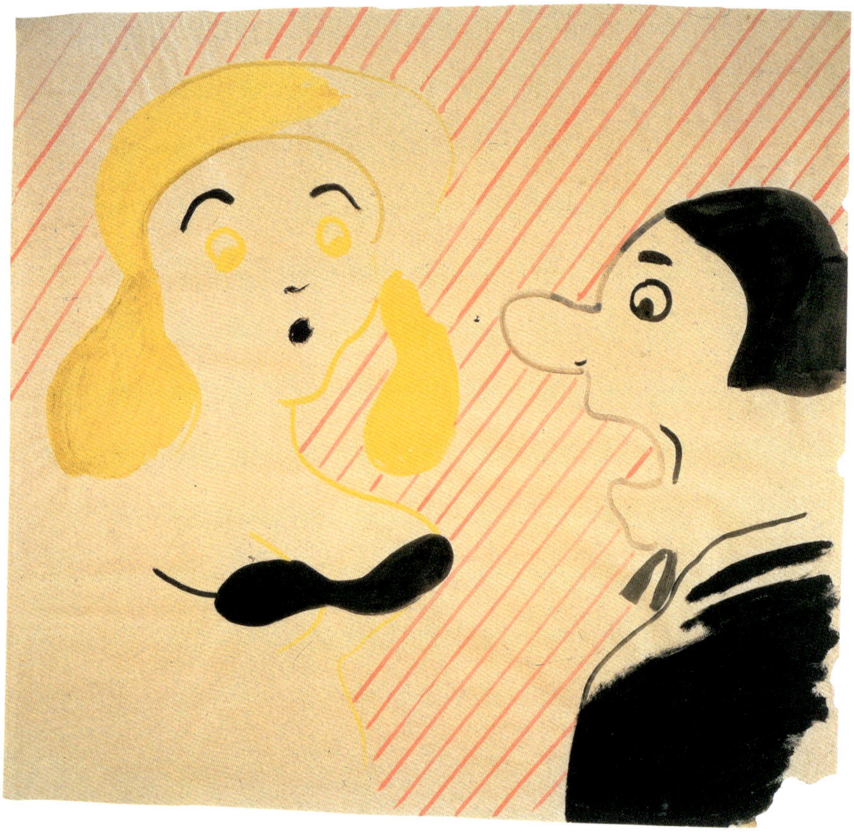

74 **SIGMAR POLKE**
Untitled, (c. 1964)
Synthetic polymer paint on paper, 29 x 29 ³⁄₈" (73.5 x 74.5 cm)
Fractional and promised gift of Anna Marie and Robert F. Shapiro
in honor of Margit Rowell, 2000

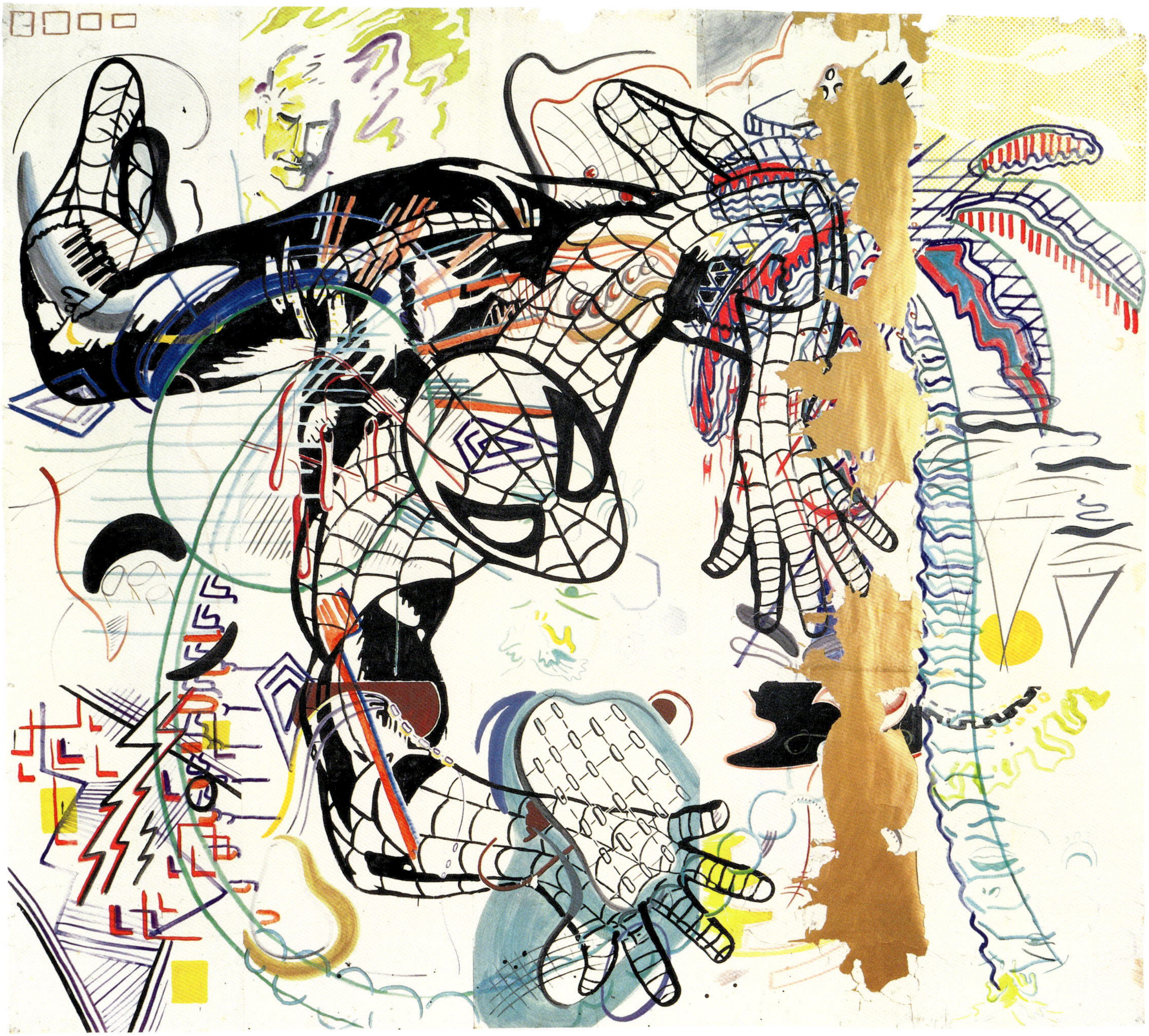

75 **SIGMAR POLKE**

Spiderman, (1971–74)

Cut-and-pasted painted paper on canvas, 9' 3 1/4" x 10' 3" (282.6 x 213.4 cm)

Purchased with funds given by Leon D. Black, Mr. and Mrs. Henry R. Kravis, Jo Carole and Ronald S. Lauder, and the Richard E. Salomon Family, 1999

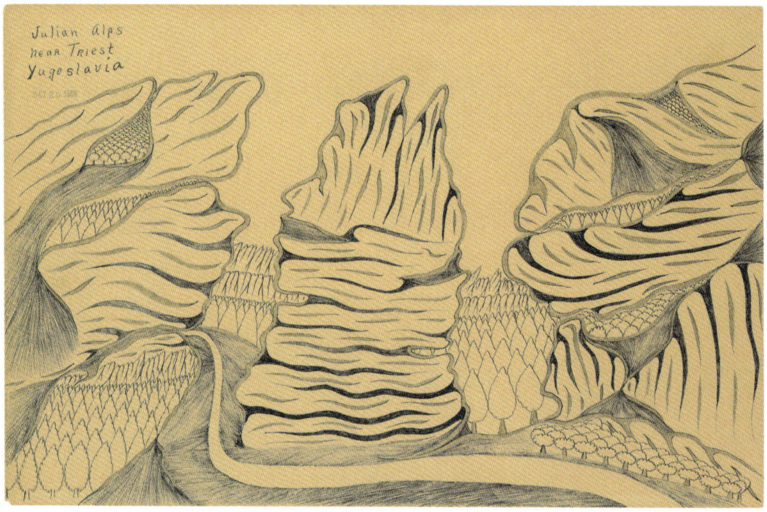

76 **JOSEPH E. YOAKUM**
Julian Alps Near Triest, Yugoslavia. (1964)
Ballpoint pen and pencil on brown paper, 12 x 18" (30.5 x 45.7 cm)
Gift of Jan Christiaan Braun in honor of Mrs. June Noble Larkin, 2004

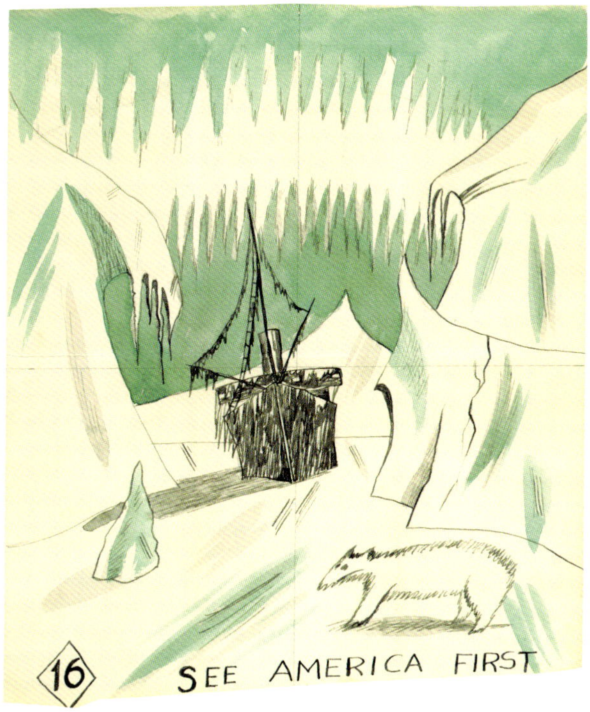

77 **H. C. WESTERMANN**
Drawing for See America First #16, (1968)
Ink, watercolor, and pencil on paper, 13 x 10 1/2" (33 x 26.7 cm)
Purchased with funds given by Sarah-Ann and
Werner H. Kramarsky, 1999

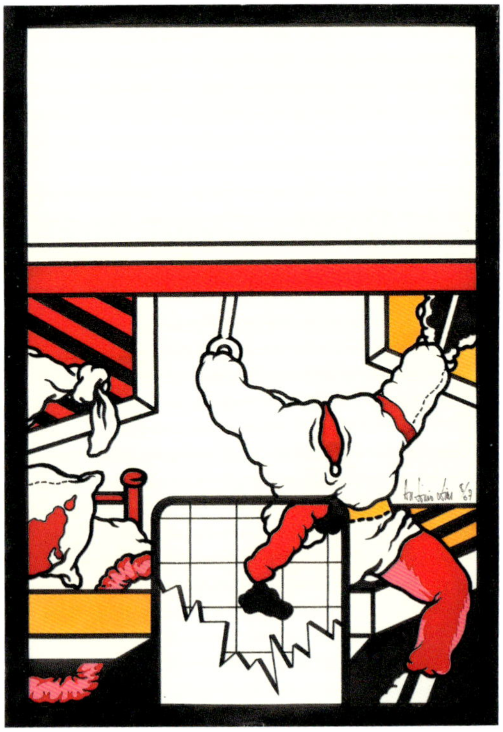

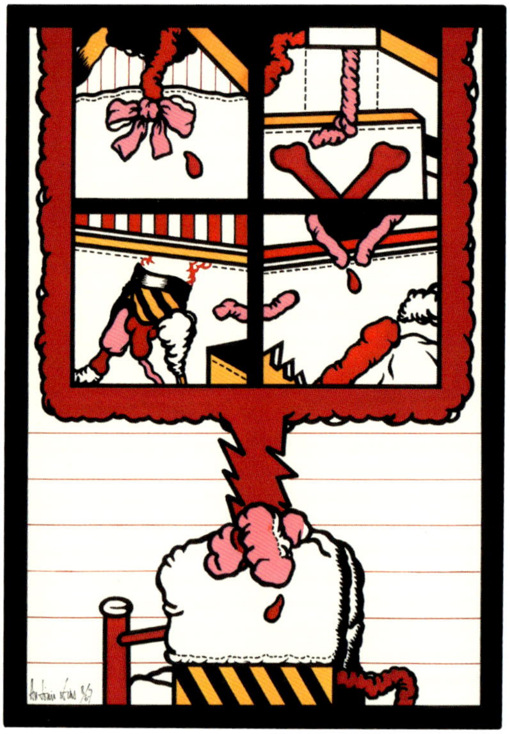

78 **ANTONIO DIAS**
Untitled, 1967
Colored ink on paper,
18 1/2 x 12 5/8" (47 x 31.9 cm)
Inter-American Fund, 1969

79 **ANTONIO DIAS**
Untitled, 1967
Gouache and colored ink on paper,
18 1/2 x 12 5/8" (47 x 31.9 cm)
Inter-American Fund, 1969

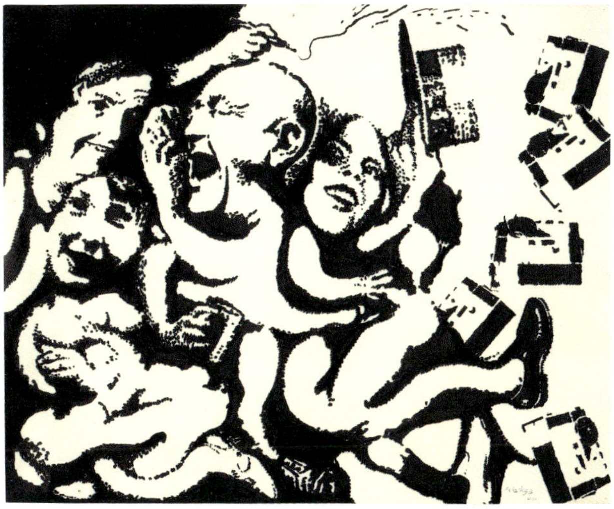

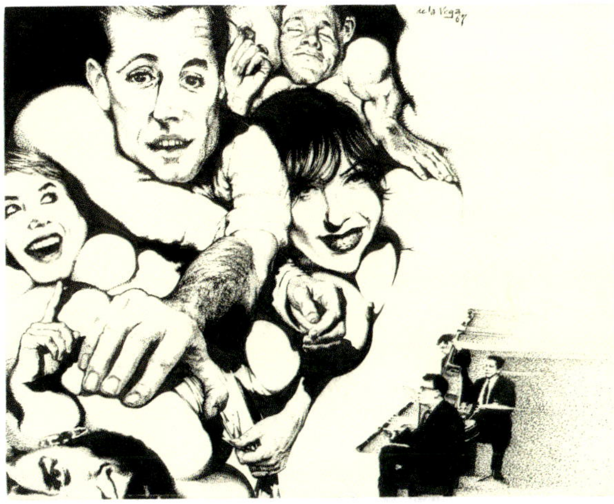

80 **JORGE DE LA VEGA**
Documentary (Documental), 1966
Ink on paper, 14 x 16 ¾" (35.5 x 42.5 cm)
Given anonymously, 1969

81 **JORGE DE LA VEGA**
Parenthesis (Paréntesis), 1967
Ink on paper, 11 x 13 ⅝" (27.9 x 34.6 cm)
Inter-American Fund, 1969

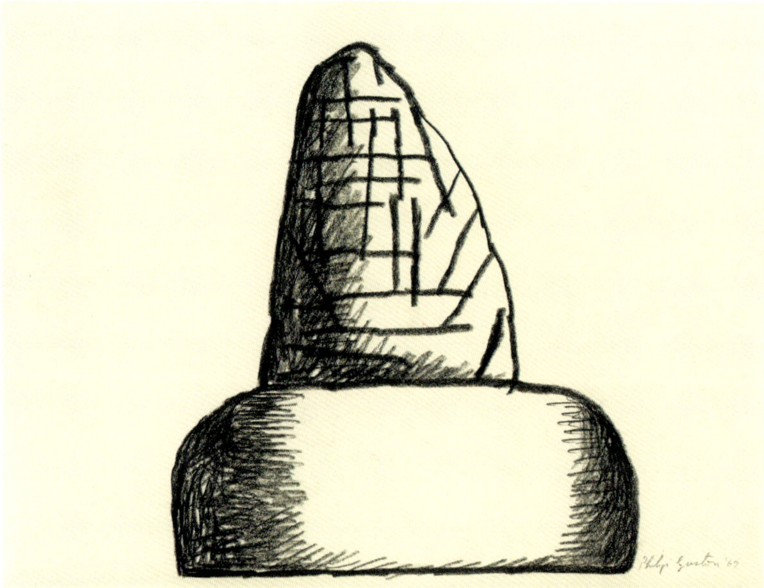

82 **PHILIP GUSTON**
Wrapped. 1969
Charcoal on paper, 17 1/4 x 21 1/2" (43.7 x 54.4 cm)
Purchase, 1983

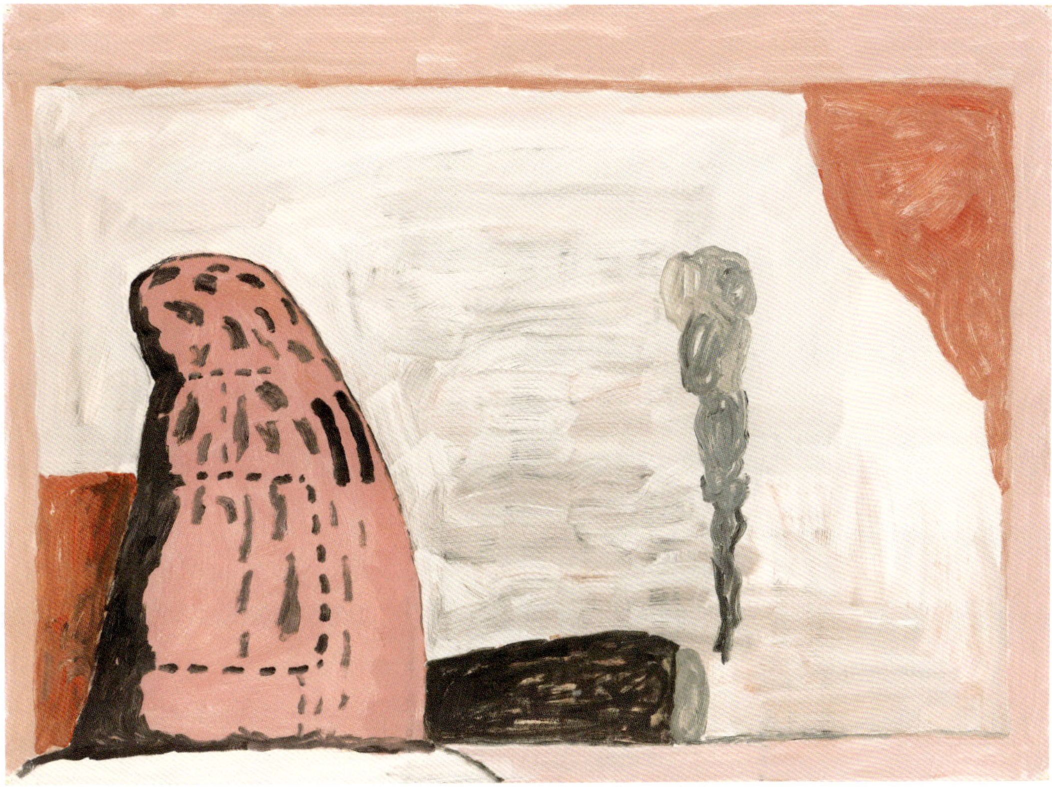

83 **PHILIP GUSTON**
Untitled (Waiting), (1972)
Oil on paper, 30 1/4 x 40" (76.8 x 101.6 cm)
Gift of Musa and Tom Mayer, 2001

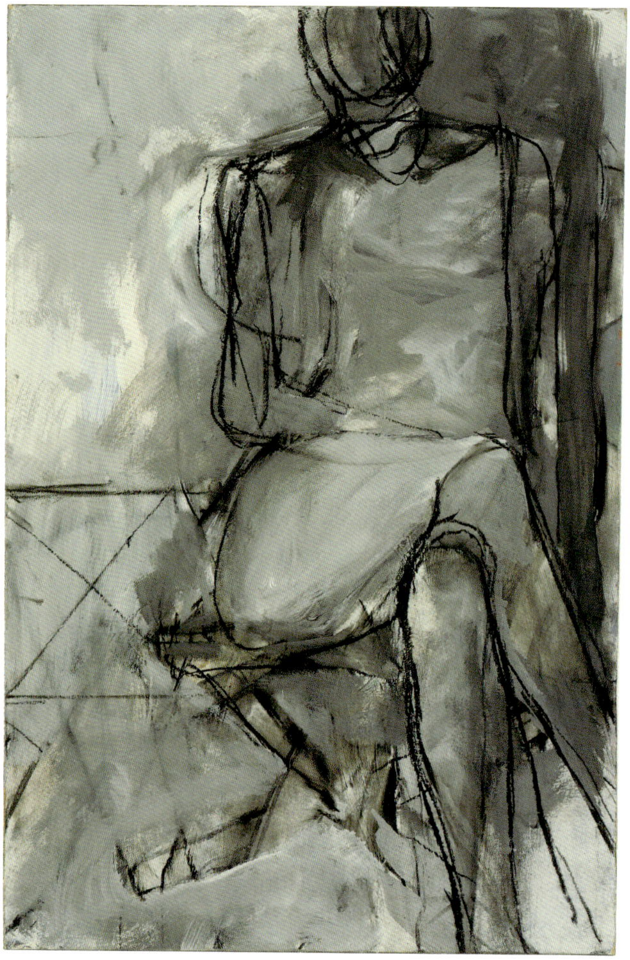

84 **RICHARD DIEBENKORN**
Seated Woman. (1966)
Synthetic polymer paint and charcoal on board,
31 x 19 7/8" (78.8 x 50.4 cm)
Gift of the artist, 1990

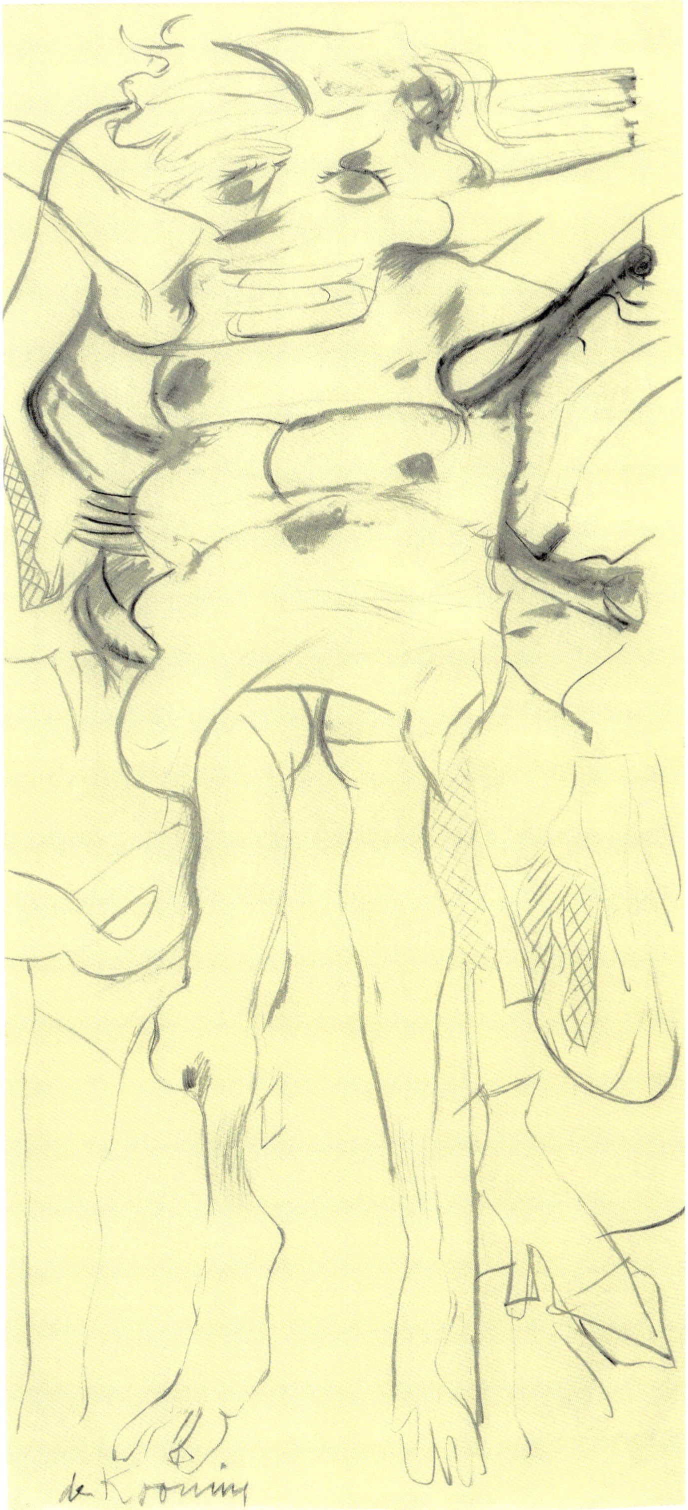

85 **WILLEM DE KOONING**

Woman, (1965)

Charcoal on transparentized paper, 6' 8" x 35 ¾" (203.2 x 90.8 cm)

Purchased with funds provided by Kathy and Richard S. Fuld, Jr., Jo Carole and Ronald S. Lauder, Thomas Weisel, Agnes Gund, Sarah-Ann and Werner H. Kramarsky and gift of The Sidney and Harriet Janis Collection (by exchange), 2000

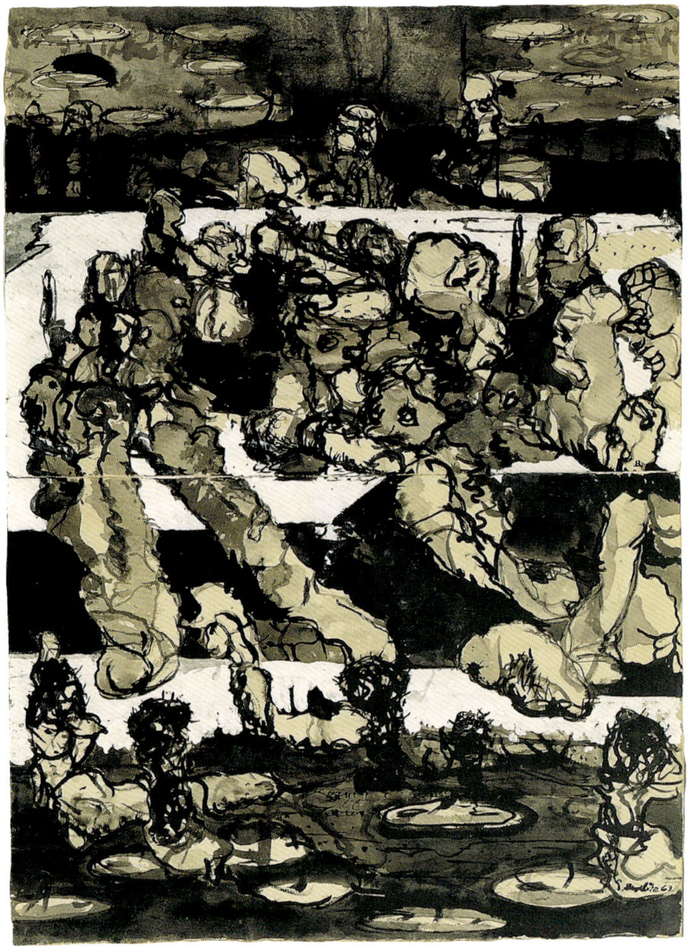

86 **GEORG BASELITZ**
P.D. Drawing (P.D. Zeichnung), 1963
Ink and gouache on two sheets of paper, 33 1/2 x 24 1/4" (85 x 61.5 cm)
Purchased with funds given by Jo Carole and Ronald S. Lauder
and Leon D. Black, 1995

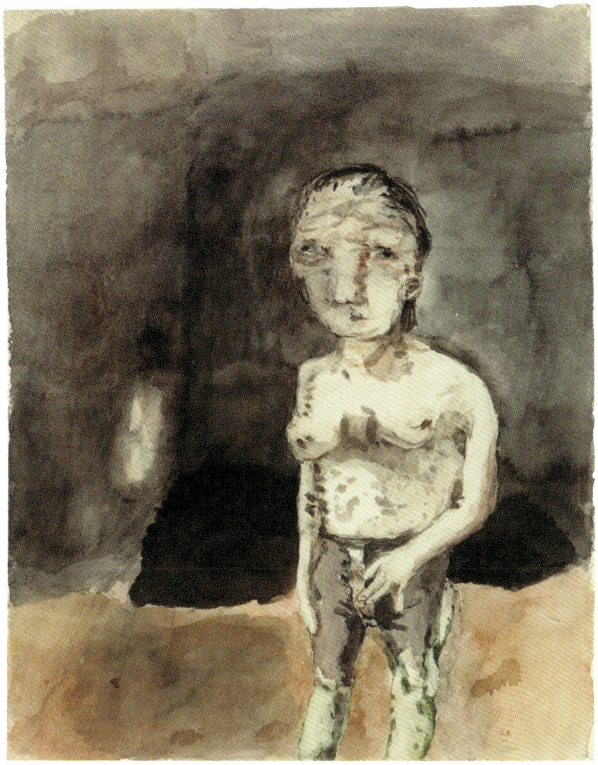

87 **GEORG BASELITZ**
Big Night Down the Drain (Die grosse Nacht im Eimer), 1963
Watercolor and pencil on paper, 24 3/4 x 19" (62.9 x 48.3 cm)
Gift of R. L. B. Tobin, 1987

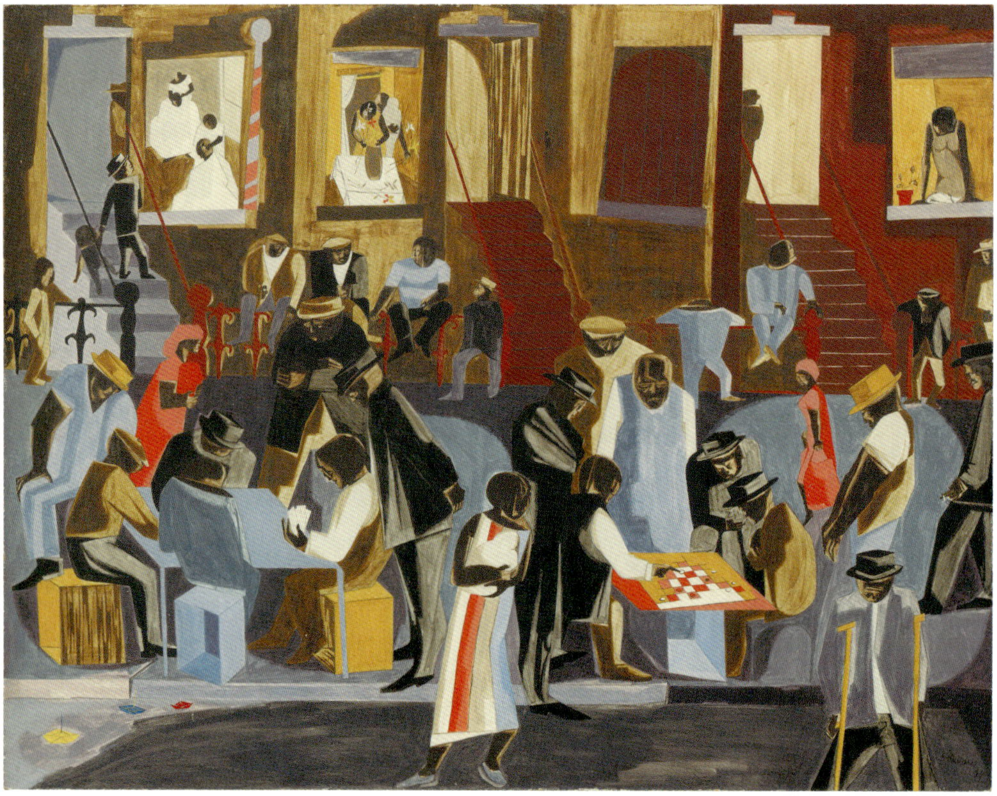

88 **JACOB LAWRENCE**
Street Shadows, 1959
Egg tempera and pencil on gessoed board, 24 x 29 7/8" (61 x 75.9 cm)
Gift of Ellen Kern and Gail Garlick in memory of their parents,
Jewel and Lewis Garlick, 2000

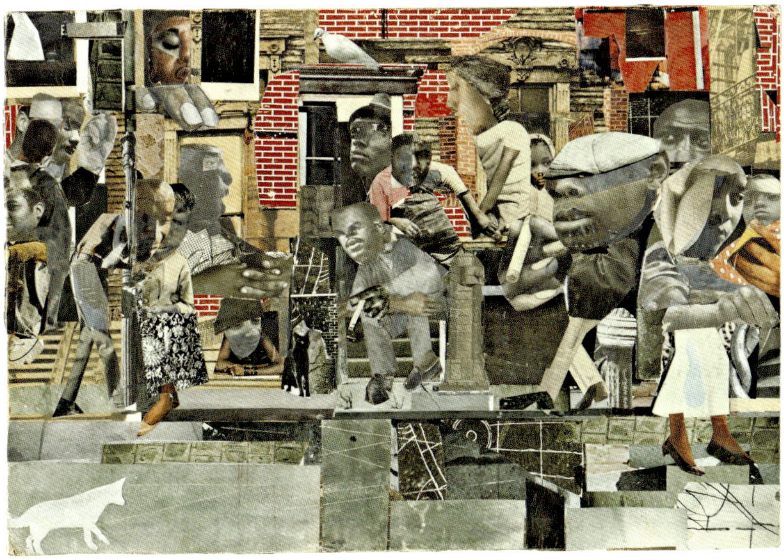

89 **ROMARE BEARDEN**
The Dove, (1964)
Cut-and-pasted printed paper, gouache, pencil, and colored pencil on board, 13 ⅜ x 18 ¾" (33.8 x 47.5 cm)
Blanchette Hooker Rockefeller Fund, 1971

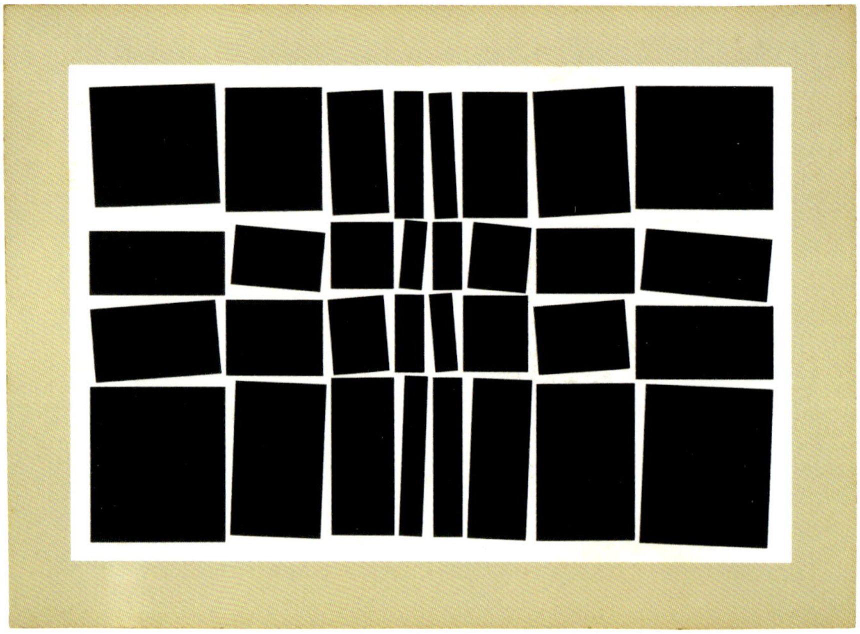

90 **HÉLIO OITICICA**
Untitled. (1959)
Gouache on board, 19 7/8 x 26 3/4" (50.5 x 68 cm)
Purchased with funds given by Patricia Phelps de Cisneros
in honor of Paulo Herkenhoff, 1997

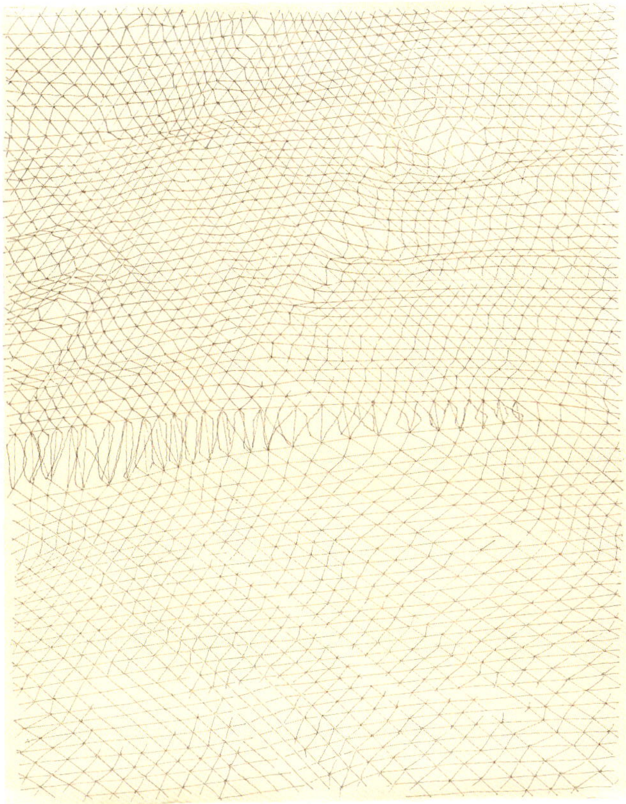

91 **GEGO**

Untitled, 1970

Colored ink on paper, 25 ¾ x 19 ¾" (65.4 x 50.2 cm)

Gift of Patricia Phelps de Cisneros in memory of Warren Lowry, 2001

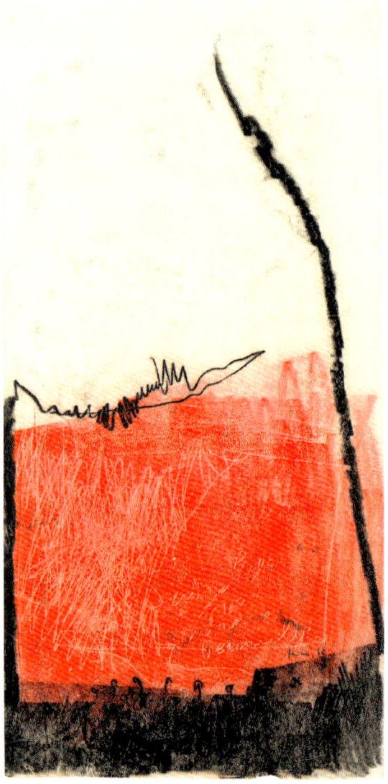

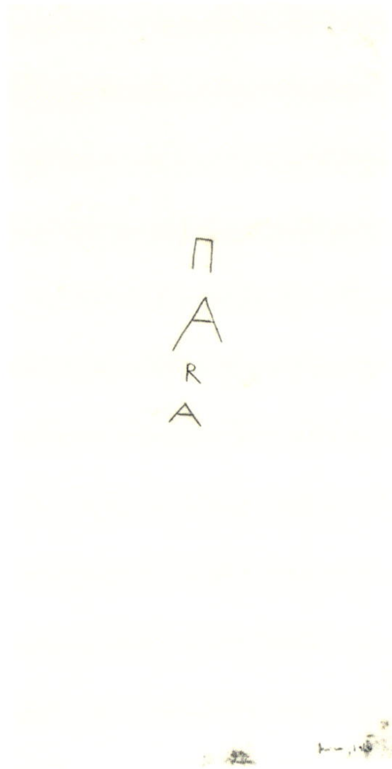

92 **MIRA SCHENDEL**
Untitled (Red). (1964)
Monotype, 18 1/2 x 9" (47 x 22.9 cm)
Gift of Luisa Strina in memory of
Lydia and Ferdinando Strina, 2001

93 **MIRA SCHENDEL**
Untitled, 1964
Monotype, 18 1/4 x 9" (46.4 x 22.9 cm)
Gift of Luisa Strina in memory of
Lydia and Ferdinando Strina, 2001

94 **LEÓN FERRARI**
Untitled, 1962
Ink on paper, 40 x 28 5/8" (101.6 x 72.7 cm)
Purchase, 2003

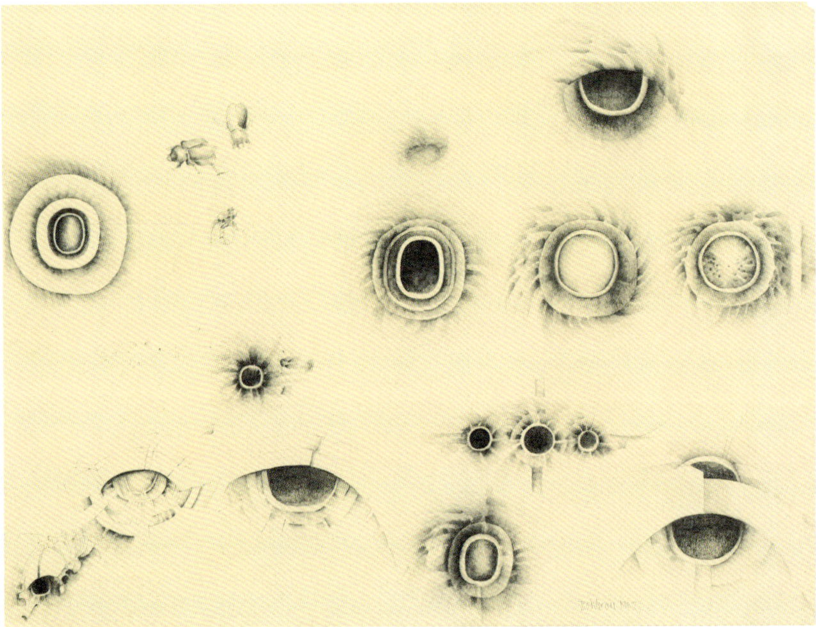

95 **LEE BONTECOU**
Untitled, 1962
Pencil on paper, 19 3/4 x 25 1/2" (50.2 x 64.8 cm)
Gift of Sarah-Ann and Werner H. Kramarsky, 2001

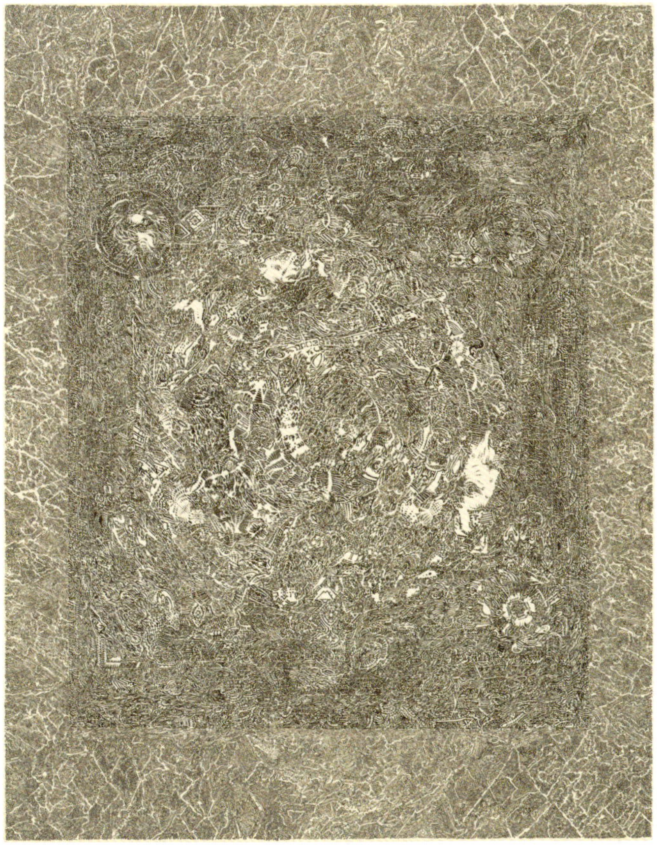

96 **BRUCE CONNER**
23 KENWOOD AVENUE, (1963)
Ink on paper, 26 x 20" (66 x 50.8 cm)
Purchase and partial gift of Achim Moeller
in memory of Paul Cummings, 2001

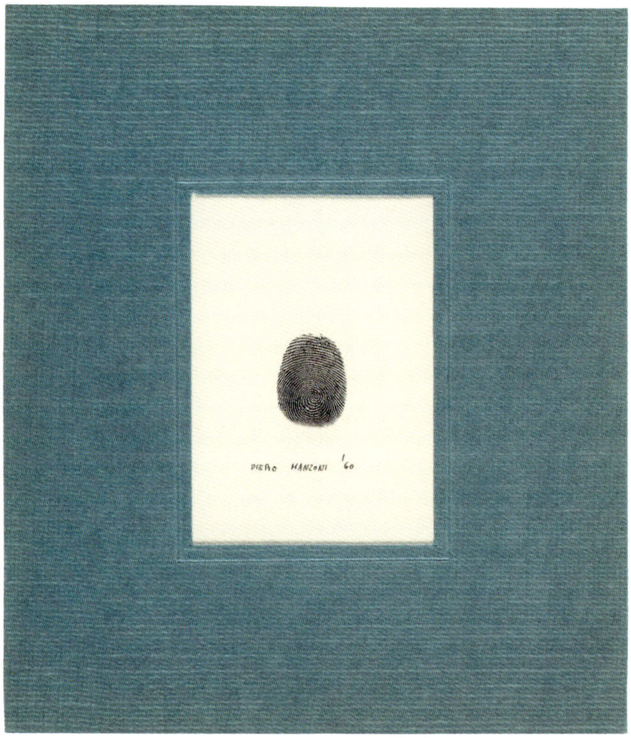

97 **PIERO MANZONI**
Thumbprint, 1960
Ink on paper, with blue mat, 8 1/4 x 7 1/8" (21 x 18 cm)
Gift of Ileana Sonnabend, 1984

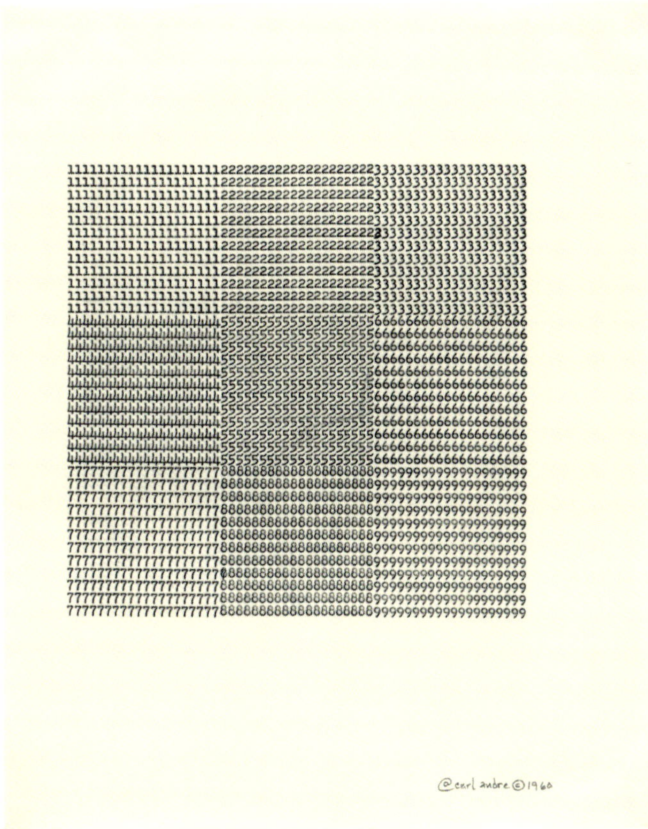

98 **CARL ANDRE**
Untitled, 1960
Typewriting on paper, 11 x 8 1/2" (27.8 x 21 cm)
Gift of Sarah-Ann and Werner H. Kramarsky, 1999

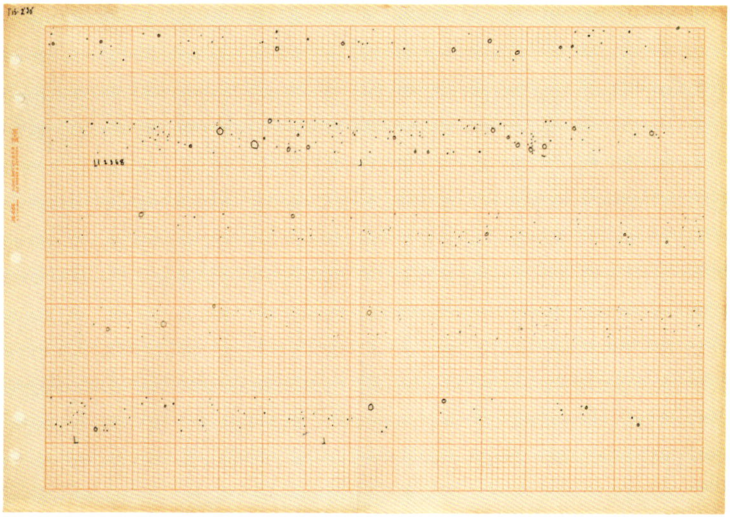

99 **JOHN CAGE**

Music for Carillon, #4, Page 3. (1961)

Ink on transparentized graph paper on board, 11 x 16⅝" (28 x 42.3 cm)

Acquired with matching funds from Gertrud A. Mellon and the National Endowment for the Arts, 1977

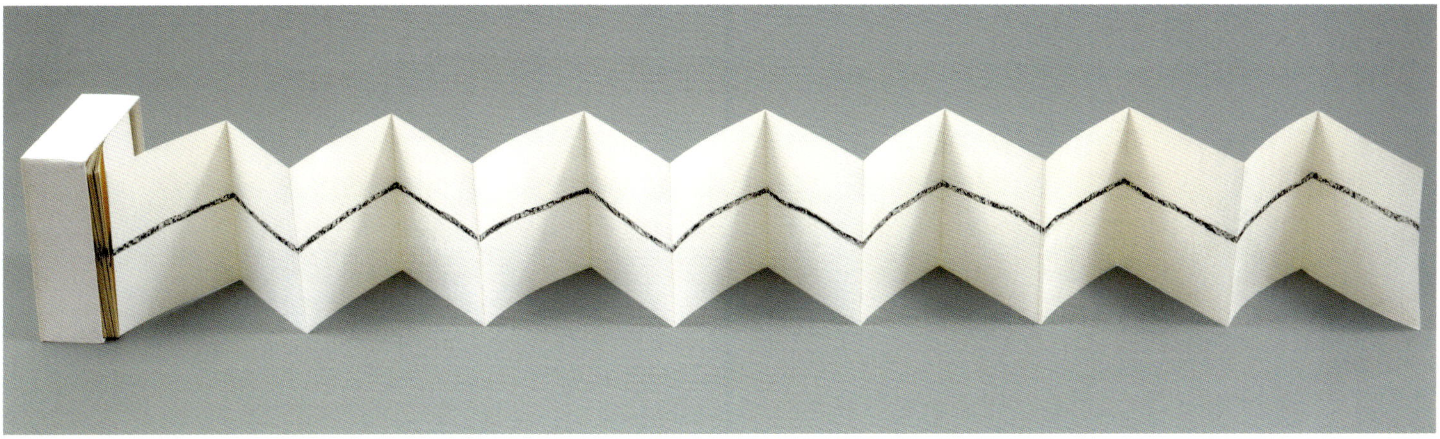

100 **JAMES LEE BYARS**

Untitled Object, (1962–64)

Crayon on Japanese paper, joined and folded, unfolded 12" x 210' 9" (30.3 cm x 64.2 m);
folded 12 x 12 x 3 3/4" (30.3 x 30.3 x 9.5 cm)

Gift of the artist, 1965

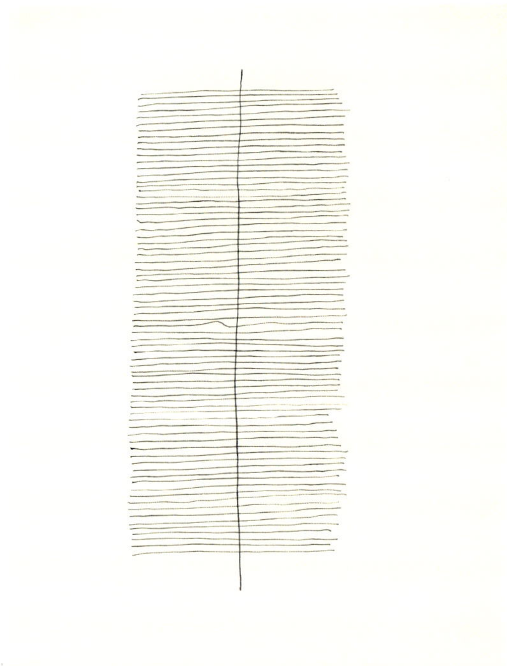

101 **JAN J. SCHOONHOVEN**

T 62-103, (1962)

Ink on paper, 19 ¾ x 15" (50.2 x 38.1 cm)

Gift of Sarah-Ann and Werner H. Kramarsky, 2001

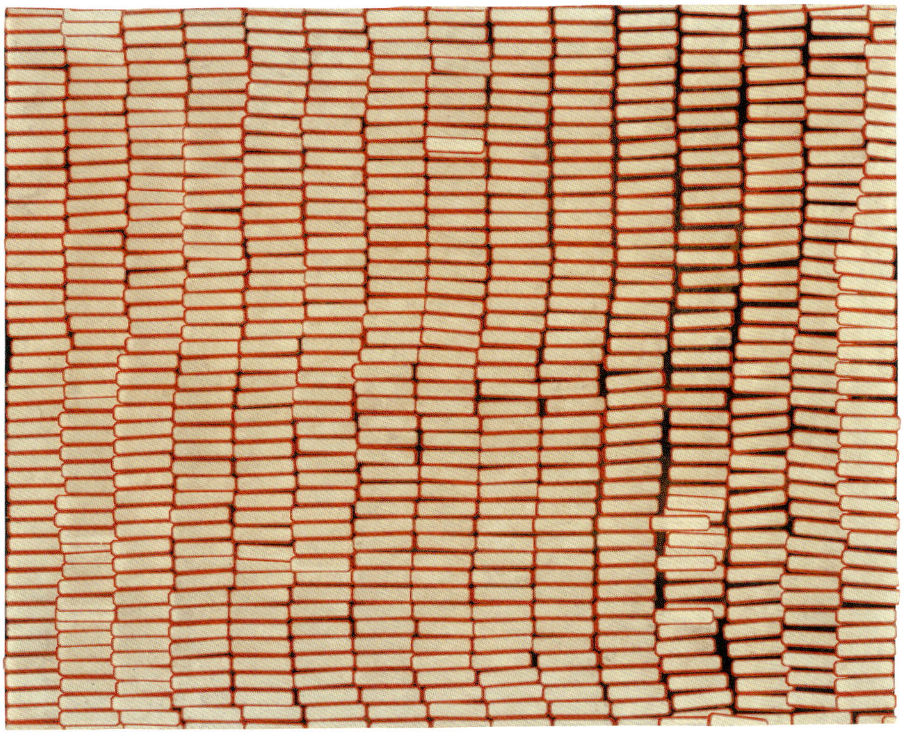

102 **YAYOI KUSAMA**
Accumulation of Stamps, 63. 1962
Pasted labels and ink on paper, 23 ¾ x 29" (60.3 x 73.6 cm)
Gift of Philip Johnson, 1970

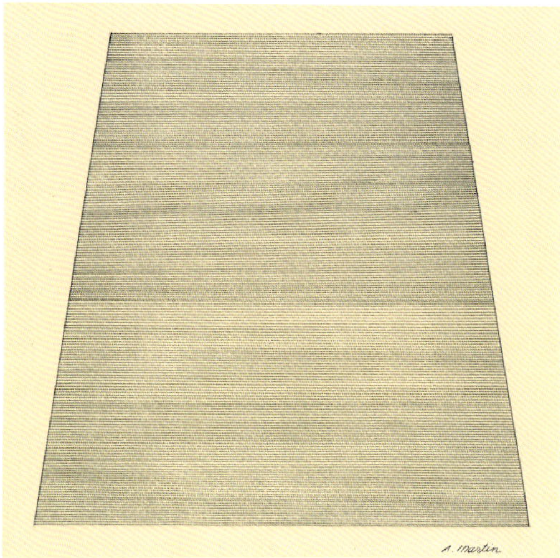

103 **AGNES MARTIN**
Mountain, (1960)
Ink and pencil on paper, 9 ⅛ x 11 ⅞" (24 x 30.2 cm),
shown 9 x 8 ½" (23 x 21.5 cm)
Ruth Vollmer Bequest, 1983

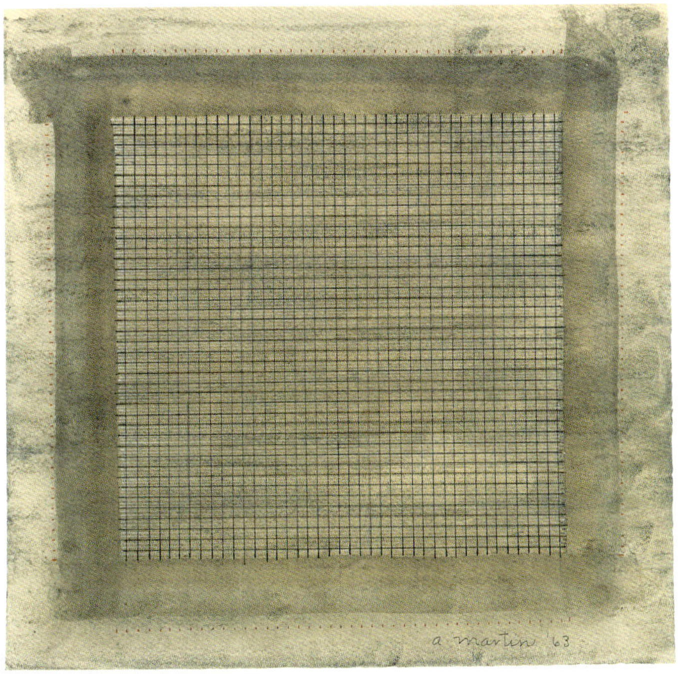

104 **AGNES MARTIN**

Wood I, 1963

Watercolor and pencil on paper, 15 x 15 ½" (38.1 x 39.4 cm)

Fractional and promised gift of Sarah-Ann and Werner H. Kramarsky, 2004

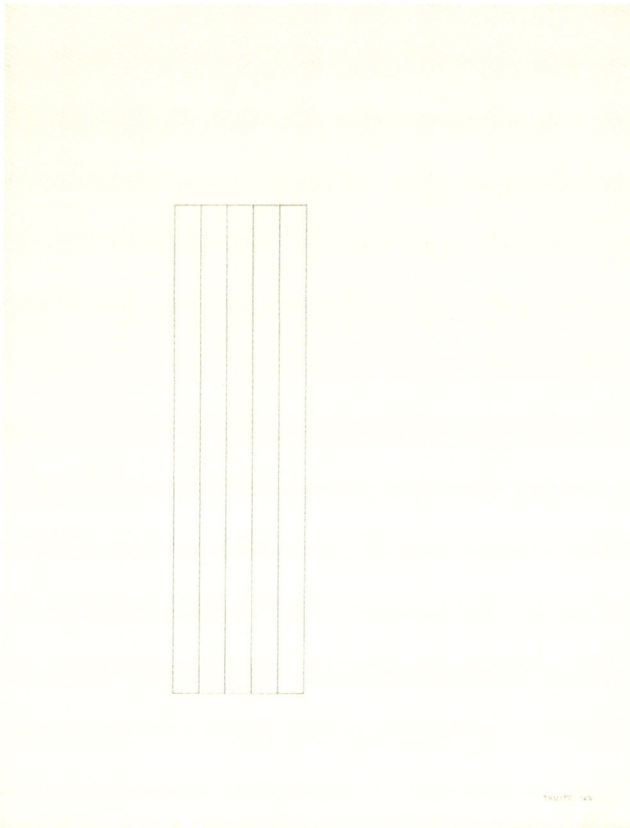

105 **ANNE TRUITT**
Untitled, 1962
Pencil on paper, 24 x 18" (61 x 45.7 cm)
Purchase, 2004

106 **JO BAER**
Rook, 1962
Gouache and pencil on paper, 6 x 6" (15.3 x 15.3 cm)
Gift of Sarah-Ann and Werner H. Kramarsky, 1999

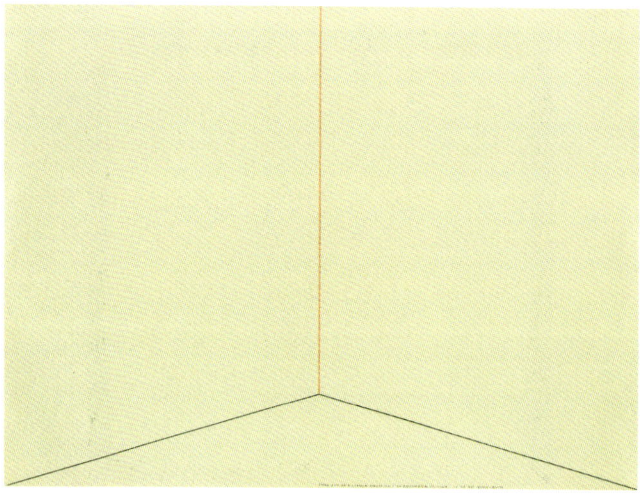

107 **DAN FLAVIN**
Pink out of a Corner from No. 1 of December 19, 1963, October 14, 1965
Pencil and crayon on colored paper, 10 x 13" (25.4 x 33 cm)
Gift of Philip Johnson, 1971

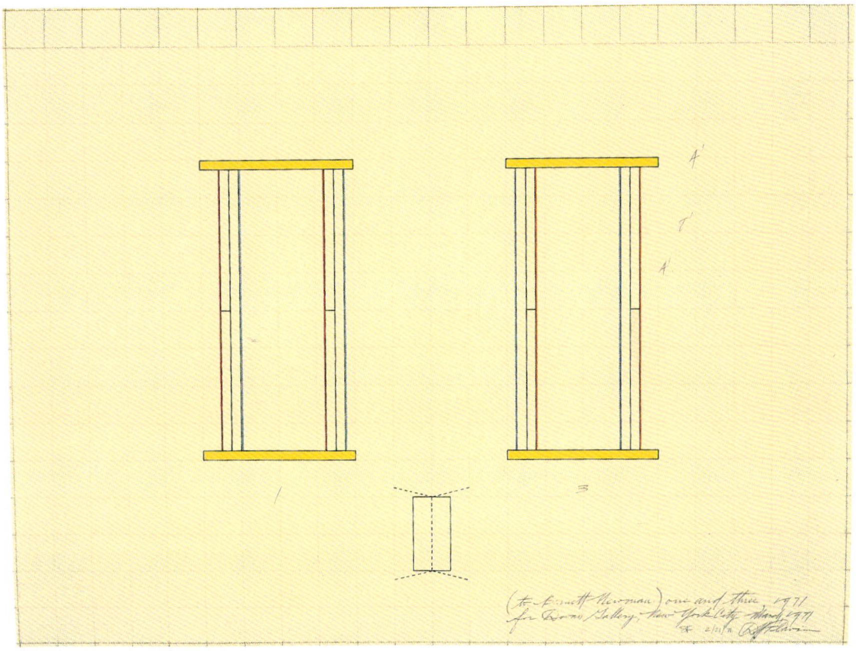

108 **DAN FLAVIN**

Untitled (to Barnett Newman) One and Three, 1971

Ink, colored pencil, and pencil on graph paper, 16 x 22" (40.6 x 55.9 cm)

Fractional and promised gift of Sarah-Ann and Werner H. Kramarsky, 2004

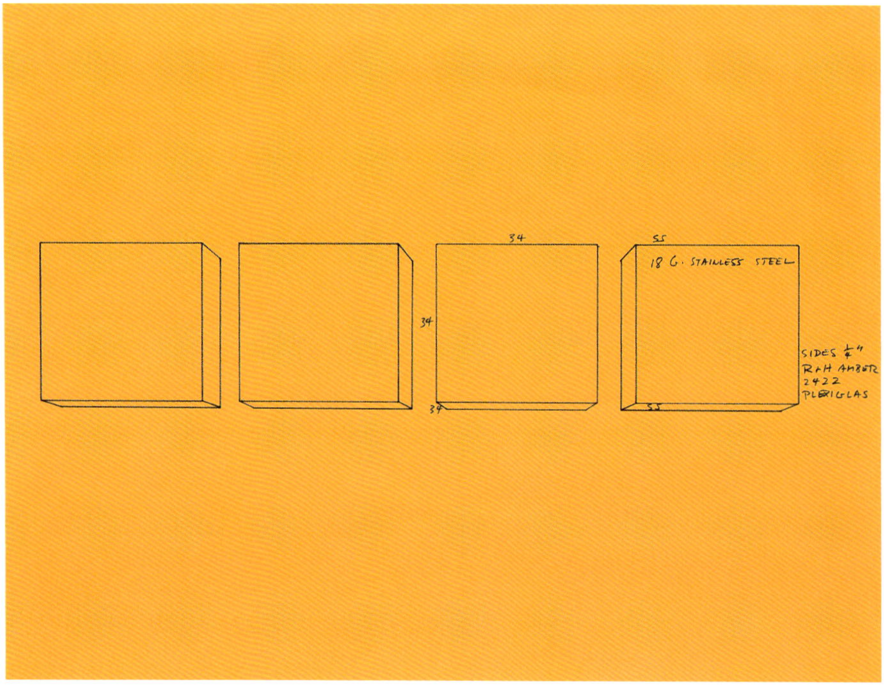

109 **DONALD JUDD**

Untitled, 1966

Felt-tip pen on yellow paper, 17 1/8 x 22" (43.5 x 56 cm)

L-B Foundation Fund, 1967

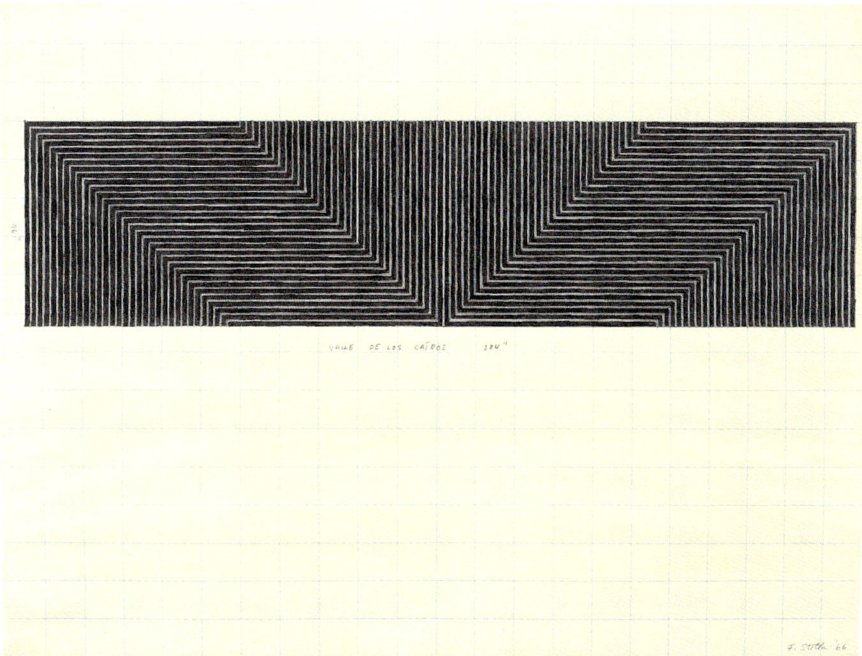

110 **FRANK STELLA**

Study for Valle de los Caídos, 1966

Felt-tip pen and pencil on graph paper, 17¼ x 22¼" (43.8 x 56.5 cm)

Fractional and promised gift of Sarah-Ann and Werner H. Kramarsky, 2004

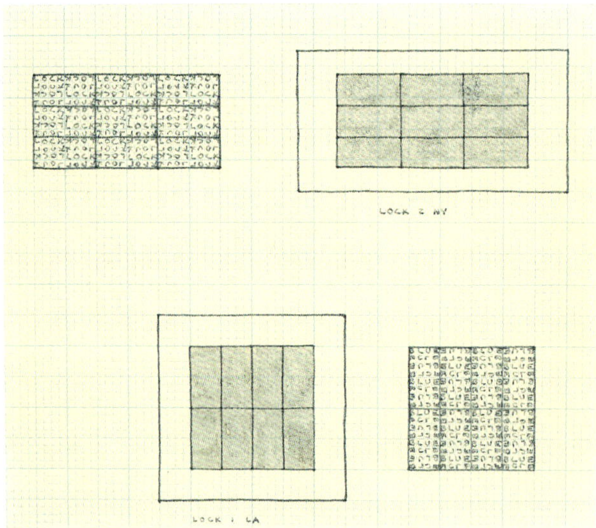

111 **CARL ANDRE**

Blue Lock, (1966)

Colored ink on graph paper, 8 ¾ x 9 ¾" (22.2 x 24.8 cm)

Fractional and promised gift of Sarah-Ann and Werner H. Kramarsky, 2004

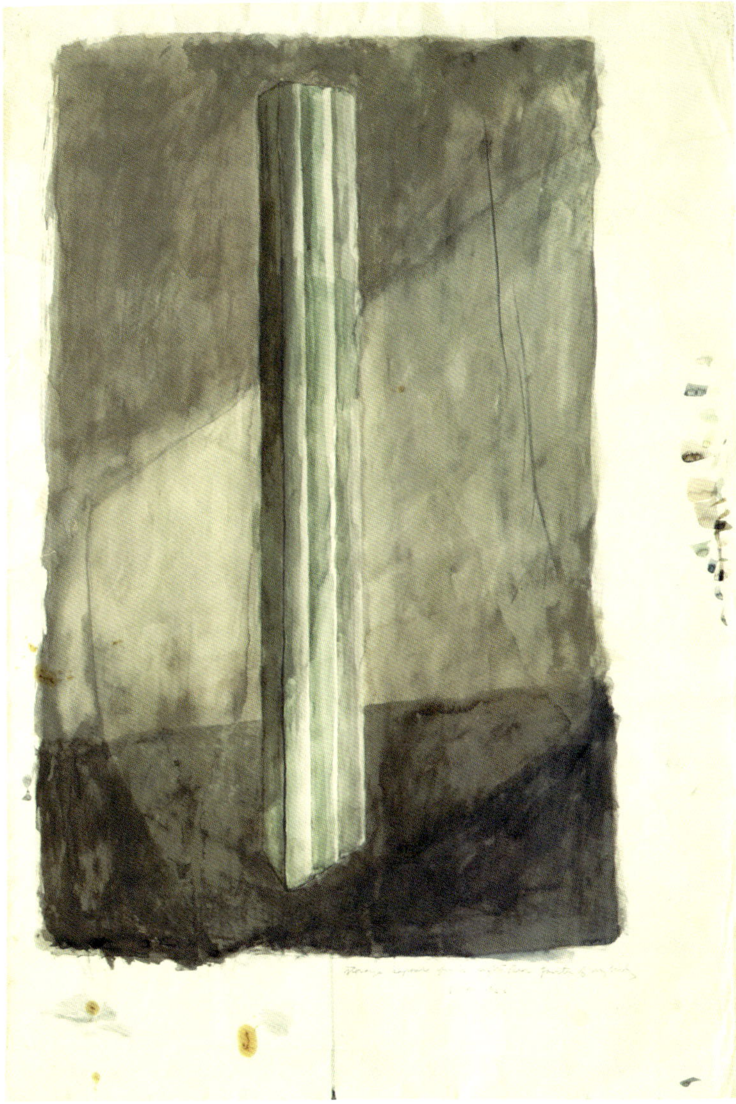

112 **BRUCE NAUMAN**
Study related to the sculpture Storage Capsule for the Right Rear Quarter of My Body, 1966
Watercolor and pencil on paper, 38 x 24 ¾" (95.5 x 63 cm)
Gift of Alexis Gregory and purchase, 1985

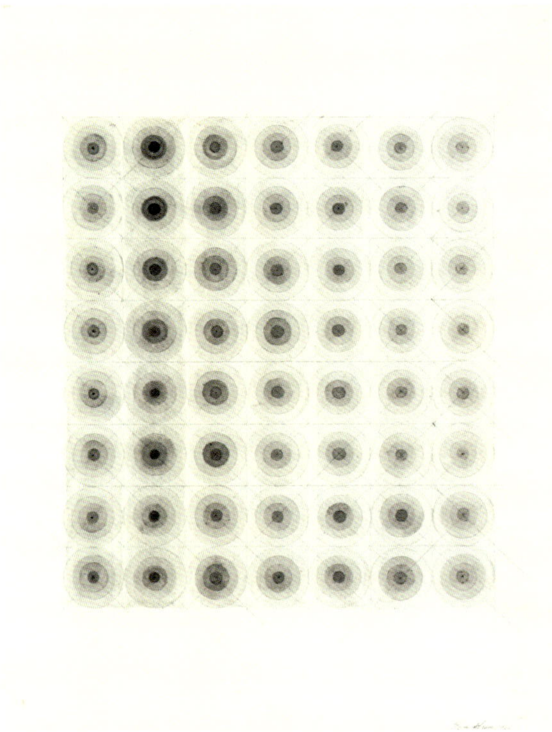

113 **EVA HESSE**
Untitled, 1966
Watercolor and pencil on paper, 11 3/4 x 9 1/8" (30 x 23.1 cm)
Gift of Mr. and Mrs. Herbert Fischbach, 1969

114 **EVA HESSE**
Untitled ("For Ruth."), 1967
Ink on graph paper, 11 7/8 x 8 1/4" (30.2 x 21 cm)
Ruth Vollmer Bequest, 1983

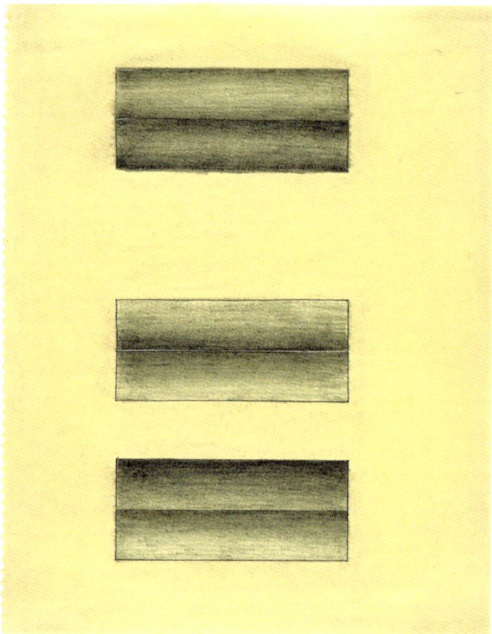

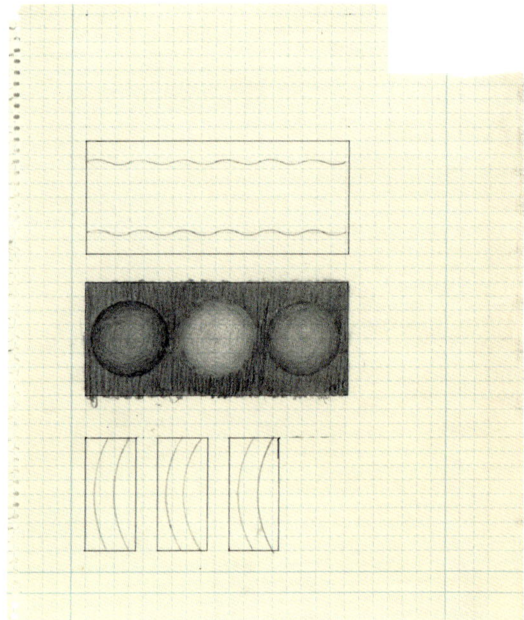

115 **LEE LOZANO**
Untitled, (c. 1965)
Pencil and ballpoint pen on yellow paper,
11 x 8 1/2" (27.9 x 21.6 cm)
Fractional and promised gift of Sarah-Ann
and Werner H. Kramarsky, 2004

116 **LEE LOZANO**
Untitled, 1965
Pencil and ballpoint pen on graph paper,
11 x 8 1/2" (27.9 x 21.6 cm)
Fractional and promised gift of Sarah-Ann
and Werner H. Kramarsky, 2004

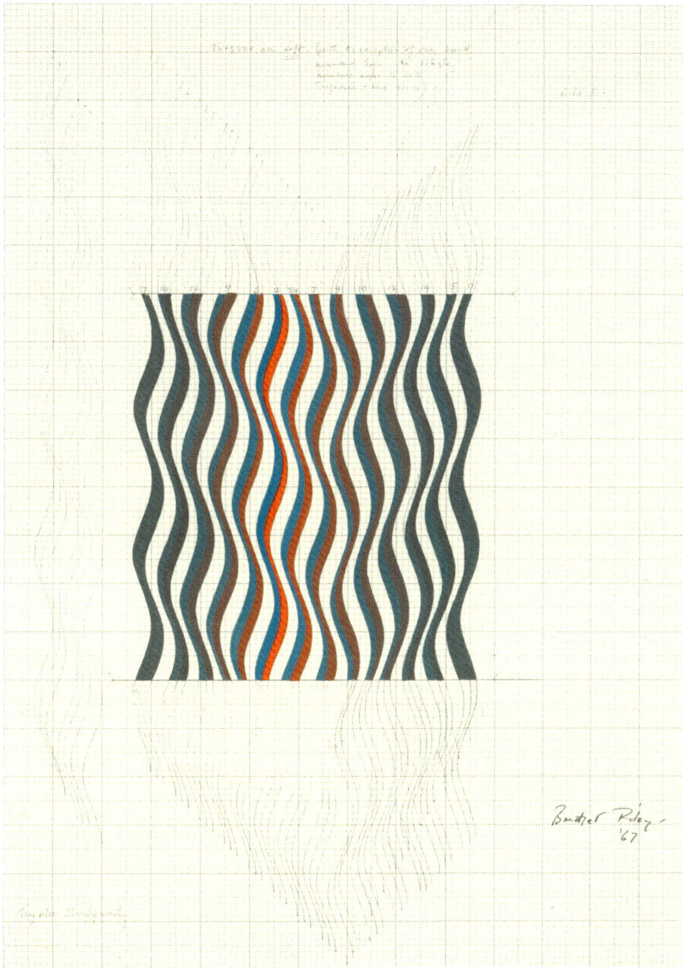

117 **BRIDGET RILEY**
Study, 1967
Gouache and pencil on graph paper, 20 1/2 x 14 1/2" (52 x 36.8 cm)
Philip Johnson Fund, 1969

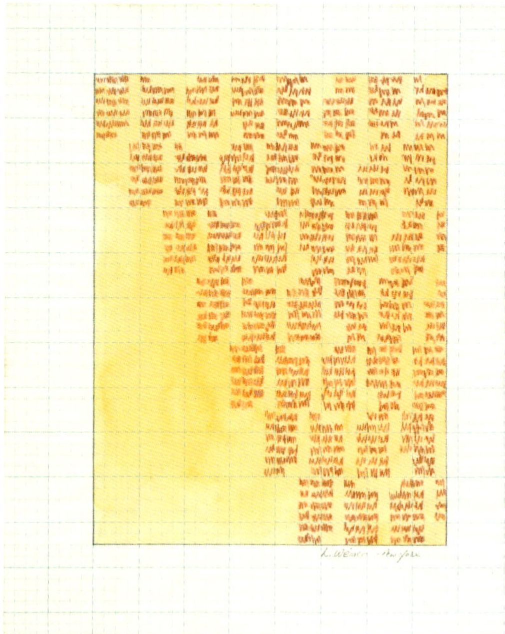

118 **LAWRENCE WEINER**
Untitled, (1965)
Watercolor, colored pencil, and pencil on graph paper, 14 x 11" (35.6 x 27.9 cm)
Bequest of Alicia Legg, 2002

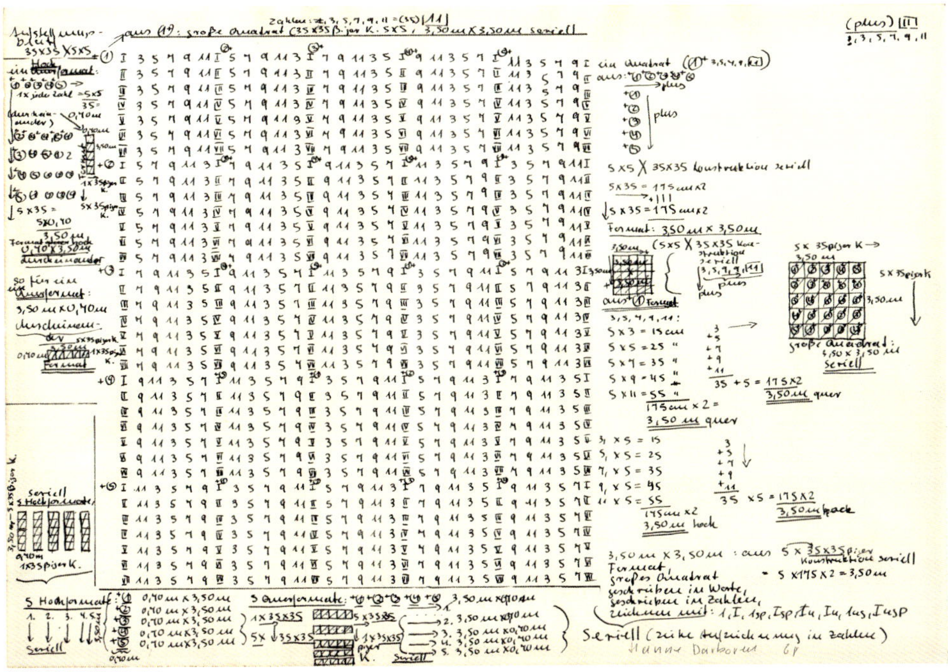

119 **HANNE DARBOVEN**

Construction Drawing (Konstruktionszeichnung), 1968

Ink on graph paper, 17 x 23 7/8" (43.2 x 60.7 cm)

Purchase, 2003

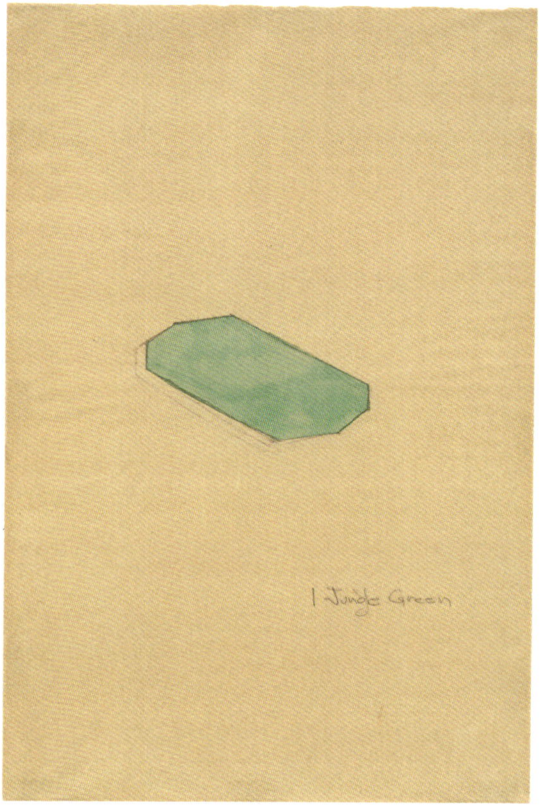

120 **RICHARD TUTTLE**
Study for First Green Octagon, (1967)
Watercolor and pencil on paper,
$17\frac{5}{8} \times 11\frac{5}{8}$" (44.9 x 29.5 cm)
Gift of Jock Truman, 1974

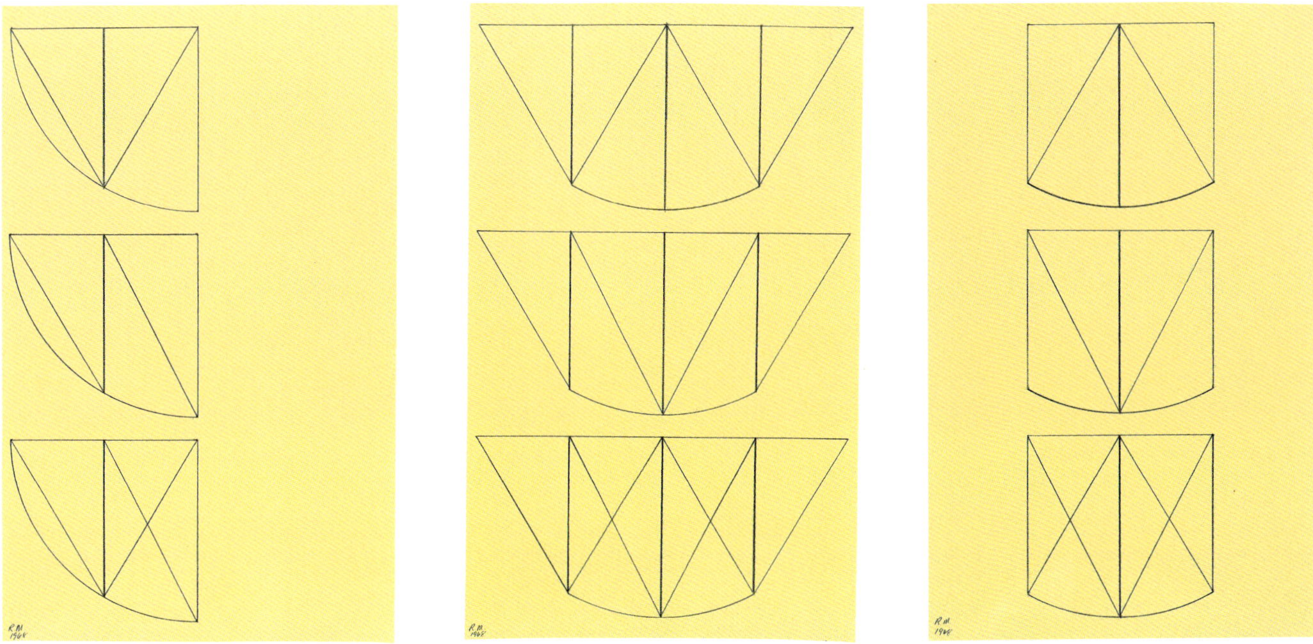

121 **ROBERT MANGOLD**
Untitled Drawing #1, #2, and #3, 1968
Pencil on paper, three sheets, each 13 7/8 x 8 1/2" (35.2 x 21.6 cm)
Fractional and promised gift of Sarah-Ann and Werner H. Kramarsky, 2004

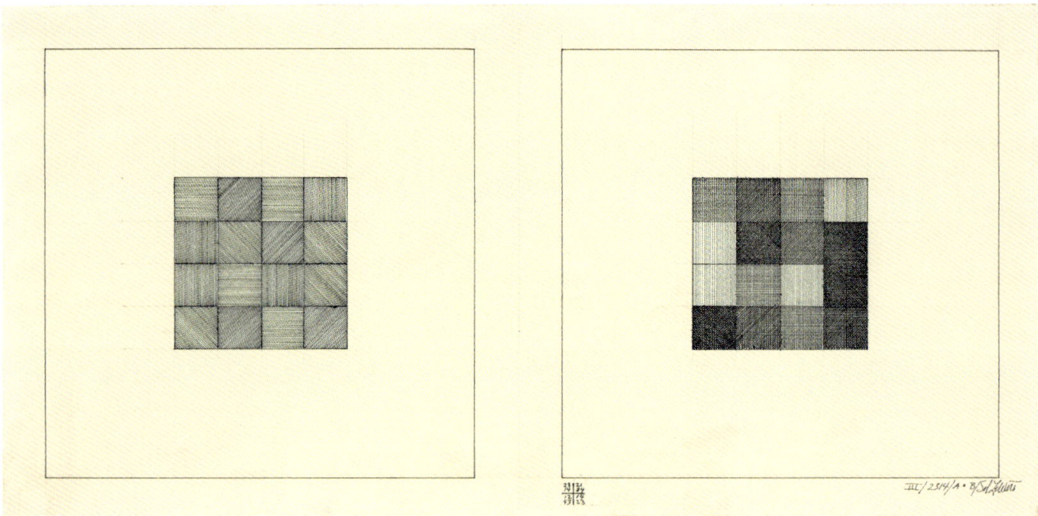

122 **SOL LEWITT**
Drawing Series III/2314/A & B. (1969)
Ink and pencil on paper, 12 x 24" (30.6 x 61 cm)
Ruth Vollmer Bequest. 1982

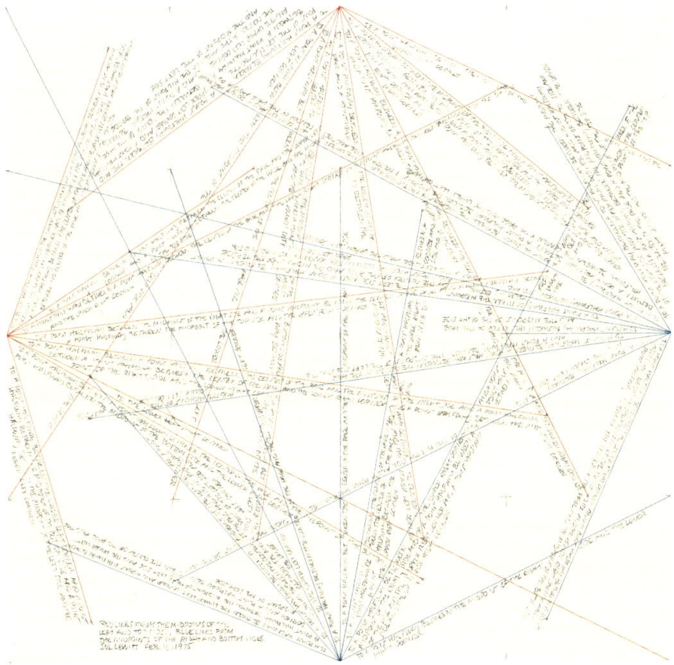

123 **SOL LEWITT**
Red Lines from the Midpoints of the Left and Top Sides, Blue Lines from the Midpoints of the Right and Bottom Sides, 1975
Pencil and colored ink on paper, 15 x 15" (38.1 x 38.1 cm)
Fractional and promised gift of Sarah-Ann and Werner H. Kramarsky, 2004

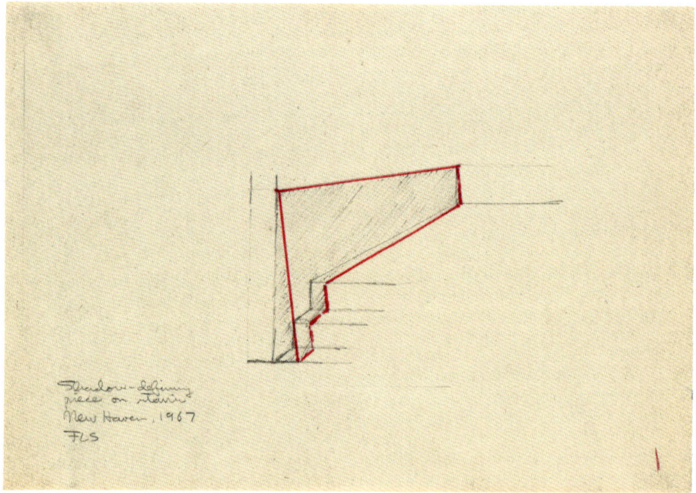

124 **FRED SANDBACK**

Shadow-defining piece on stairs, 1967

Pencil and felt-tip pen on paper, 7⅝ x 10⅝" (19.4 x 27 cm)

Gift of Jan Christiaan Braun in honor of Werner H. Kramarsky, 2003

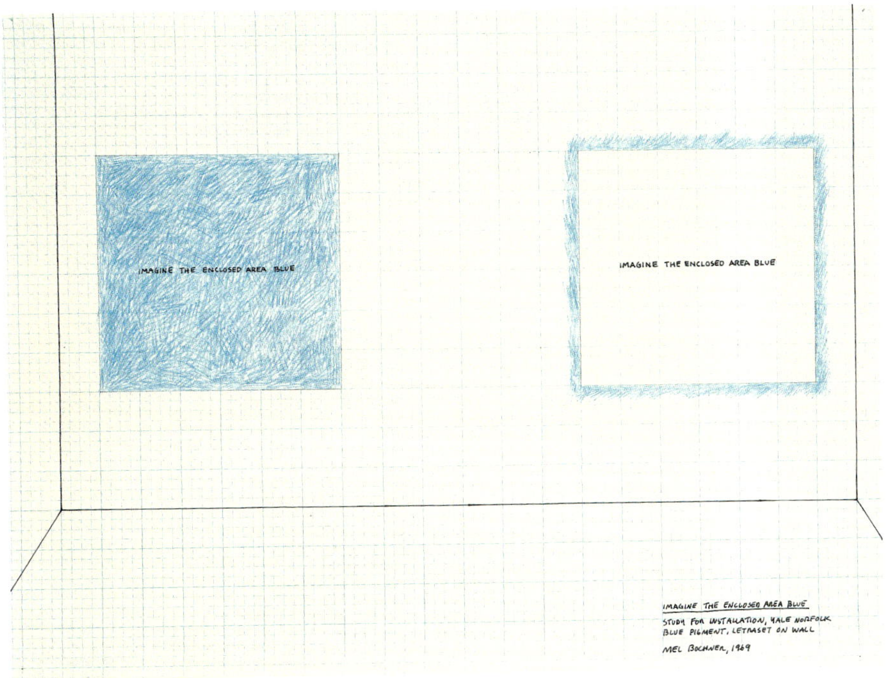

125 **MEL BOCHNER**
Imagine the Enclosed Area Blue (Study for Installation, Yale, Norfolk), 1968
Blue carpenter's chalk and ink on paper, 16 x 22" (40.6 x 55.9 cm)
Fractional and promised gift of Sarah-Ann and Werner H. Kramarsky, 2004

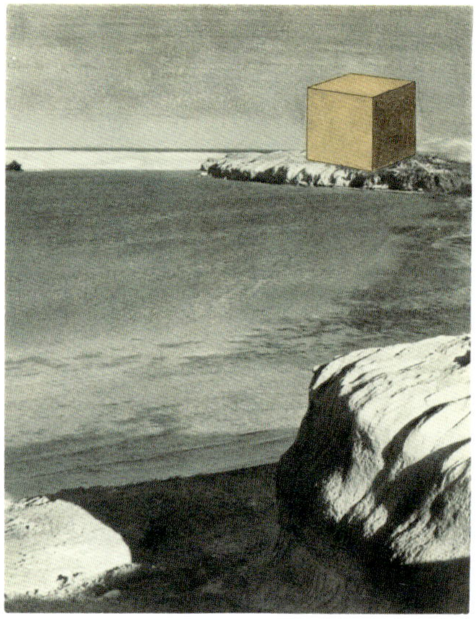

126 **ROBERT SMITHSON**

Proposal for a Monument on the Red Sea, (1966)

Cut-and-pasted printed paper and pencil on gravure,

8 1/4 x 6 1/2" (21 x 16.7 cm)

Elmer A. Johnson, Jr. Bequest, 1994

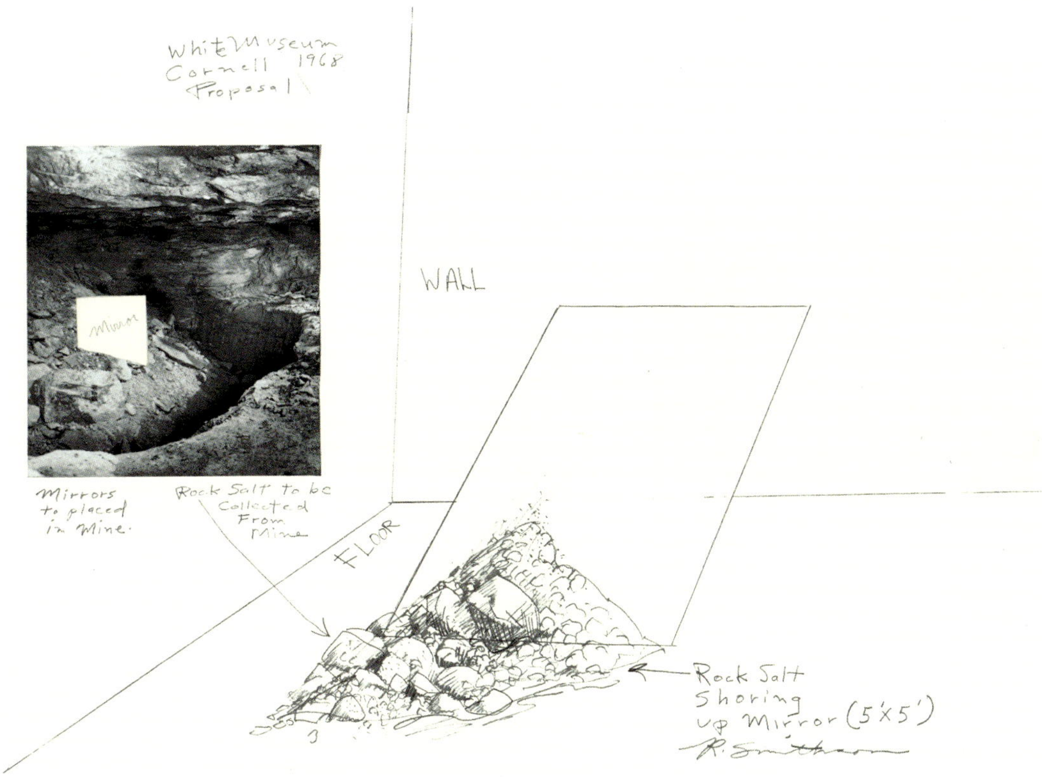

127 **ROBERT SMITHSON**

Mirror with Rock Salt (Salt Mine and Museum Proposal), 1968

Pencil, cut-and-pasted gelatin silver print, and cut-and-pasted paper on paper,

17 3/4 x 24" (45.1 x 60.8 cm)

Gift of Mrs. John de Cuevas, 1971

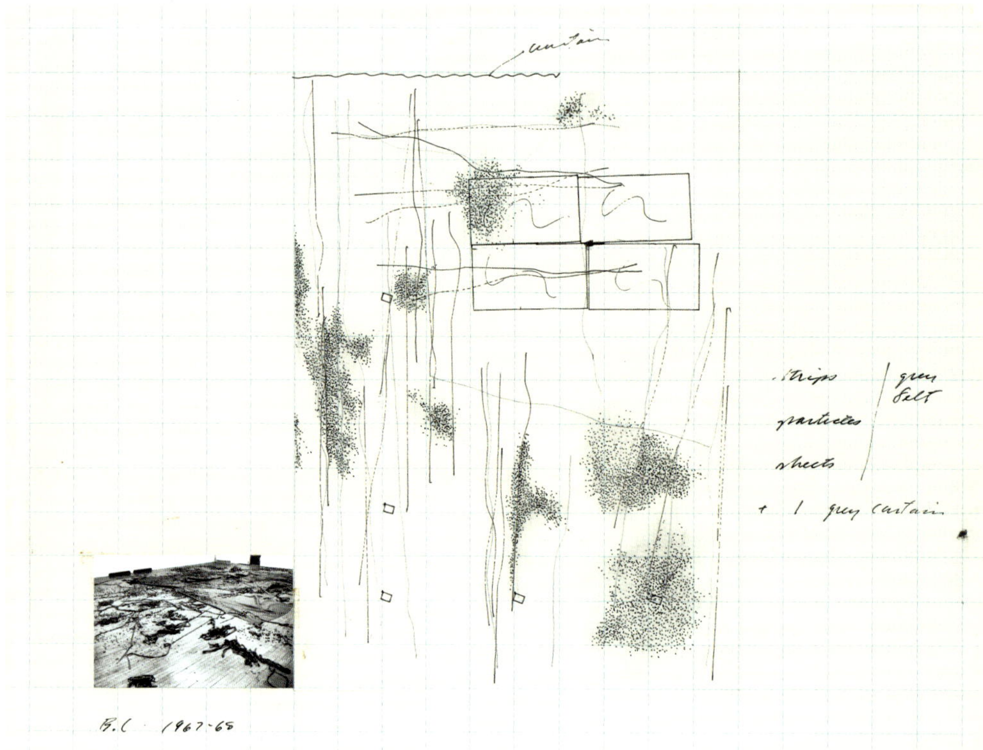

128 **BARRY LE VA**

Strips, Sheets, Particles, 1967–68

Ink, gelatin silver print, and pencil on graph paper,

$17\frac{1}{8} \times 21\frac{5}{8}$" (43.5 x 55.1 cm)

Philip Johnson Fund, 1971

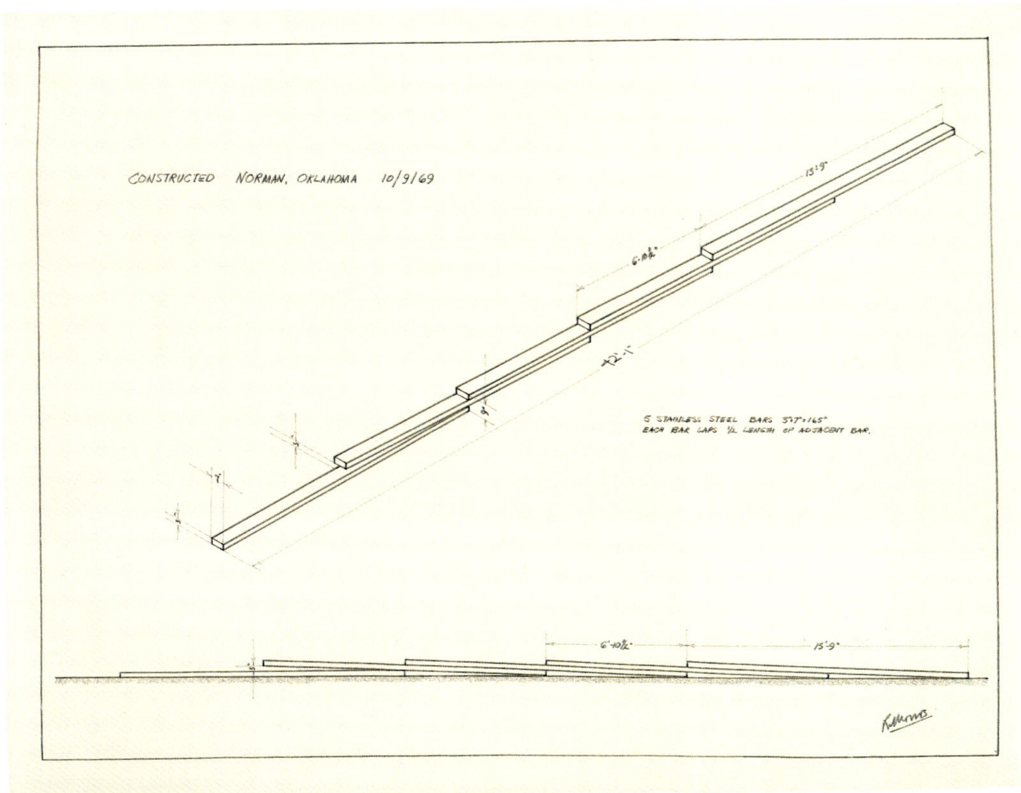

129 **ROBERT MORRIS**

Untitled, 1969

Ink on paper, 20 x 25 ½" (50.8 x 64.8 cm)

Fractional and promised gift of Sarah-Ann and Werner H. Kramarsky, 2004

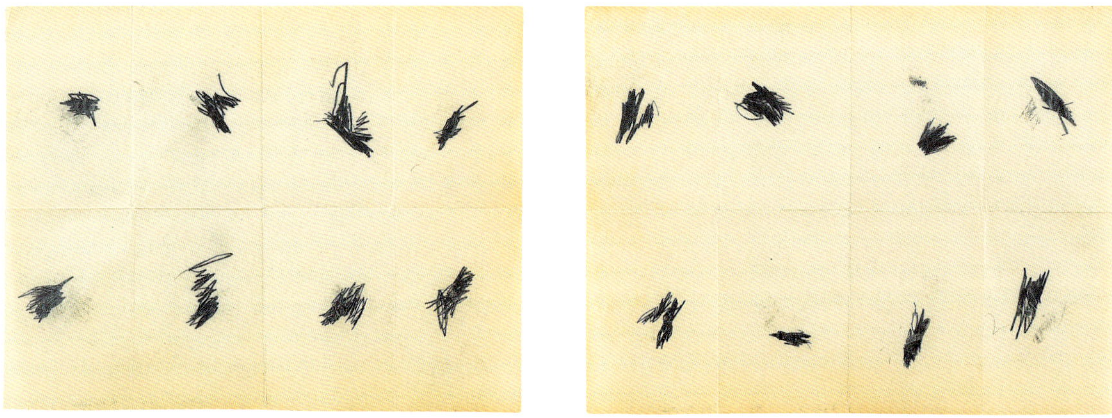

130 **WILLIAM ANASTASI**

Untitled (Pocket Drawings), 1969

Pencil on vellum, two sheets, each 10⅞ x 14" (27.6 x 35.6 cm)

Fractional and promised gift of Sarah-Ann and Werner H. Kramarsky, 2004

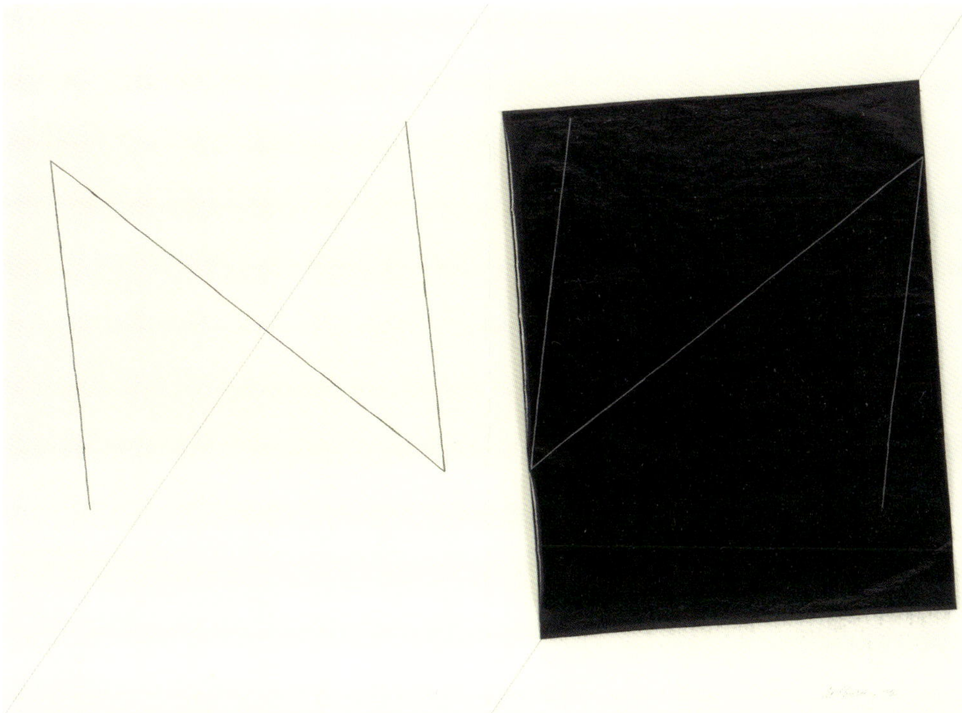

131 **DOROTHEA ROCKBURNE**

Drawing Which Makes Itself, 1972

Carbon, carbon transfer, and pencil on paper, 22 ½ x 30" (57.2 x 76.2 cm)

The Riklis Collection of McCrory Corporation, 1983

132 **BRICE MARDEN**
Untitled, 1970–72
Graphite and wax on paper, 26 x 40" (66.1 x 101.6 cm)
The Werner and Elaine Dannheisser Collection, 1996

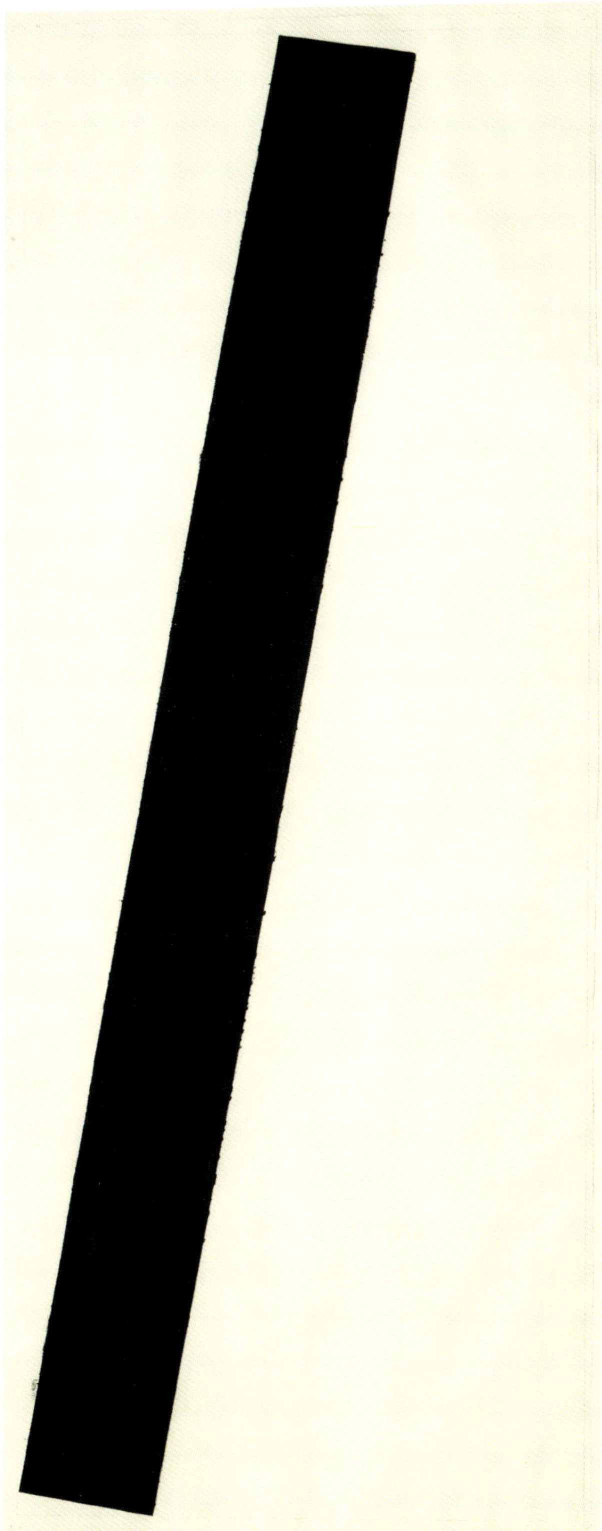

133 **RICHARD SERRA**

Heir. (1973)

Paintstik and graphite on paper, 9' 6 5/8" x 42 1/4" (291.2 x 107.2 cm)
Acquired with matching funds from Mr. and Mrs. S. I. Newhouse, Jr. and the National Endowment for the Arts, 1974

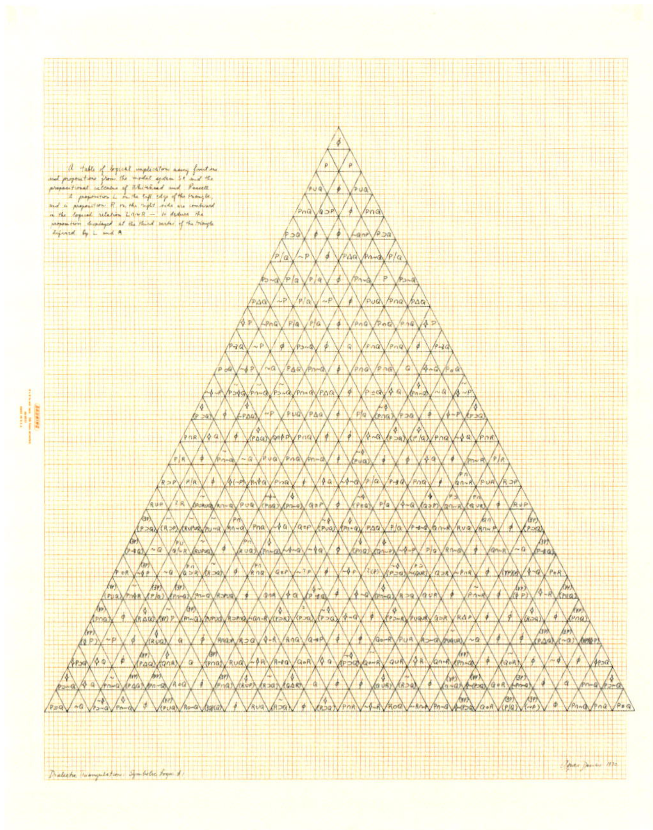

134 **AGNES DENES**

The Human Argument, 1969–70

Ink on transparentized graph paper, 20 7/8 x 16 7/8" (53 x 42.9 cm)

Gift of the artist in honor of Agnes Gund, 2002

135 **WALTERCIO CALDAS**
Japan (Japão), 1972
Ink, metallic ink, and transfer type on paper, 19 x 17 ½" (48.3 x 44.4 cm)
Gift of Gilberto Chateaubriand in memory of Monroe Wheeler, Francisco Masjuan and John Brady, 1995

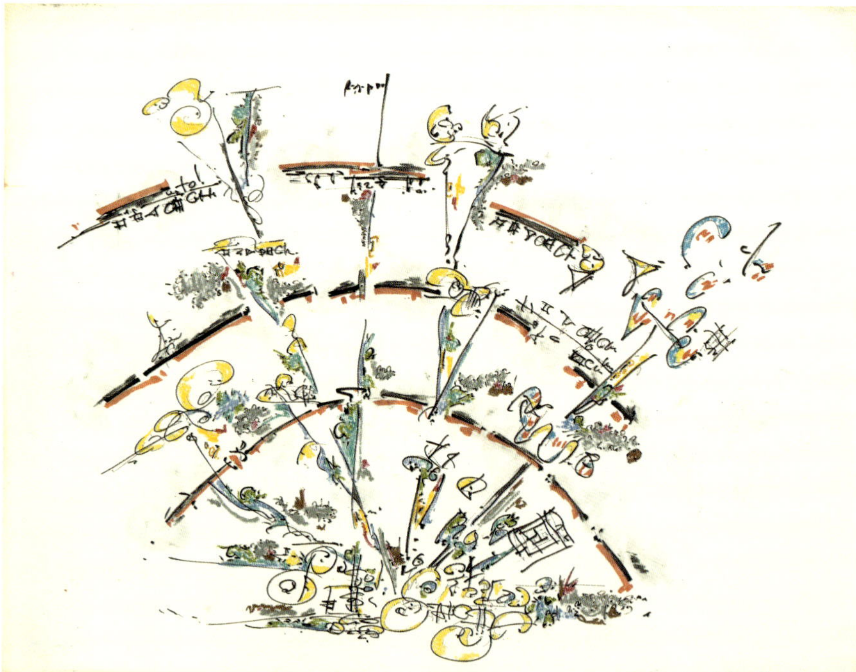

136 **GORDON MATTA-CLARK**
Untitled (Energytree), (1972–73)
Crayon, felt-tip pen, and ballpoint pen on paper, 22 ½ x 28 ½" (57 x 72 cm)
Gift of the artist's estate, 1999

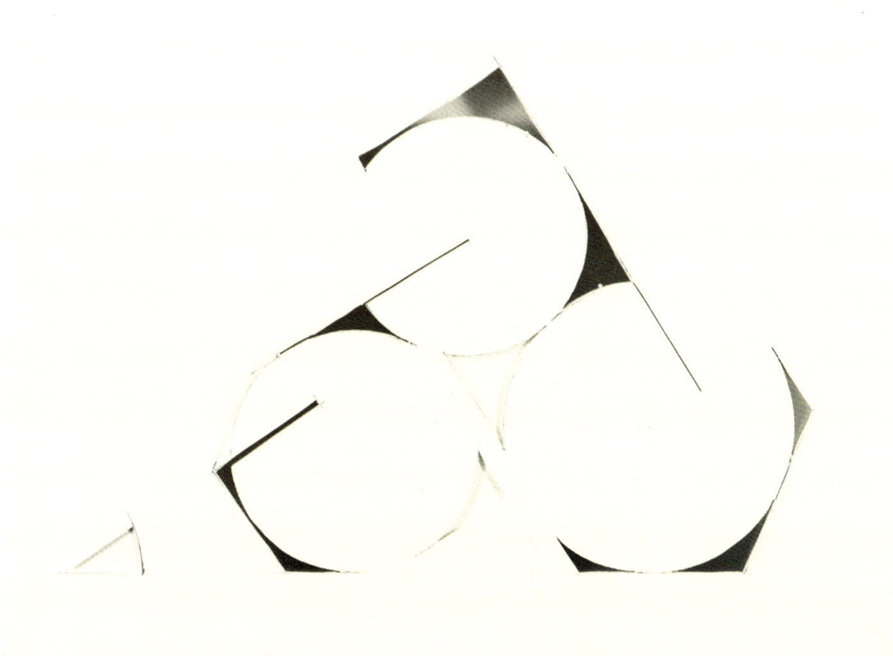

137 **GORDON MATTA-CLARK**
Untitled (Cut Drawing). (1976–77)
Pencil on layers of cut paper, 22 ½ x 29 ½ x ½" (57 x 74 x 1.3 cm)
Purchase through the Vincent D'Aquila and Harry Soviak Bequest Fund, The Judith Rothschild Foundation and Purchase Fund, 1999

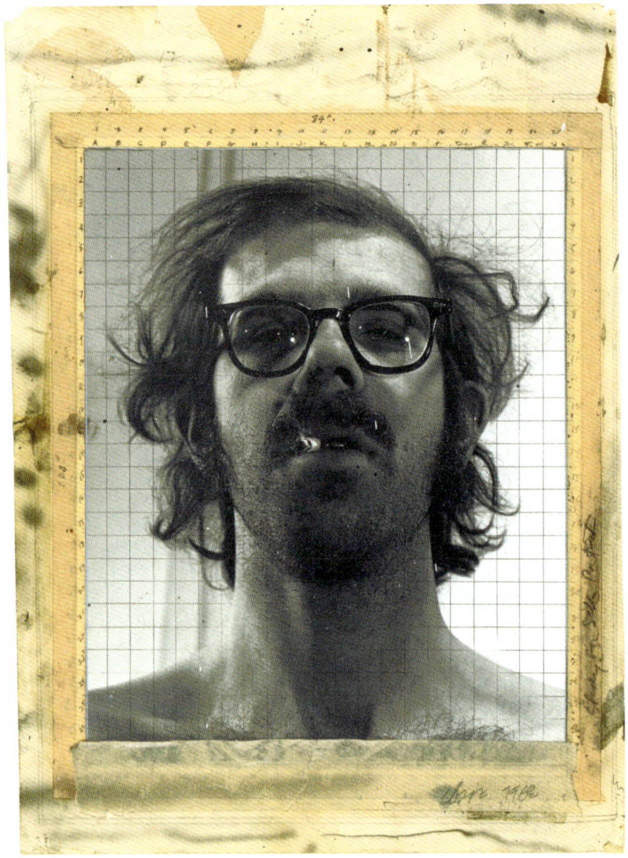

138 **CHUCK CLOSE**
Study for **Self-Portrait**, 1968
Gelatin silver print, ink, pencil, and pressure-sensitive tape on board, 18⅝ x 13⅜" (47.2 x 33.9 cm)
Gift of Norman Dubrow, 1978

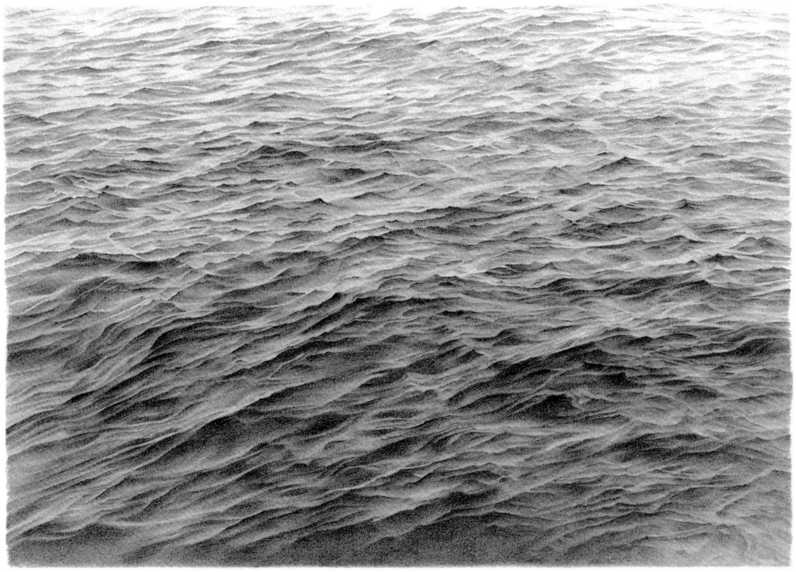

139 **VIJA CELMINS**
Untitled (Ocean), 1970
Pencil on paper, 14 ⅛ x 18 ⅞" (36 x 48 cm)
Mrs. Florene M. Schoenborn Fund, 1970

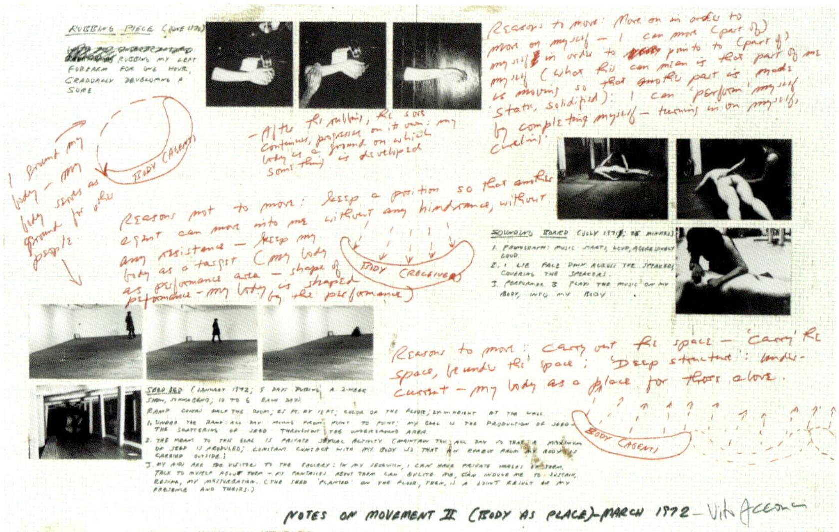

140 **VITO ACCONCI**

Notes on Movement II (Body As Place), March 1972

Felt-tip pen and cut-and-pasted gelatin silver prints on two sheets of graph paper on board, 21 ⅞ x 34" (55.4 x 86.4 cm)

Gift of Charles Cowles, 1974

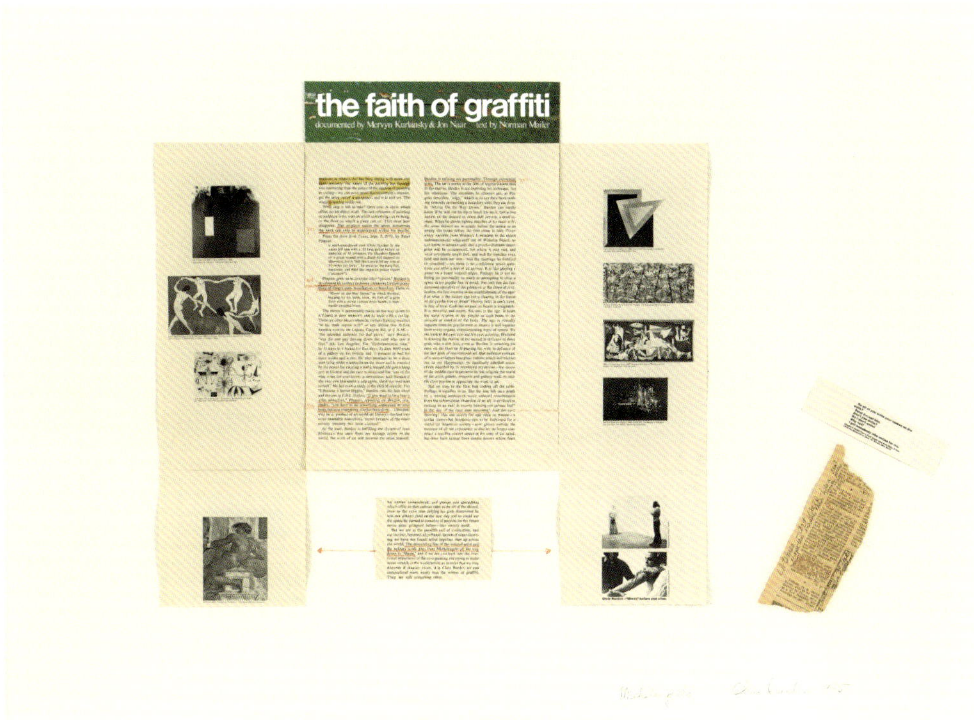

141 **CHRIS BURDEN**

Michelangelo, 1975

Cut-and-pasted printed paper with felt-tip pen and ink on board,

30 x 40" (76.2 x 101.6 cm)

From the Collection of Laura-Lee and Robert Woods, 1991

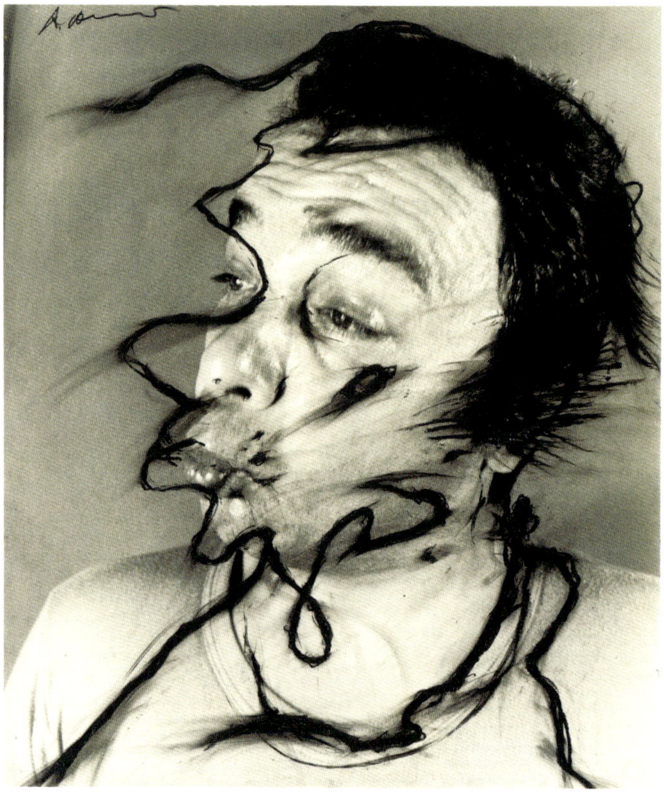

142 **ARNULF RAINER**
Untitled, (1969–74)
Oil stick on gelatin silver print, 23 x 19" (58.4 x 48.4 cm)
Gift of Joan and Lester Avnet (by exchange), 1988

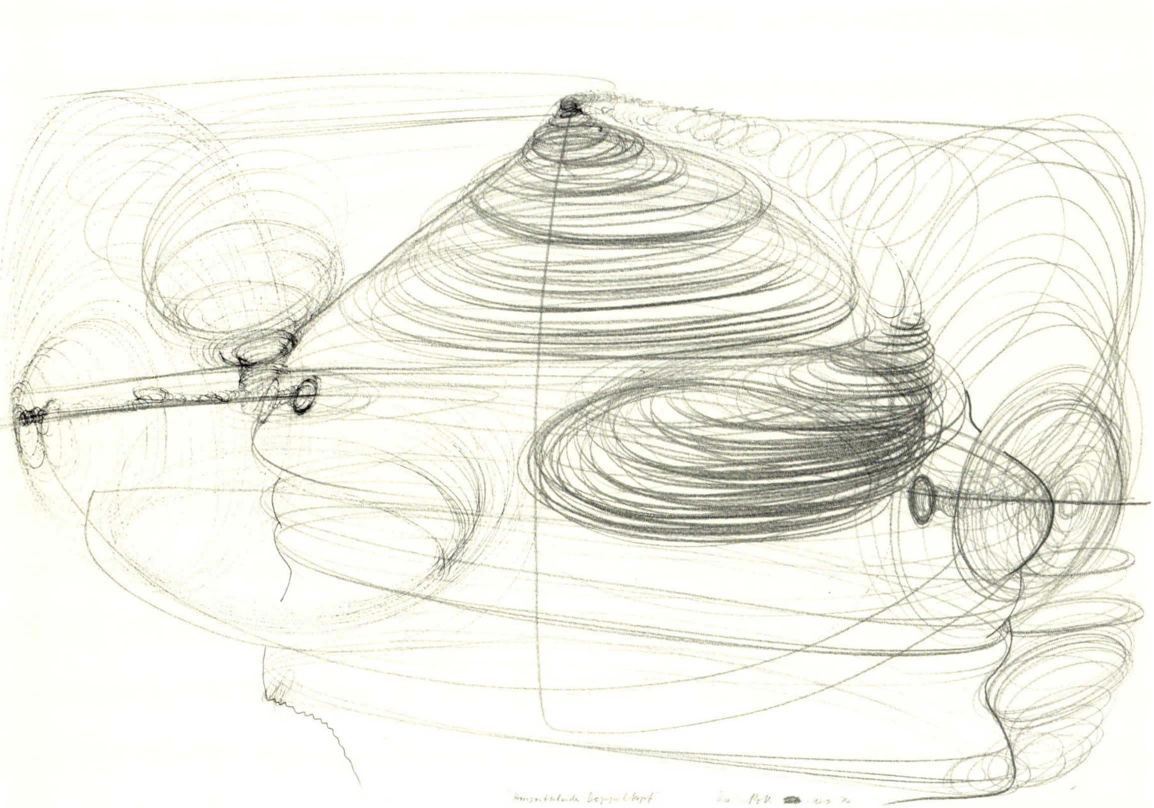

143 **DIETER ROTH**

Doublehead Viewing Horizon (Horizontsehender Doppelkopf). (1974)

Pencil and ink on paper, 24 x 33 ¾" (61 x 85.7 cm)

Purchase, 2004

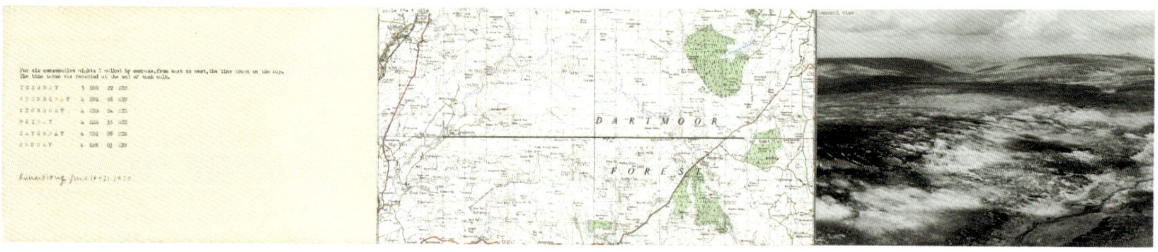

 RICHARD LONG

Walking a Straight 10-Mile Line, Dartmoor, England, 1970

Typewritten sheet, lithograph, and gelatin silver print, each mounted to board on board, overall $8\frac{7}{8}$ x $39\frac{1}{2}$" (22.5 x 100.3 cm)

Charles Simon Fund, 1970

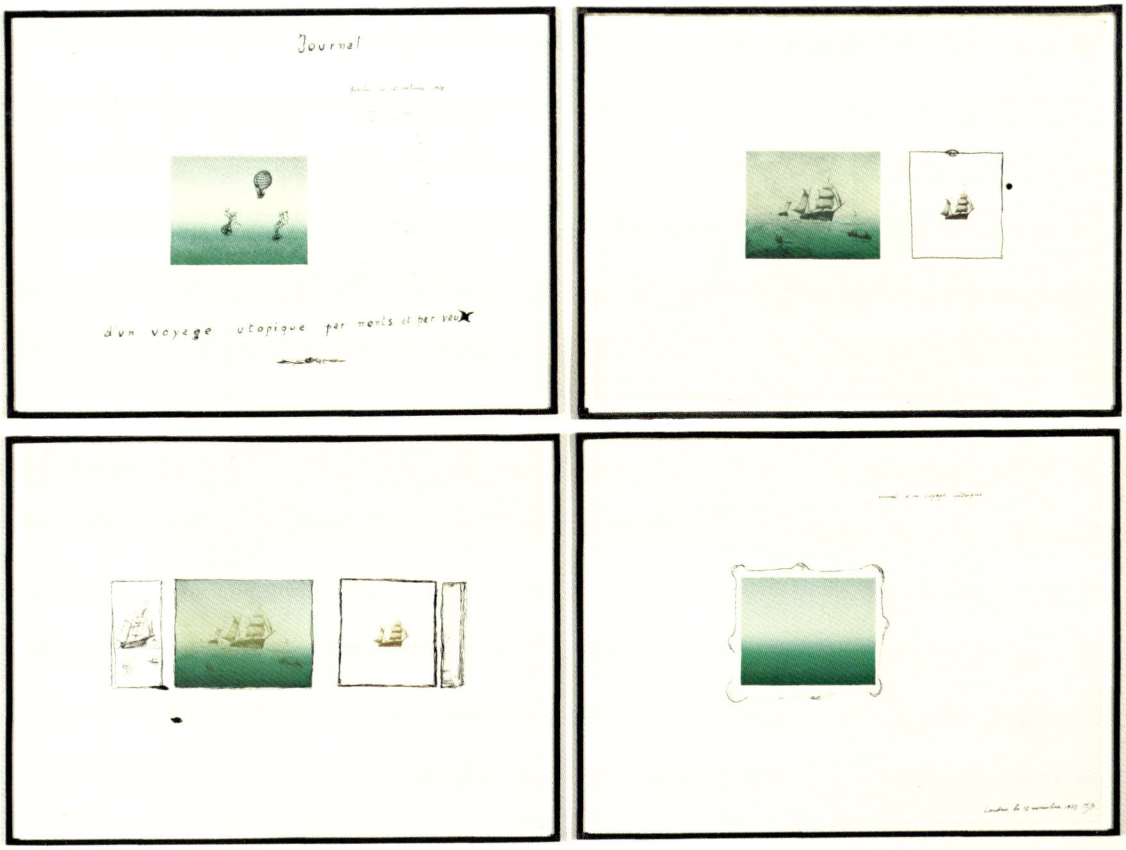

145 **MARCEL BROODTHAERS**
Journal d'un voyage utopique, 1973
Ink, colored ink, and lithograph, each sheet framed between board and acrylic sheet with pressure-sensitive tape and mounted to board, overall 37 ½ x 47 ⅜" (95 x 120.4 cm)
Gift of Samuel I. Rosenman (by exchange), 1985

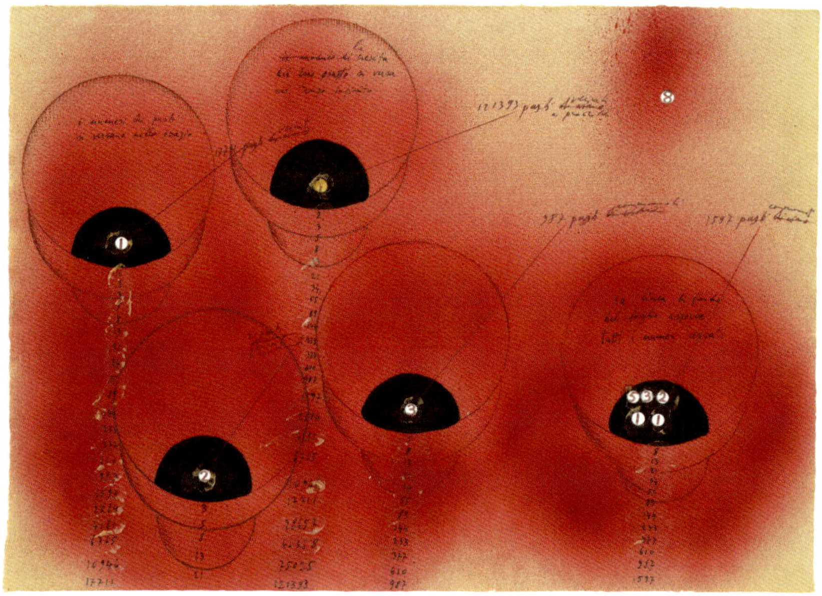

146 **MARIO MERZ**

Berlin Cup (Berliner Tasse), 1974

Spray paint, ink, pencil, and fat on paper,
one of seven drawings, 19 x 26 1/4" (48.3 x 66.7 cm)
Purchased with funds given by Jo Carole and Ronald S. Lauder,
Maria-Gaetana Matisse, and the Committee on Drawings, 1996

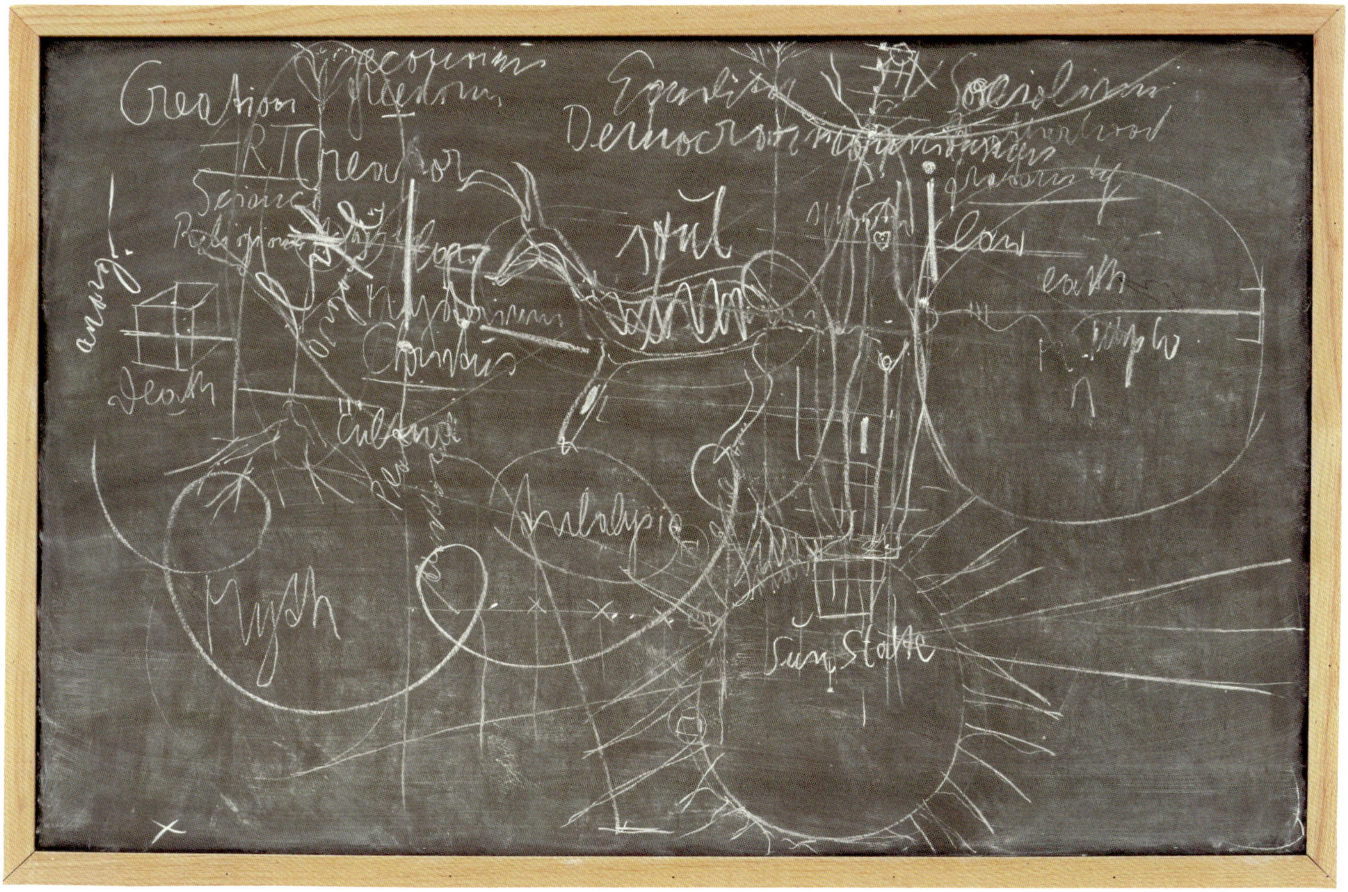

147 **JOSEPH BEUYS**

Untitled (Sun State). (1974)

Chalk on painted board with wood frame, $47\frac{1}{2} \times 71\frac{1}{8}$" (120.7 x 180.7 cm)

Gift of Abby Aldrich Rockefeller (by exchange) and acquired through the Lillie P. Bliss Bequest (by exchange), 1984

CHECKLIST

In this alphabetical list of artists, each checklist entry includes full cataloguing information. Parentheses around the date of a work indicate that the date is not inscribed on the work itself. Unless otherwise noted, dimensions refer to the whole sheet, with height preceding width. The Museum of Modern Art accession number, including the year a work was acquired, appears at the end of the entry.

VITO ACCONCI (American, born 1940)

Notes on Movement II (Body As Place), March 1972
Felt-tip pen and cut-and-pasted gelatin silver prints on two sheets of graph paper on board, 21 7/8 x 34" (55.4 x 86.4 cm)
Gift of Charles Cowles. 1361.1974
Page 188

WILLIAM ANASTASI (American, born 1933)

Untitled (Pocket Drawings), 1969
Pencil on vellum, two sheets, each 10 7/8 x 14" (27.6 x 35.6 cm)
Fractional and promised gift of Sarah-Ann and Werner H. Kramarsky. 71.2004.1–2
Page 178

CARL ANDRE (American, born 1935)

Untitled, 1960
Typewriting on paper, 11 x 8 1/2" (27.8 x 21 cm)
Gift of Sarah-Ann and Werner H. Kramarsky. 371.1999
Page 147

Blue Lock, (1966)
Colored ink on graph paper, 8 3/4 x 9 3/4" (22.2 x 24.8 cm)
Fractional and promised gift of Sarah-Ann and Werner H. Kramarsky. 74.2004
Page 160

RICHARD ARTSCHWAGER (American, born 1923)

Table and Two Chairs, 1965
Charcoal on paper, 19 x 25" (48.3 x 63.6 cm)
Gift of Paul Bianchini. 808.1969
Page 110

JO BAER (American, born 1929)

Rook, 1962
Gouache and pencil on paper, 6 x 6" (15.3 x 15.3 cm)
Gift of Sarah-Ann and Werner H. Kramarsky. 372.1999
Page 155

GEORG BASELITZ (German, born 1938)

P.D. Drawing (P.D. Zeichnung), 1963
Ink and gouache on two sheets of paper, 33 1/2 x 24 1/4" (85 x 61.5 cm)
Purchased with funds given by Jo Carole and Ronald S. Lauder and Leon D. Black. 694.1995.a–b
Page 136

Big Night Down the Drain (Die grosse Nacht im Eimer), 1963
Watercolor and pencil on paper, 24 3/4 x 19" (62.9 x 48.3 cm)
Gift of R. L. B. Tobin. 253.1987
Page 137

ROMARE BEARDEN (American, 1911–1988)

The Dove, (1964)
Cut-and-pasted printed paper, gouache, pencil, and colored pencil on board, 13 3/8 x 18 3/4" (33.8 x 47.5 cm)
Blanchette Hooker Rockefeller Fund. 377.1971
Page 139

JOSEPH BEUYS (German, 1921–1986)

Untitled, (1947) and (1970s)
Pencil on four sheets of paper on painted wood panel, with frame, 31 1/2 x 45 1/2" (80 x 115.5 cm)
Gift of Agnes Gund, and Jo Carole and Ronald S. Lauder. 249.1990.a–d
Page 75

Untitled (Skull on Ur-Sled), 1957
Watercolor, dirt, and metallic paint on tracing paper, 9 5/8 x 12 7/8" (24.5 x 32.8 cm)
Gift of Barbara G. Pine and purchase. 41.1985
Page 76

Dynamis 3, Dynamis, 1960
Oil, pencil, and ink on two sheets of paper on black paper, 16 3/8 x 11 5/8" (41.5 x 29.5 cm)
Purchase. 652.1983
Page 77

Untitled (Sun State), (1974)
Chalk on painted board with wood frame, 47 1/2 x 71 1/8" (120.7 x 180.7 cm)
Gift of Abby Aldrich Rockefeller (by exchange) and acquired through the Lillie P. Bliss Bequest (by exchange). 369.1984
Page 195

MEL BOCHNER (American, born 1940)
Imagine the Enclosed Area Blue
(Study for Installation, Yale, Norfolk), 1968
Blue carpenter's chalk and ink on paper, 16 x 22"
(40.6 x 55.9 cm)
Fractional and promised gift of Sarah-Ann and
Werner H. Kramarsky. 82.2004
Page 173

LEE BONTECOU (American, born 1931)
Untitled, 1962
Pencil on paper, 19 3/4 x 25 1/2" (50.2 x 64.8 cm)
Gift of Sarah-Ann and Werner H. Kramarsky. 2580.2001
Page 144

LOUISE BOURGEOIS (American, born France, 1911;
to United States 1938)
Untitled, (1950)
Gouache, pencil, and colored pencil on blue-green
paper, 28 x 21 3/8" (71.1 x 54.3 cm)
Purchase through the Vincent d'Aquila and
Harry Soviak Bequest Fund. 178.1995
Page 69

MARCEL BROODTHAERS (Belgian, 1924–1976)
Journal d'un voyage utopique, 1973
Ink, colored ink, and lithograph, each sheet framed
between board and acrylic sheet with pressure-
sensitive tape and mounted to board, overall
37 1/2 x 47 3/8" (95 x 120.4 cm)
Gift of Samuel I. Rosenman (by exchange). 42.1985.a–d
Page 193

CHRIS BURDEN (American, born 1946)
Michelangelo, 1975
Cut-and-pasted printed paper with felt-tip pen and ink
on board, 30 x 40" (76.2 x 101.6 cm)
From the Collection of Laura-Lee and Robert Woods.
411.1991
Page 189

JAMES LEE BYARS (American, 1932–1997; in Japan
1958–67)
Untitled Object, (1962–64)
Crayon on Japanese paper, joined and folded,
unfolded 12" x 210' 9" (30.3 cm x 64.23 m);
folded 12 x 12 x 3 3/4" (30.3 x 30.3 x 9.5 cm)
Gift of the artist. 47.1965
Page 149

JOHN CAGE (American, 1912–1992)
Music for Carillon, #4, Page 3, (1961)
Ink on transparentized graph paper on board,
11 x 16 5/8" (28 x 42.3 cm)
Acquired with matching funds from Gertrud A. Mellon
and the National Endowment for the Arts. 5.1977
Page 148

WALTERCIO CALDAS (Brazilian, born 1946)
Japan (Japão), 1972
Ink, metallic ink, and transfer type on paper,
19 x 17 1/2" (48.3 x 44.4 cm)
Gift of Gilberto Chateaubriand in memory of Monroe
Wheeler, Francisco Masjuan and John Brady. 182.1995
Page 183

VIJA CELMINS (American, born Latvia, 1938;
to United States 1948)
Untitled (Ocean), 1970
Pencil on paper, 14 1/8 x 18 7/8" (36 x 48 cm)
Mrs. Florene M. Schoenborn Fund. 585.1970
Page 187

CHRISTO (CHRISTO JAVACHEFF) (American,
born Bulgaria, 1935; to France 1958–64, to
United States 1964) and **JEANNE-CLAUDE
(JEANNE-CLAUDE DE GUILLEBON)**
(American, born Morocco, 1935; to France 1957–64,
to United States 1964)
"The Museum of Modern Art Packed Project", 1968
Cut-and-pasted gelatin silver prints (by Ferdinand
Boesch) with oil on board, pencil, colored pencil,
cut-and-pasted tracing paper, and pressure-sensitive
tape on board, 21 3/4 x 15 1/2" (55.2 x 39.5 cm)
Gift of D. and J. de Menil. 869.1968
Page 113

CHUCK CLOSE (American, born 1940)
Study for Self-Portrait, 1968
Gelatin silver print, ink, pencil, and pressure-sensitive
tape on board, 18 5/8 x 13 3/8" (47.2 x 33.9 cm)
Gift of Norman Dubrow. 732.1978
Page 186

BRUCE CONNER (American, born 1933)
23 KENWOOD AVENUE, (1963)
Ink on paper, 26 x 20" (66 x 50.8 cm)
Purchase and partial gift of Achim Moeller
in memory of Paul Cummings. 2401.2001
Page 145

JOSEPH CORNELL (American, 1903–1972)
Allegory of Innocence, (1956)
Cut-and-pasted printed paper on paper mounted on board in wood frame with antique glass, 15 1/4 x 12 1/4 x 2 1/4" (38.5 x 31 x 5.8 cm)
Purchase. 464.1980
Page 84

HANNE DARBOVEN (German, born 1941)
Construction Drawing (Konstruktionszeichnung), 1968
Ink on graph paper, 17 x 23 7/8" (43.2 x 60.7 cm)
Purchase. 142.2003
Page 167

AGNES DENES (American, born Hungary, 1938; to United States 1954)
The Human Argument, 1969–70
Ink on transparentized graph paper, 20 7/8 x 16 7/8" (53 x 42.9 cm)
Gift of the artist in honor of Agnes Gund. 393.2002
Page 182

ANTONIO DIAS (Brazilian, born 1944)
Untitled, 1967
Colored ink on paper, 18 1/2 x 12 5/8" (47 x 31.9 cm)
Inter-American Fund. 817.1969
Page 130

Untitled, 1967
Gouache and colored ink on paper, 18 1/2 x 12 5/8" (47 x 31.9 cm)
Inter-American Fund. 818.1969
Page 130

RICHARD DIEBENKORN (American, 1922–1993)
Seated Woman, (1966)
Synthetic polymer paint and charcoal on board, 31 x 19 7/8" (78.8 x 50.4 cm)
Gift of the artist. 253.1990
Page 134

SARI DIENES (American, born Hungary, 1898–1992; to United States 1939)
Tomb, (1950)
Crayon on paper, painted textile, torn paper with ink, and torn board, 36 x 24" (91.4 x 61 cm)
Gift of the Sari Dienes Foundation, Inc. 376.1999
Page 90

JIM DINE (American, born 1935)
Untitled (Five-bladed Saw) from Untitled Tool Series, 1973
Graphite, charcoal, and crayon on paper, 25 5/8 x 19 3/4" (65.1 x 50.2 cm)
Gift of the Robert Lehman Foundation, Inc. 484.1976.1
Page 114

ÖYVIND FAHLSTRÖM (Swedish, born Brazil, 1928–1976; to Sweden 1939, to United States 1961)
Notes 4 (C. I. A. Brand Bananas), 1970
Synthetic polymer paint and ink on paper, 16 5/8 x 14" (42.2 x 35.3 cm)
Mrs. Bertram Smith Fund. 430.1971
Page 124

LEÓN FERRARI (Argentine, born 1920)
Untitled, 1962
Ink on paper, 40 x 28 5/8" (101.6 x 72.7 cm)
Purchase. 379.2003
Page 143

DAN FLAVIN (American, 1933–1996)
Pink out of a Corner from No. 1 of December 19, 1963, October 14, 1965
Pencil and crayon on colored paper, 10 x 13" (25.4 x 33 cm)
Gift of Philip Johnson. 619.1971
Page 156

Untitled (to Barnett Newman) One and Three, 1971
Ink, colored pencil, and pencil on graph paper, 16 x 22" (40.6 x 55.9 cm)
Fractional and promised gift of Sarah-Ann and Werner H. Kramarsky. 103.2004
Page 157

LUCIO FONTANA (Italian, born Argentina, 1899–1968; worked in Italy and Argentina; to Italy 1948)
Spatial Concept (Concetto spaziale), 1957
Ink and pencil on paper on canvas, with punctures and scrapes, 55" x 7' 6 7/8" (139.7 x 200.4 cm)
Gift of Morton G. Neumann. 701.1976
Page 74

SAM FRANCIS (American, 1923–1994)
Untitled, (1958)
Watercolor on paper, 27 x 40 1/8" (68.6 x 101.9 cm)
Gift of Udo M. Reinach Estate. 28.1960
Page 71

LUCIAN FREUD (British, born Germany, 1922; to England 1933)
Girl with Leaves, (1948)
Pastel on gray paper, 18 7/8 x 16 1/2" (47.9 x 41.9 cm)
Purchase. 240.1948
Page 82

GEGO (GERTRUDE GOLDSCHMIDT) (Venezuelan, born Germany, 1912–1994; to Venezuela 1939)
Untitled, 1970
Colored ink on paper, 25 3/4 x 19 3/4" (65.4 x 50.2 cm)
Gift of Patricia Phelps de Cisneros in memory of Warren Lowry. 2418.2001
Page 141

ALBERTO GIACOMETTI (Swiss, 1901–1966; to France 1922)
Annette, (1954)
Pencil on paper, 16 5/8 x 11 3/4" (42 x 29.8 cm)
The Sidney and Harriet Janis Collection. 602.1967
Page 83

ARSHILE GORKY (American, born Armenia, 1904–1948; to United States 1920)
Summation, (1947)
Pencil, pastel, charcoal, and gouache on paper mounted on composition board, 6' 7 5/8" x 8' 5 3/4" (202.1 x 258.2 cm)
Nina and Gordon Bunshaft Fund. 234.1969
Page 55

PHILIP GUSTON (American, born Canada, 1913–1980; to United States 1919)
Drawing, 1953
Ink on paper, 17 3/4 x 23 3/4" (45.1 x 60.3 cm)
Promised gift of an anonymous donor in celebration of The Museum of Modern Art's 75th anniversary. 437.2004
Page 65

Wrapped, 1969
Charcoal on paper, 17 1/4 x 21 1/2" (43.7 x 54.4 cm)
Purchase. 305.1983
Page 132

Untitled (Waiting), (1972)
Oil on paper, 30 1/4 x 40" (76.8 x 101.6 cm)
Gift of Musa and Tom Mayer. 2583.2001
Page 133

RICHARD HAMILTON (British, born 1922)
The Solomon R. Guggenheim – Architect's visual, 1965
Crayon, pastel, synthetic polymer paint, and ink on paper, 20 x 23" (50.7 x 58.4 cm)
Gift of Charles B. Benenson. 2114.1967
Page 112

EVA HESSE (American, born Germany, 1936–1970; to United States 1939)
Untitled, 1966
Watercolor and pencil on paper, 11 3/4 x 9 1/8" (30 x 23.1 cm)
Gift of Mr. and Mrs. Herbert Fischbach. 1016.1969
Page 162

Untitled ("For Ruth."), 1967
Ink on graph paper, 11 7/8 x 8 1/4" (30.2 x 21 cm)
Ruth Vollmer Bequest. 1101.1983
Page 163

DAVID HOCKNEY (British, born 1937; to United States 1963)
Beverly Hills Interior, 1966
Colored pencil on paper, 13 3/8 x 20 1/8" (34 x 51.1 cm)
Promised gift of Joel Wachs, and purchase. 112.2004
Page 111

JASPER JOHNS (American, born 1930)
Flag, 1955
Graphite and graphite wash on prepared paper, 8 1/2 x 10 1/8" (21.6 x 25.7 cm)
Gift of Edgar Kaufmann, Jr. (by exchange) and purchase. 438.2004
Page 94

Jubilee, (1960)
Graphite wash on paper, 31 1/8 x 25" (79 x 63.5 cm)
The Joan and Lester Avnet Collection. 105.1978
Page 95

No, 1964
Graphite, charcoal, and tempera on paper, 20 1/4 x 17 1/2" (51.4 x 44.5 cm)
Fractional and promised gift of Sarah-Ann and Werner H. Kramarsky. 114.2004
Page 96

Diver, 1962–63
Charcoal, pastel, and watercolor on paper mounted on canvas, two panels, 7' 2 1/2" x 71 3/4" (219.7 x 182.2 cm)
Partial gift of Kate Ganz and Tony Ganz in memory of their parents, Victor and Sally Ganz, and in memory of Kirk Varnedoe; Mrs. John Hay Whitney Bequest Fund; gift of Edgar Kaufmann, Jr. (by exchange); and purchase. Acquired by the Trustees of The Museum of Modern Art in memory of Kirk Varnedoe. 377.2003.a–b
Page 97

RAY JOHNSON (American, 1927–1995)
Caged, (1959)
Cut-and-pasted painted paper on brown-paper-surfaced board mounted on painted board, 17 3/4 x 13 1/2" (45 x 34.2 cm)
Larry Aldrich Foundation Fund. 289.1965
Page 120

DONALD JUDD (American, 1928–1994)
Untitled, 1966
Felt-tip pen on yellow paper, 17 1/8 x 22" (43.5 x 56 cm)
L-B Foundation Fund. 468.1967
Page 158

ALEX KATZ (American, born 1927)
Ada, 1973
Pencil on paper, 19 3/4 x 26" (50.3 x 66.2 cm)
Gift of Edgar B. Howard. 312.1980
Page 115

ELLSWORTH KELLY (American, born 1923)
Study for **Window, Museum of Modern Art, Paris**, (1949)
Ink and pencil on paper, 16 1/2 x 12" (41.9 x 30.8 cm)
Gift of Sarah-Ann and Werner H. Kramarsky. 504.1997
Page 86

Study for **Meschers**, (1951)
Cut-and-pasted printed paper, 19 1/2 x 19 1/2" (49.5 x 49.5 cm)
Gift of the artist. 502.1997
Page 87

Study for **Black Ripe**, (1954)
Ink and pencil on paper, 20 x 19 1/4" (52.4 x 48.9 cm)
Purchased with funds given by Mr. and Mrs. Edmond J. Safra in honor of Mr. and Mrs. Henry R. Kravis. 7.1998
Page 88

Wild Grape, (1960)
Pencil on two sheets of paper, 28 1/2 x 45" (72.4 x 114.3 cm)
Gift of Kathy and Richard S. Fuld, Jr. in honor of Ellsworth Kelly's 80th birthday. 145.2003
Page 89

YVES KLEIN (French, 1928–1962)
Untitled (**fire-color painting**), (1962)
Dry pigment in synthetic resin with gold paint on asbestos-coated paper on board, partially charred, 24 1/2 x 19" (62.1 x 48.3 cm)
Gift of the Scaler Foundation and purchase. 133.1984
Page 81

FRANZ KLINE (American, 1910–1962)
Untitled II, (c. 1952)
Ink and oil on cut-and-pasted telephone book pages on paper on board, 11 x 9" (28.1 x 23 cm)
Purchase. 309.1983
Page 64

WILLEM DE KOONING (American, born the Netherlands, 1904–1997; to United States 1927)
Valentine, (1947)
Oil and enamel on paper on board, 36 3/8 x 24 1/4" (92.2 x 61.5 cm)
Gift of Mr. and Mrs. Gifford Phillips. 1093.1969
Page 57

Seated Woman, (1953–54)
Pencil on paper, 14 x 12" (35.6 x 30.5 cm)
Estate of Stella Waitzkin given in loving memory of Bill Waitzkin and promised gift of an anonymous donor in celebration of The Museum of Modern Art's 75th anniversary. 439.2004
Page 60

Seated Woman, (1952)
Pencil, pastel, and oil on two sheets of paper, 12 1/8 x 9 1/2" (30.8 x 24.2 cm)
The Lauder Foundation Fund. 33.1975
Page 61

Woman, (1965)
Charcoal on transparentized paper, 80 x 35 3/4" (203.2 x 90.8 cm)
Purchased with funds provided by Kathy and Richard S. Fuld, Jr., Jo Carole and Ronald S. Lauder, Thomas Weisel, Agnes Gund, Sarah-Ann and Werner H. Kramarsky and gift of The Sidney and Harriet Janis Collection (by exchange). 1607.2000
Page 135

YAYOI KUSAMA (Japanese, born 1929; in United States 1957–73)

Flower, 1953 and (1963)
Ink, gouache, and pastel on paper, 15 3/4 x 13 1/4" (40.1 x 33.8 cm)
Purchased with funds given by Sheldon H. Solow. 210.1996
Page 80

Accumulation of Stamps, 63, 1962
Pasted labels and ink on paper, 23 3/4 x 29" (60.3 x 73.6 cm)
Gift of Philip Johnson. 510.1970
Page 151

JACOB LAWRENCE (American, 1917–2000)

Street Shadows, 1959
Egg tempera and pencil on gessoed board, 24 x 29 7/8" (61 x 75.9 cm)
Gift of Ellen Kern and Gail Garlick in memory of their parents, Jewel and Lewis Garlick. 1631.2000
Page 138

BARRY LE VA (American, born 1941)

Strips, Sheets, Particles, 1967–68
Ink, gelatin silver print, and pencil on graph paper, 17 1/8 x 21 5/8" (43.5 x 55.1 cm)
Philip Johnson Fund. 101.1971
Page 176

SOL LEWITT (American, born 1928)

Drawing Series III/2314/A & B, (1969)
Ink and pencil on paper, 12 x 24" (30.6 x 61 cm)
Ruth Vollmer Bequest. 187.1982
Page 170

Red Lines from the Midpoints of the Left and Top Sides, Blue Lines from the Midpoints of the Right and Bottom Sides, 1975
Pencil and colored ink on paper, 15 x 15" (38.1 x 38.1 cm)
Fractional and promised gift of Sarah-Ann and Werner H. Kramarsky. 119.2004
Page 171

ROY LICHTENSTEIN (American, 1923–1997)

Baked Potato, (1962)
Ink and synthetic polymer paint on paper, 22 1/4 x 30 1/8" (56.6 x 76.5 cm)
Gift of Abby Aldrich Rockefeller (by exchange). 385.1984
Page 102

Study for Tension, (1964)
Pencil and colored pencil on paper, 5 3/4 x 5 3/4" (14.6 x 14.6 cm)
Purchased with funds provided by the Frances Keech Fund and the Vincent D'Aquila and Harry Soviak Drawings Bequest Fund. 120.2004
Page 103

Thumbprint, (1964)
Pencil on paper, 5 3/4 x 5 3/4" (14.6 x 14.6 cm)
Fractional and promised gift of Jan Cowles and Charles Cowles to honor the memory of Roy Lichtenstein. 1372.1974
Page 104

Brushstrokes, 1966–68
Pencil and tusche pochoir on paper, 22 1/8 x 29 7/8" (56.5 x 75.5 cm)
Gift of Leo Castelli in memory of Toiny Castelli. 626.1987
Page 105

RICHARD LONG (British, born 1945)

Walking a Straight 10-Mile Line, Dartmoor, England, 1970
Typewritten sheet, lithograph, and gelatin silver print, each mounted to board on board, overall 8 7/8 x 39 1/2" (22.5 x 100.3 cm)
Charles Simon Fund. 394.1970.a–c
Page 192

LEE LOZANO (American, 1930–1999)

Untitled, 1965
Pencil and ballpoint pen on graph paper, 11 x 8 1/2" (27.9 x 21.6 cm)
Fractional and promised gift of Sarah-Ann and Werner H. Kramarsky. 124.2004
Page 164

Untitled, (c. 1965)
Pencil and ballpoint pen on yellow paper, 11 x 8 1/2" (27.9 x 21.6 cm)
Fractional and promised gift of Sarah-Ann and Werner H. Kramarsky. 126.2004
Page 164

ROBERT MANGOLD (American, born 1937)

Untitled Drawing #1, #2, and #3, 1968
Pencil on paper, three sheets, each 13 7/8 x 8 1/2" (35.2 x 21.6 cm)
Fractional and promised gift of Sarah-Ann and Werner H. Kramarsky. 129.2004.a–c
Page 169

PIERO MANZONI (Italian, 1933–1963)
Thumbprint, 1960
Ink on paper, with blue mat, 8 1/4 x 7 1/8" (21 x 18 cm)
Gift of Ileana Sonnabend. 386.1984
Page 146

BRICE MARDEN (American, born 1938)
Untitled, 1970–72
Graphite and wax on paper, 26 x 40" (66.1 x 101.6 cm)
The Werner and Elaine Dannheisser Collection.
211.1996
Page 180

AGNES MARTIN (American, born Canada, 1912–2004; to United States 1932)
Mountain, (1960)
Ink and pencil on paper, 9 3/8 x 11 7/8" (24 x 30.2 cm)
Ruth Vollmer Bequest. 318.1983
Page 152

Wood I, 1963
Watercolor and pencil on paper, 15 x 15 1/2"
(38.1 x 39.4 cm)
Fractional and promised gift of Sarah-Ann and
Werner H. Kramarsky. 135.2004
Page 153

HENRI MATISSE (French, 1869–1954)
The Necklace (Le collier), May 1950
Ink on paper, 20 7/8 x 16 1/8" (52.8 x 40.7 cm)
The Joan and Lester Avnet Collection. 131.1978
Page 185

GORDON MATTA-CLARK (American, 1945–1978)
Untitled (Energytree), (1972–73)
Crayon, felt-tip pen, and ballpoint pen on paper,
22 1/2 x 28 1/2" (57 x 72 cm)
Gift of the artist's estate. 140.1999
Page 184

Untitled (Cut Drawing), (1976–77)
Pencil on layers of cut paper, 22 1/2 x 29 1/2 x 1/2"
(57 x 74 x 1.3 cm)
Purchase through the Vincent D'Aquila and
Harry Soviak Bequest Fund, The Judith Rothschild
Foundation and Purchase Fund. 141.1999
Page 185

MARIO MERZ (Italian, 1925–2003)
Berlin Cup (Berliner Tasse), 1974
Spray paint, ink, pencil, and fat on paper,
one of seven drawings, 19 x 26 1/4" (48.3 x 66.7 cm)
Purchased with funds given by Jo Carole and
Ronald S. Lauder, Maria-Gaetana Matisse,
and the Committee on Drawings. 213.1996.7
Page 194

HENRI MICHAUX (French, born Belgium, 1899–1984)
Mescaline Drawing (Mescaline dessin), (1960)
Ink on paper, 12 5/8 x 9 1/2" (32 x 23.9 cm)
Gift of Philip Johnson. 789.1969
Page 78

ROBERT MORRIS (American, born 1931)
Untitled, 1969
Ink on paper, 20 x 25 1/2" (50.8 x 64.8 cm)
Fractional and promised gift of Sarah-Ann and
Werner H. Kramarsky. 139.2004
Page 177

ROBERT MOTHERWELL (American, 1915–1991)
Elegy to the Spanish Republic No. 1, (1948)
Ink on paper, 10 3/4 x 8 1/2" (27.3 x 21.8 cm)
Gift of the artist. 639.1987
Page 62

BRUCE NAUMAN (American, born 1941)
Study related to the sculpture Storage Capsule for the Right Rear Quarter of My Body, 1966
Watercolor and pencil on paper, 38 x 24 3/4"
(95.5 x 63 cm)
Gift of Alexis Gregory and purchase. 46.1985
Page 161

BARNETT NEWMAN (American, 1905–1970)
Untitled, (1946)
Ink on paper, 24 x 18" (61 x 45.8 cm)
Gift of the Committee on Drawings in honor of
Richard E. Oldenburg. 530.1994
Page 63

JIM NUTT (American, born 1938)
Rosie Comon, (1968)
Pencil, cut-and-pasted printed paper, pressure-sensitive tape, and gouache on paper, 38 x 25"
(96.5 x 63.5 cm)
Purchased with funds provided by Jo Carole and
Ronald S. Lauder. 1370.2001
Page 123

HÉLIO OITICICA (Brazilian, 1937–1980)

Untitled, (1959)
Gouache on board, 19⅞ x 26¾" (50.5 x 68 cm)
Purchased with funds given by Patricia Phelps de Cisneros in honor of Paulo Herkenhoff. 176.1997
Page 140

CLAES OLDENBURG (American, born Sweden, 1929; to United States 1936)

Flag to Fold in the Pocket, (1960)
Ink and crayon on butcher paper, 29½ x 47" (74.9 x 119.4 cm) (irreg.)
Purchase. 658.1983
Page 116

Empire Sign – With M and I Deleted, (1960)
Casein on cut-and-pasted corrugated cardboard, 54¾ x 23⅞" (139.1 x 60.7 cm) (irreg.)
Gift of Agnes Gund. 657.1987
Page 117

Store Poster, Torn Out Letters Newspaper Pie Cup Cakes and Hot Dog, 1961
Cut-and-pasted paper and printed paper, watercolor, and crayon on paper, 20 x 26" (50.8 x 66.1 cm)
Purchased with funds given by Mr. and Mrs. Henry R. Kravis. 215.1996
Page 118

Colossal Fagend, Dream State, 1967
Pencil on paper, 30 x 22" (76.1 x 56.1 cm)
Gift of Lily Auchincloss, Charles B. Benenson, Jo Carole and Ronald S. Lauder, and purchase. 48.1988
Page 119

SIGMAR POLKE (German, born 1941)

Young Man Come Back Soon (Junge komm bald wieder), (1963)
Ballpoint pen and watercolor on brown paper, 11¾ x 8½" (29.8 x 21 cm)
Gift by exchange: Heinz Berggruen and Klaus Perls in memory of Frank Perls, Glickstein Foundation, and Mrs. Alfred P. Shaw. 39.1997
Page 125

Untitled (Head with Dots), (1963)
Ballpoint pen, oil, and gouache on brown paper, 11⅝ x 8½" (29.6 x 21 cm)
By exchange from the Joan and Lester Avnet Collection and John S. Newberry Collection. 40.1997
Page 125

Untitled, (c. 1964)
Synthetic polymer paint on paper, 29 x 29⅜" (73.5 x 74.5 cm)
Fractional and promised gift of Anna Marie and Robert F. Shapiro in honor of Margit Rowell. 252.2000
Page 126

Spiderman, (1971–74)
Cut-and-pasted painted paper on canvas, 9' 3¼" x 10' 3" (282.6 x 213.4 cm)
Purchased with funds given by Leon D. Black, Mr. and Mrs. Henry R. Kravis, Jo Carole and Ronald S. Lauder, and the Richard E. Salomon Family. 411.1999
Page 127

JACKSON POLLOCK (American, 1912–1956)

Untitled, 1945
Pastel, gouache, and ink on paper, 30⅝ x 22⅜" (77.7 x 56.9 cm)
Blanchette Hooker Rockefeller Fund. 13.1958
Page 56

Untitled, (c. 1950)
Ink on paper, 17½ x 22¼" (44.5 x 56.6 cm)
Gift of Jo Carole and Ronald S. Lauder in honor of Eliza Parkinson Cobb. 448.1982
Page 58

Untitled, (c. 1951)
Black and colored ink on Japanese paper, 24⅜ x 34⅜" (62.1 x 87.3 cm)
The Joan and Lester Avnet Collection. 153.1978
Page 59

ARNULF RAINER (Austrian, born 1929)

Untitled, (1969–74)
Oil stick on gelatin silver print, 23 x 19" (58.4 x 48.4 cm)
Gift of Joan and Lester Avnet (by exchange). 214.1988
Page 190

ROBERT RAUSCHENBERG (American, born 1925)

Untitled (Mirror), (1952)
Oil, solvent transfer, watercolor, crayon, pencil, and cut-and-pasted paper on paper, 10½ x 8½" (26.7 x 21.6 cm)
Fractional and promised gift of Sarah-Ann and Werner H. Kramarsky. 162.2004
Page 91

Canto XV: Circle Seven, Round 3, The Violent Against Nature from the series Thirty-Four Illustrations for Dante's Inferno, (1959–60)
Transfer drawing, gouache, watercolor, and pencil on paper, 14½ x 11½" (36.8 x 29.2 cm)
Given anonymously. 346.1963.15
Page 92

Canto XXX: Circle Eight, Bolgia 10, The Falsifiers: The Evil Impersonators, Counterfeiters, and False Witnesses from the series Thirty-Four Illustrations for Dante's Inferno, (1959–60)
Transfer drawing, watercolor, gouache, and pencil on paper, 14½ x 11½" (36.8 x 29.3 cm)
Given anonymously. 346.1963.30
Page 93

BRIDGET RILEY (British, born 1931)
Study, 1967
Gouache and pencil on graph paper, 20½ x 14½" (52 x 36.8 cm)
Philip Johnson Fund. 841.1969
Page 165

DOROTHEA ROCKBURNE (Canadian, born 1934; to United States 1951)
Drawing Which Makes Itself, 1972
Carbon, carbon transfer, and pencil on paper, 22½ x 30" (57.2 x 76.2 cm)
The Riklis Collection of McCrory Corporation. 946.1983
Page 179

DIETER ROTH (Swiss, born Germany, 1930–1998; to Switzerland 1943)
Doublehead Viewing Horizon (Horizontsehender Doppelkopf), (1974)
Pencil and ink on paper, 24 x 33¾" (61 x 85.7 cm)
Purchase. 168.2004
Page 191

EDWARD RUSCHA (American, born 1937)
Smash, 1964
Powdered graphite on three sheets of paper, overall 11¾ x 31½" (29.8 x 80 cm)
Purchased with funds given by Agnes Gund, Mr. and Mrs. James R. Hedges IV, Jo Carole and Ronald S. Lauder, and the General Drawings Fund. 119.2000.a–c
Page 106

Normandie, 1965
Powdered graphite and pencil on paper, 14⅛ x 22½" (36 x 57.2 cm)
Purchased with funds given by Agnes Gund, Mr. and Mrs. James R. Hedges IV, Ronald S. Lauder, and the General Drawings Fund. 118.2000
Page 107

Self, 1967
Pastel and gunpowder on paper, 14½ x 22½" (36.8 x 57.2 cm)
Fractional and promised gift of Sarah-Ann and Werner H. Kramarsky. 170.2004
Page 108

Blood Strip, 1973
Gunpowder and blood on paper, 11½ x 29" (29.2 x 73.7 cm)
Purchased with funds given by Agnes Gund, Mr. and Mrs. James R. Hedges IV, Jo Carole and Ronald S. Lauder, and the General Drawings Fund. 112.2000
Page 109

LUCAS SAMARAS (American, born Greece, 1936; to United States 1948)
Untitled, 1961
Pastel on red paper, 12 x 8⅞" (30.5 x 22.8 cm)
D. S. and R. H. Gottesman Foundation Fund. 270.1966
Page 121

FRED SANDBACK (American, 1943–2003)
Shadow-defining piece on stairs, 1967
Pencil and felt-tip pen on paper, 7⅝ x 10⅝" (19.4 x 27 cm)
Gift of Jan Christiaan Braun in honor of Werner H. Kramarsky. 248.2003
Page 172

MIRA SCHENDEL (Brazilian, born Switzerland, 1919–1988)
Untitled (Red), (1964)
Monotype, 18½ x 9" (47 x 22.9 cm)
Gift of Luisa Strina in memory of Lydia and Ferdinando Strina. 2453.2001
Page 142

Untitled, 1964
Monotype, 18¼ x 9" (46.4 x 22.9 cm)
Gift of Luisa Strina in memory of Lydia and Ferdinando Strina. 2454.2001
Page 142

JAN J. SCHOONHOVEN (Dutch, 1914–1994)

T 62-103, (1962)
Ink on paper, 19 3/4 x 15" (50.2 x 38.1 cm)
Gift of Sarah-Ann and Werner H. Kramarsky. 2595.2001
Page 150

RICHARD SERRA (American, born 1939)

Heir, (1973)
Paintstik and graphite on paper, 9' 6 5/8" x 42 1/4" (291.2 x 107.2 cm)
Acquired with matching funds from Mr. and Mrs. S. I. Newhouse, Jr. and the National Endowment for the Arts. 122.1974
Page 181

DAVID SMITH (American, 1906–1965)

Untitled (Tank Totems), 1953
Ink and gouache on paper, 29 3/4 x 42 3/8" (75.6 x 107.6 cm)
Gift of Alexis Gregory. 255.1976
Page 66

Untitled 5/28/55, 1955
Oil crayon on paper, 29 3/4 x 42 3/8" (75.6 x 107.6 cm)
Gift of Barbara G. Pine in memory of Morris Goldman. 331.1989
Page 67

TONY SMITH (American, 1912–1980)

Untitled, (1953–55)
Charcoal on brown paper, 31 1/2 x 39 1/8" (80 x 99.4 cm)
Purchased with funds given by Sarah-Ann and Werner H. Kramarsky. 220.1996
Page 70

ROBERT SMITHSON (American, 1938–1973)

Proposal for a Monument on the Red Sea, (1966)
Cut-and-pasted printed paper and pencil on gravure, 8 1/4 x 6 1/2" (21 x 16.7 cm)
Elmer A. Johnson, Jr. Bequest. 532.1994
Page 174

Mirror with Rock Salt (Salt Mine and Museum Proposal), 1968
Pencil, cut-and-pasted gelatin silver print, and cut-and-pasted paper on paper, 17 3/4 x 24" (45.1 x 60.8 cm)
Gift of Mrs. John de Cuevas. 622.1971
Page 175

FRANK STELLA (American, born 1936)

Study for Valle de los Caídos, 1966
Felt-tip pen and pencil on graph paper, 17 1/4 x 22 1/4" (43.8 x 56.5 cm)
Fractional and promised gift of Sarah-Ann and Werner H. Kramarsky. 179.2004
Page 159

MYRON STOUT (American, 1908–1987)

Untitled, (1950)
Charcoal and pastel on paper, 25 x 19" (63.4 x 48.2 cm)
The Riklis Collection of McCrory Corporation. 962.1983
Page 68

MARK TOBEY (American, 1890–1976)

Space Wall, 1960
Gouache on board mounted on board, 5 1/2 x 5 3/4" (14 x 14.5 cm)
Gift of Mrs. Henry Ives Cobb. 226.1985
Page 79

ANNE TRUITT (American, 1921–2004)

Untitled, 1962
Pencil on paper, 24 x 18" (61 x 45.7 cm)
Purchase. 440.2004
Page 154

RICHARD TUTTLE (American, born 1941)

Study for First Green Octagon, (1967)
Watercolor and pencil on paper, 17 5/8 x 11 5/8" (44.9 x 29.5 cm)
Gift of Jock Truman. 124.1974
Page 168

CY TWOMBLY (American, born 1928; to Italy 1957)

Untitled, (1955)
Pencil on paper, 24 3/8 x 36 1/8" (62 x 91.7 cm)
Gift of Jo Carole and Ronald S. Lauder. 503.1992
Page 72

Untitled, 1957
Oil, pencil, and crayon on gessoed board on paper-faced canvas, 19 5/8 x 27 5/8" (49.8 x 70.2 cm)
Gift of Carol O. Selle, the Denise and Andrew Saul Fund, and Abby Aldrich Rockefeller (by exchange). 403.1984
Page 73

JORGE DE LA VEGA (Argentine, 1930–1971)

Documentary (Documental), 1966
Ink on paper, 14 x 16 3/4" (35.5 x 42.5 cm)
Given anonymously. 814.1969
Page 131

Parenthesis (Paréntesis), 1967
Ink on paper, 11 x 13 5/8" (27.9 x 34.6 cm)
Inter-American Fund. 815.1969
Page 131

JACQUES DE LA VILLEGLÉ (French, born 1926)

122 rue du temple, 1968
Torn-and-pasted printed paper on canvas, 62 5/8" x 6' 10 3/4" (159.2 x 210.3 cm)
Gift of Joachim Aberbach (by exchange). 229.1988
Page 122

ANDY WARHOL (American, 1928–1987)

Unknown Female, (c. 1957)
Gold leaf and ink on paper, 23 1/8 x 15 1/2" (58.7 x 39.4 cm)
Gift of Sarah-Ann and Werner H. Kramarsky. 328.1998
Page 98

Untitled (City Text), (c. 1962)
Pencil and gouache on paper, 29 x 23" (73.7 x 58 cm)
Purchased with funds given by The Edward John Noble Foundation and Purchase Fund. 34.1999
Page 99

Coca-Cola, (1962)
Mimeograph stencil, 14 x 9" (35.6 x 22.9 cm)
Purchase. 16.2004
Page 100

Soup n' sandwich!, (1962)
Mimeograph stencil, 14 x 9" (35.6 x 22.9 cm)
Purchase. 19.2004
Page 100

Roll of Bills, (1962)
Pencil, crayon, and felt-tip pen on paper, 40 x 30" (101.6 x 76.2 cm)
Purchase. 151.1984
Page 101

LAWRENCE WEINER (American, born 1942)

Untitled, (1965)
Watercolor, colored pencil, and pencil on graph paper, 14 x 11" (35.6 x 27.9 cm)
Bequest of Alicia Legg. 415.2002
Page 166

H. C. WESTERMANN (American, 1922–1981)

Drawing for See America First #16, (1968)
Ink, watercolor, and pencil on paper, 13 x 10 1/2" (33 x 26.7 cm)
Purchased with funds given by Sarah-Ann and Werner H. Kramarsky. 39.1999
Page 129

JOSEPH E. YOAKUM (American, 1890–1972)

Julian Alps Near Triest, Yugoslavia, (1964)
Ballpoint pen and pencil on brown paper, 12 x 18" (30.5 x 45.7 cm)
Gift of Jan Christiaan Braun in honor of Mrs. June Noble Larkin. 20.2004
Page 128

COMPILED BY
Francesca Pietropaolo

SELECTED BIBLIOGRAPHY

The following three-part bibliography focuses primarily on exhibition catalogues and other publications on modern drawing. The first section references sources that examine modern drawing's history, beginning in the late nineteenth century, as well as selected general texts. The second section concentrates specifically on developments from 1945 to 1975. The last section focuses on the artists featured in the catalogue, emphasizing recent scholarship on works on paper, and includes selected artists' statements on drawing practices.

MODERN DRAWING: GENERAL

Benjamin, Walter. "Painting and the Graphic Arts" (1917) and "Painting, or Signs and Marks" (1917). Trans. Rodney Livingstone. In Marcus Bullock and Michael W. Jennings, eds., *Walter Benjamin: Selected Writings, 1913–1926*, 82 and 83–86. Vol. 1. Cambridge, Mass., and London: The Belknap Press of Harvard University Press, 1996. Published as "Malerei und Graphik" and "Über die Malerei oder Zeichen und Mal," in *Walter Benjamin: Gesammelte Schriften*, ed. Rolf Tiedemann and Hermann Schweppenhäuser, vol. 2. (Frankfurt: Suhrkamp, 1977), 602–07.

Bernadac, Marie-Laure, et al. *Du trait à la ligne*. Paris: Éditions du Centre Georges Pompidou, 1995.

———. *Dessins: Acquisitions 1992–1996*. Paris: Centre Georges Pompidou, Musée national d'art moderne, Cabinet d'art graphique, 1996.

Bernadac, Marie-Laure, Dieter Koepplin, and Rudolf Velhagen. *De Beuys à Trockel. Dessins contemporains du Kunstmuseum de Bâle*. Paris: Centre Georges Pompidou, Musée national d'art moderne, Cabinet d'art graphique, 1996.

Bolger, Doreen, et al. *American Pastels in The Metropolitan Museum of Art*. New York: The Metropolitan Museum of Art, 1989.

Brettell, Richard R., et al. *Nineteenth- and Twentieth-Century European Drawings in the Robert Lehman Collection*. New York: The Metropolitan Museum of Art, in association with Princeton University Press, 2002.

Brockelman, Thomas P. *The Frame and the Mirror: On Collage and the Postmodern*. Evanston, Ill.: Northwestern University Press, 2001.

Brodie, Judith, and Andrew Robison, eds. *A Century of Drawing: Works on Paper from Degas to LeWitt*. Washington, D.C.: National Gallery of Art, 2001.

Carrieri, Raffaele. *Il disegno italiano contemporaneo*. Milan: Damiani, 1945.

Cassou, Jean, and Philippe Jaccottet. *Le dessin français au XXe siècle*. Lausanne: Mermod, 1951.

Champa, Kermit S. "Modern Drawing." *Art Journal* 25, no. 3 (spring 1966): 226–33.

Charcoal Drawings, 1880–1985. Houston: Janie C. Lee Gallery, 1985.

Clayton, Martin. *Holbein to Hockney. Drawings from the Royal Collection*. London: Royal Collection Enterprises, 2004.

Cogniat, Raymond. *Twentieth-Century Drawings and Watercolors*. New York: Crown, 1966.

Collischan Van Wagner, Judy K., et al. *Lines of Vision: Drawings by Contemporary Women*. New York: Hudson Hills Press, 1989.

Craig-Martin, Michael. *Drawing the Line: Reappraising Drawing Past and Present*. London: South Bank Centre, 1995.

Crispolti, Enrico, et al. *Disegno italiano del Novecento*. Milan: Electa, 1993.

Cummings, Paul. *American Drawings: The Twentieth Century*. New York: Viking Press, 1976.

———. *Sculptors' Drawings 1910–1980: Selections from the Permanent Collection*. New York: Whitney Museum of American Art, 1984.

———. *Twentieth-Century American Drawings: The Figure in Context*. Washington, D.C.: International Exhibitions Foundation, 1984.

———. *Twentieth-Century Drawings from the Whitney Museum of American Art*. New York: Whitney Museum of American Art, 1987.

De Grazia, Diane, and Carter E. Foster, eds. *Master Drawings from The Cleveland Museum of Art*. Cleveland: The Cleveland Museum of Art, 2000.

Delcarte, Françoise, et al. "Dossier: Le Dessin." Special issue on drawing. *La Part de l'Œil*, no. 6 (1990).

Den Gedanken auf der Spur bleiben. Zeichnungen 1960 bis 1990 aus der Sammlung des Kaiser Wilhelm Museums. Krefeld, Germany: Museum Haus Lange and Museum Haus Esters, 1991.

Dethloff, Diana, ed. *Drawing: Masters and Methods. Raphael to Redon*. London: Philip Wilson Publishers in association with the Royal Academy of Arts, 1992.

Di Castro, Federica, ed. *Disegni del XX secolo nella collezione del Gabinetto delle Stampe*. Rome: De Luca Editore, 1980.

Dubary, Fred, and John Willats. *Perspective and Other Drawing Systems*. New York: Van Nostrand Reinhold, 1972.

Eisler, Colin T. *Sculptors' Drawings over Six Centuries, 1400–1950*. New York: The Drawing Center, 1981.

Elderfield, John. *The Modern Drawing: One Hundred Works on Paper from The Museum of Modern Art*. New York: The Museum of Modern Art, 1983.

———. "Works on Paper." In Gary Garrels, ed., *Celebrating Modern Art: The Anderson Collection*, 287–98. San Francisco: San Francisco Museum of Modern Art, 2000.

Elderfield, John, ed. "American Drawing in the Mid-Twentieth Century." Special issue. *Master Drawings* 40, no. 1 (spring 2002).

Finch, Christopher. *Twentieth-Century Watercolors*. New York: Abbeville Press, 1988.

Flam, Jack. "The Modern Drawing." In Flam et al., *New York Collects: Drawings and Watercolors, 1900–1950*, 8–30. New York: The Pierpont Morgan Library, 1999.

Foster, Carter E., et al. *Drawing Modern: Works from the Agnes Gund Collection*. Cleveland: The Cleveland Museum of Art, 2003.

Gallo, Francesco, ed. *Disegno italiano del Novecento*. Milan: Electa, 1990.

Garberi, Mercedes, et al. *Da Modigliani a Fontana. Disegno italiano del XX secolo nelle Civiche Raccolte d'Arte di Milano*. Milan: Mazzotta, 1991.

Gettings, Frank. *Drawings 1974–1984*. Washington, D.C.: Hirshhorn Museum and Sculpture Garden, Smithsonian Institution, 1984.

Godfrey, Tony. *Drawing Today: Draughtsmen in the Eighties*. Oxford: Phaidon, 1990.

Haverkamp-Begemann, Egbert, and Carolyn Logan. *Creative Copies: Interpretive Drawings from Michelangelo to Picasso*. New York: The Drawing Center, 1988.

Hayes, Bartlett H., Jr. *The American Line: 100 Years of Drawing*. Andover, Mass.: Addison Gallery of American Art, 1959.

———. *American Drawings*. New York: Shorewood Publishers, 1965.

Hayt, Elizabeth. "The Artist as Reproducer." In *Paste-Up: Past and Present*, unpag. New York: Kent Gallery, 1995.

Hoffman, Katherine, ed. *Collage: Critical Views*. Ann Arbor and London: UMI Research Press, 1989.

Hofmann, Werner, et al. *Von Dürer bis Baselitz: Deutsche Zeichnungen aus dem Kupferstichkabinett der Hamburger Kunsthalle*. Hamburg: Hamburger Kunsthalle, 1989.

Hopps, Walter, et al. *Cinquante ans de dessins américains 1930–1980*. Houston: The Menil Foundation; Paris: École nationale supérieure des Beaux-Arts, 1985.

Johnson, Una E. *Twentieth-Century Drawings: 1900–1940*. Vol. 1. New York: Shorewood Publishers, 1964.

———. *Twentieth-Century Drawings: 1940 to the Present*. Vol. 2. New York: Shorewood Publishers, 1964.

Jones, Caroline A. *Twentieth-Century Drawings from the Anderson Collection: Auguste Rodin to Elizabeth Murray*. Stanford, Calif.: Stanford University Museum of Art, 1988.

Krauss, Rosalind E. "The Crisis of the Easel Picture." In Kirk Varnedoe and Pepe Karmel, eds., *Jackson Pollock: New Approaches, 155–79*. New York: The Museum of Modern Art, 1999.

Kushner, Marilyn. *The Modernist Tradition in American Watercolors 1911–1939*. Chicago: Mary and Leigh Block Gallery, Northwestern University, 1991.

Lambert, Susan. *Drawing: Technique and Purpose*. London: Victoria and Albert Museum, 1981.

———. *Reading Drawings: An Introduction to Looking at Drawings*. New York: The Drawing Center, 1984.

Lebel, Jean-Jacques, Ewald Rathke, and Vittorio Fagone. *Il disegno del nostro secolo. Da Klimt a Wols*. Milan: Mazzotta, 1994.

Lecointre, Yves, et al. *Dessiner une collection d'art contemporain*. Paris: FRAC Picardie, Musée du Luxembourg, 1994.

Leymarie, Jean, Geneviève Monnier, and Bernice Rose. *History of an Art: Drawing*. Trans. Barbara Bray. New York: Rizzoli, 1979.

Lieberman, William S. *A Treasury of Modern Drawing: The Joan and Lester Avnet Collection in The Museum of Modern Art*. New York: The Museum of Modern Art, 1978.

Master Drawings, Pissarro to Lichtenstein. New York: Bianchini Gallery in association with the Cincinnati Contemporary Arts Center, 1966.

Mendelowitz, Daniel. *Drawing*. New York: Holt, Rinehart & Winston, 1967.

Merleau-Ponty, Maurice. "Eye and Mind." Trans. Carleton Dallery. In Merleau-Ponty, *The Primacy of Perception and Other Essays on Phenomenological Psychology, the Philosophy of Art, History and Politics*, ed. James M. Edie, 159–90. Evanston, Ill.: Northwestern University Press, 1964. Published as *L'Œil et l'esprit* (Paris: Gallimard, 1964). Originally published in *Art de France: Revue annuelle de l'art ancien et moderne* 1, no. 1 (1961): 187–208.

Mitchell-Innes, Lucy. *Master Drawings of the Twentieth Century*. New York: Mitchell-Innes & Nash, 1998.

Mongan, Agnes. "On Left-Handedness." In Walter Strauss and Tracie Felker, eds., *Drawings Defined*, 160–64. New York: Abaris Books, 1987.

Mongan, Agnes, ed. *One Hundred Master Drawings*. Cambridge, Mass.: Harvard University Press, 1949.

Naginski, Erika, et al. "Forum: Writing on Drawing." *Representations*, no. 72 (fall 2000): 64–166.

Newman, Avis. *The Stage of Drawing: Gesture and Act. Selected from the Tate Collection*. Ed. Catherine de Zegher. New York: The Drawing Center, 2003.

Oberhuber, Konrad, et al. *From Dürer to Rauschenberg: A Quintessence of Drawing. Masterworks from the Albertina and the Guggenheim*. Milan: Electa, 1997.

Petherbridge, Deanna. *The Primacy of Drawing: An Artist's View*. London: The South Bank Centre, 1991.

Philbin, Ann, and Jack Shear, eds. *Drawn from Artists' Collections*. New York: The Drawing Center, 1999.

Pignatti, Terisio. *Master Drawings*. Trans. Sylvia Mulcahy. New York: Harry N. Abrams, 1982.

Poling, Clark V. *Surrealist Vision and Technique: Drawings and Collages from the Pompidou Center and the Picasso Museum, Paris*. Atlanta: Michael C. Carlos Museum, Emory University, 1996.

Princeton Alumni Collections: Works on Paper. Princeton, N.J.: The Art Museum of Princeton University in association with Princeton University Press, 1981.

Ragon, Michel. *Les maîtres du dessin satirique en France de 1830 à nos jours*. Paris: P. Horay, 1972.

Rawson, Philip S. *Drawing*. Philadelphia: University of Pennsylvania Press, 1987.

Reaves, Wendy Wick, et al. *Eye Contact: Modern American Drawings from the National Portrait Gallery*. Washington, D.C.: National Portrait Gallery, Smithsonian Institution, in association with the University of Washington Press, 2002.

Reid, Martine, ed. "Boundaries: Writing and Drawing." Special issue on drawing. *Yale French Studies*, no. 84 (1994).

Reynolds, Graham. *Twentieth-Century Drawings*. London: Pleiades Books, 1946.

Rosand, David. *Drawing Acts: Studies in Graphic Expression and Representation*. Cambridge: Cambridge University Press, 2002.

Rose, Bernice. *A Century of Modern Drawing from The Museum of Modern Art, New York*. New York: The Museum of Modern Art, 1982.

———. *Allegories of Modernism: Contemporary Drawing*. New York: The Museum of Modern Art, 1992.

Rose, Bernice, Keinosuke Murata, and Akira Tatehata. *Drawing As Itself*. Osaka: The National Museum of Art, 1989.

Salmon, Béatrice. *Face à face*. Paris: Centre Georges Pompidou, Musée national d'art moderne, Cabinet d'art graphique, 1994.

Schwarz, Dieter, ed. *Von Edgar Degas bis Gerhard Richter: Arbeiten auf Papier aus der Sammlung des Kunstmuseums Winterthur*. Winterthur, Switzerland: Kunstmuseum Winterthur, 2000.

Shapiro, Meyer. "On Some Problems in the Semiotics of Visual Art: Field and Vehicle in Image-Signs." In *Theory and Philosophy of Art: Style, Artist, and Society*, 1–32. New York: George Braziller, 1994. Originally published in Semiotica 1 (1969): 223–42.

Shone, Richard. *From Figure to Object. A Century of Sculptors' Drawings*. London: Frith Street Gallery and Karsten Schubert, 1996.

Simon, Sidney, and Emily Rauh. *Twentieth-Century Master Drawings*. Cambridge, Mass.: The Fogg Art Museum, Harvard University, 1963.

Smith, Roberta. "Drawing Now (and Then)." *Artforum* 14, no. 8 (April 1976): 52–59.

Stebbins, Theodore E., Jr. *American Master Drawings and Watercolors: A History of Works on Paper from Colonial Times to the Present*. New York: Harper & Row, 1976.

Stoops, Susan L. *Contemporary Drawing: Existence, Passage, and the Dream*. Waltham, Mass.: Rose Art Museum, Brandeis University, 1991.

Storr, Robert. *Modern Art despite Modernism*. New York: The Museum of Modern Art, 2000.

Storsve, Jonas, and Guy Tosatto, eds. *Au fil du trait: De Matisse à Basquiat*. Paris: Centre Georges Pompidou, Musée national d'art moderne; Nîmes: Carré d'art, 1998.

Taylor, Brendon. *Collage. The Making of Modern Art*. New York: Thames & Hudson, 2004.
Tillim, Sidney. "Representing Paper." *Artforum* 25, no. 4 (December 1986): 90–91.
Viatte, Françoise, and Lizzie Boubli. *Réserves: Les Suspens du dessin*. Paris: Musée du Louvre, 1995.
Waldman, Diane. *Twentieth-Century American Drawing: Three Avant-Garde Generations*. New York: Solomon R. Guggenheim Museum, 1976.
Wedewer, Rolf, Fred Jahn, and David Nolan. *Amerikanische Zeichnungen in den 80er Jahren/ American Drawings of the '80s*. Vienna: Graphische Sammlung Albertina, 1990.

MODERN DRAWING: 1945–1975

Ades, Dawn. *Photomontage*. New York: Pantheon Books, 1976.
Alloway, Lawrence. *American Drawings*. New York: Solomon R. Guggenheim Museum, 1964.
American Drawings of the Sixties: A Selection. New York: New School Art Center, 1969.
Anderson, Lisa, et al. *Minimalism and Post-Minimalism: Drawing Distinctions*. Hanover, N.H.: Hood Museum of Art, Dartmouth College, 1990.
Anderson, Richard E. *New Dimensions in Drawing, 1950–1980*. Ridgefield, Conn.: Aldrich Museum of Contemporary Art, 1981.
Ashton, Dore. *One Hundred Contemporary American Drawings*. Ann Arbor: The University of Michigan Museum of Art, 1965.
Aust, Gunter. *The Art of German Drawing VII. Free Abstraction*. London: Goethe-Institut; Edinburgh: Scottish National Gallery of Modern Art, 1990.
Beck, Martha, and Marie Keller. *New Drawing in America*. New York: The Drawing Center, 1982.
Buchloh, Benjamin H. D. "Villeglé: From Fragment to Detail." In *Neo-Avantgarde and Culture Industry. Essays on European and American Art from 1955 to 1975*, 433–60. Cambridge, Mass.: The MIT Press, 2000. First published in *October* 56 (spring 1991): 99–110.
Butler, Cornelia H., and Pamela M. Lee. *Afterimage: Drawing through Process*. Los Angeles: Museum of Contemporary Art; Cambridge, Mass.: The MIT Press, 1999.
Coplans, John. *Five Europeans: Bacon, Balthus, Dubuffet, Giacometti, Morandi: Paintings and Drawings*. Irvine: University of California, 1966.
Corà, Bruno, et al. *"Bildhauerzeichnungen."* Graz, Austria: Grazer Kunstverein, 1987.
Delehanty, Suzanne. *Painting, Drawing, and Sculpture of the '60s and the '70s from the Dorothy and Herbert Vogel Collection*. Philadelphia: Institute of Contemporary Art, University of Pennsylvania, 1975.
Dietrich-Boorsch, Dorothea. *German Drawings of the '60s*. New Haven, Conn.: Yale University Art Gallery, 1982.
Drawings by Five Abstract Expressionist Painters: Arshile Gorky, Willem de Kooning, Jackson Pollock, Franz Kline, Philip Guston. Cambridge, Mass.: Hayden Gallery, Massachusetts Institute of Technology, 1975.
Drawings for Outdoor Sculpture, 1946–1977. New York: John Weber Gallery, 1977.
Dreishpoon, Douglas. *Between Transcendence and Brutality: American Sculptural Drawings from the 1940s and 1950s: Louise Bourgeois, Dorothy Dehner, Herbert Ferber, Seymour Lipton, Isamu Noguchi, Theodore Roszak, David Smith*. Tampa: Tampa Museum of Art, 1994.
Duncan, Barbara, Damián Bayón, and Ana M. Casciero. *Recent Latin American Drawings, 1969–1976: Lines of Vision*. Washington, D.C.: International Exhibitions Foundation, 1977.
Gercken, Günther, and Uwe M. Schneede. *Zeichen setzen durch Zeichnen. Baselitz, Beuys, Palermo, Penck, Pichler, Polke, Rainer, Schmit*. Hamburg: Kunstverein, 1979.
Ginsburg, Susan. *3D into 2D. Drawing for Sculpture*. New York: New York Cultural Center, 1972.
Green, Nancy E. *Surrealist Drawings from the Drukier Collection*. Ithaca, N.Y.: Herbert F. Johnson Museum of Art, Cornell University, 2003.
Greenberg, Clement. "The Pasted Paper Revolution." In John O'Brian, ed., *The Collected Essays and Criticism: Clement Greenberg*, 61–66. Vol. 4. Chicago: University of Chicago Press, 1993. Originally published in *Art News* 57, no. 5 (September 1958): 46–49.
Heckmanns, Friedrich Wilhelm. *Zeichner in Düsseldorf, 1955–1985*. Düsseldorf: Kunstmuseum Düsseldorf, 1985.

Helfenstein, Josef, and Jonathan Fineberg, eds. *Drawings of Choice from a New York Collection*. Champaign: Kranner Art Museum, University of Illinois at Urbana-Champaign; Little Rock, Ark.: Arkansas Arts Center, 2002.

Hodermarsky, Elisabeth. *The Synthetic Century: Collage from Cubism to Postmodernism. Selections from the Collection*. New Haven, Conn.: Yale University Art Gallery, 2002.

Hopkins, Henry T., and Peter Plagens. *Drawings: An Exhibition of Contemporary American Drawings*. Fort Worth: Fort Worth Art Center Museum, 1969.

Infinite Possibilities: Serial Imagery in Twentieth-Century Drawings. Wellesley, Mass.: Davis Museum and Cultural Center, Wellesley College, 2004.

Kozloff, Max. *Contemporary Drawings: Pop, Op, and Other Trends*. New York: American Federation of Arts, 1968.

Krauss, Rosalind. *Line As Language: Six Artists Draw*. Princeton, N.J.: The Art Museum, Princeton University, 1974.

———. *Works on Paper: American Art 1945–1975*. Seattle: The Washington Art Consortium, 1977.

Kren, Alfred, ed. *Drawing Distinctions: American Drawings of the Seventies*. Humlebæk, Denmark: Louisiana Museum of Modern Art, 1981.

Lee, Pamela, and Christine Mehring. *Drawing Is Another Kind of Language: Recent American Drawings from a New York Private Collection*. Cambridge, Mass.: Harvard University Art Museums; Stuttgart: G. Blaese, 1997.

Lippard, Lucy R. *Grids Grids Grids*. Philadelphia: Institute of Contemporary Art, University of Pennsylvania, 1972.

Madesani, Angela, ed. *Il disegno nell'arte italiana dal 1945 al 1975. Da Morandi al Concettuale*. Busto Arsizio, Italy: Fondazione Bandera, 2004.

McDaniel, Robert. *Abstract Expressionist Drawings, 1941–1955*. New York: Janie C. Lee Master Drawings, 1988.

Mel Bochner, Barry Le Va, Dorothea Rockburne, Richard Tuttle. Cincinnati: Contemporary Arts Center, 1975.

Messinger, Lisa Mintz. *Abstract Expressionism: Works on Paper. Selections from The Metropolitan Museum of Art*. New York: The Metropolitan Museum of Art, 1992.

Oxenaar, Rudolf, and Carter Ratcliff. *Diagrams and Drawings*. Otterlo, the Netherlands: Rijksmuseum Kröller-Müller, 1972.

Piché, Thomas, Jr., Mark Alice Durant, and Melissa Pearl Friedling. *Some Assembly Required. Collage Culture in Post-War America*. Syracuse, N.Y.: Everson Museum of Art, 2002.

Plagens, Peter. "The Possibilities of Drawing." *Artforum* (October 1969): 50–55.

Plous, Phyllis. *Contemporary Drawings/New York*. Santa Barbara: University of California Art Museum, 1978.

Poot, Jurrie, ed. *Drawings since 1960*. Amsterdam: Stedelijk Museum, 1989.

Ramírez, Mari Carmen, ed. *Re-Aligning Vision: Alternative Currents in South American Drawing*. Austin: Archer M. Huntington Art Gallery, The University of Texas at Austin, 1997.

Rice, Shelley. *Schemes: A Decade of Installation Drawings*. New York: Elise Meyer, 1981.

Rose, Bernice. *Drawing Now*. New York: The Museum of Modern Art, 1976.

Schimmel, Paul, ed. *The Interpretive Link: Abstract Surrealism into Abstract Expressionism. Works on Paper, 1938–1948*. Newport Beach, Calif.: Newport Harbor Art Museum, 1986.

Seymour, Anne. *Drawings towards painting, II*. London: Arts Council of Great Britain, 1967.

Solomon, Elke M. *American Drawings 1963–1973*. New York: Whitney Museum of American Art, 1973.

———. *Recent Drawings: William Allan, James Bishop, Vija Celmins, Brice Marden, Jim Nutt, Alan Saret, Pat Steir, Richard Tuttle*. New York: The American Federation of Arts, 1975.

Storck, Gerhard. *Zeichnungen der 50er bis 70er Jahre aus dem Kaiser Wilhelm Museum Krefeld. Graphische Sammlung und Sammlung Helga und Walther Lauffs*. Krefeld, Germany: Kaiser Wilhelm Museum, 1980.

Venn, Beth. *Collage in America*. New York: Whitney Museum of American Art, 1999.

Wedewer, Rolf. *Zeichnungen 3: USA*. Leverkusen, Germany: Städtisches Museum, Schloß Morsbroich, 1975.

Weiermair, Peter. *Vom Zeichnen: Aspekte der Zeichnung, 1960–1985*. Frankfurt am Main: Frankfurter Kunstverein, 1985.

Zeichnungen amerikanischer Künstler. Cologne: Galerie Ricke, 1970.

ARTISTS' BIBLIOGRAPHY

VITO ACCONCI

Kirshner, Judith Russi. *Vito Acconci: A Retrospective.* Chicago: Museum of Contemporary Art, 1980.

Linker, Kate. *Vito Acconci.* New York: Rizzoli, 1994.

Ruzicka, Joseph. "Lines to Be Filled in Later: An Interview with Vito Acconci." *On Paper* 1, no. 6 (July/August 1997): 26–30.

WILLIAM ANASTASI

Fausing, Bent, and Thomas McEvilley. *William Anastasi. A Retrospective.* Copenhagen: Nikolaj Copenhagen Contemporary Art Center, 2001.

Neff, Eileen, and John Hanhardt. *William Anastasi. A Retrospective, 1960–1995.* Philadelphia: The Galleries at Moore, Moore College of Art and Design, 1995.

William Anastasi. A Selection of Works from 1960 to 1989. With interview of Anastasi by Thomas McEvilley. New York: Scott Hanson Gallery, 1989.

CARL ANDRE

Andre, Carl. Interview by Paul Cummings. In Cummings, *Artists in Their Own Words,* 173–95. New York: St. Martin's Press, 1979.

Morris, Lynda. "Carl Andre: Poems, 1958–74." *Studio International* 190, no. 977 (September–October 1975): 160–61.

Sartorius, Rita, ed. *Carl Andre.* The Hague, the Netherlands: Haags Gemmentemuseum, 1987.

RICHARD ARTSCHWAGER

Corrin, Lisa G. "Artschwager's Way: An Introduction to the Notebooks of Richard Artschwager." In Melitta Kliege, et al., *Richard Artschwager: Up and Across,* 63–70. Nuremberg: Verlag für moderne Kunst in association with Neues Museum; London: Serpentine Gallery; and Vienna: MAK-Austrian Museum of Applied Arts, 2001.

Eckman, Carol. "An Interview with Richard Artschwager." In *Richard Artschwager: Drawings,* 5–11. New York: Nolan/Eckman Gallery, 1993.

Noever, Peter, et al. *Richard Artschwager: The Hydraulic Door Check. Skulptur, Malerei, Zeichnung/ Sculpture, Painting, Drawing.* Vienna: MAK-Austrian Museum of Applied Arts in association with Walther König, 2002.

Semff, Michael, and Dieter Schwarz. *Richard Artschwager: Zeichnungen/Drawings 1960–2002.* Winterthur, Switzerland: Kunstmuseum Winterthur, 2003.

JO BAER

Cooke, Lynne. *Jo Baer: The Minimalist Years, 1960–1975.* Brochure. New York: Dia Center for the Arts, 2002.

Haskell, Barbara. *Jo Baer.* New York: Whitney Museum of American Art, 1975.

GEORG BASELITZ

Bernadac, Marie-Laure, and Fabrice Hergott. *Georg Baselitz: Dessins 1962–1992.* Paris: Centre Georges Pompidou, Musée national d'art moderne, 1993.

Koepplin, Dieter. *Georg Baselitz: Zeichnungen und druckgraphische Werke aus dem Kupferstichkabinett Basel.* Basel: Kunsthalle, 1989.

Koepplin, Dieter, and Rudi Fuchs. *Georg Baselitz: Zeichnungen 1958–1983.* Basel: Kunstmuseum Basel, 1984.

Waldman, Diane. *Georg Baselitz.* New York: Solomon R. Guggenheim Museum, 1995.

ROMARE BEARDEN

Campbell, Mary Schmidt, and Sharon F. Patton. *Memory and Metaphor: The Art of Romare Bearden, 1940–1987.* New York: The Studio Museum in Harlem, 1991.

Fine, Ruth, et al. *The Art of Romare Bearden.* Washington, D.C.: National Gallery of Art in association with Harry N. Abrams, 2003.

Patton, Sharon F. "Romare Bearden: Narrations." In *Romare Bearden: Narrations,* Lucinda H. Gedeon and Dede Young, 4–16. Purchase, N.Y.: Neuberger Museum of Art, Purchase College, State University of New York, 2002.

JOSEPH BEUYS

Bastian, Heiner. *Joseph Beuys: Dibujos/Drawings.* Madrid: Fundacion Caja de Pensiones, 1985.

Compton, Ann, et al. *Joseph Beuys: Drawings.* London: Victoria and Albert Museum, 1983.

Cooke, Lynne, and Karen Kelly, eds. *Joseph Beuys: Drawings After the Codices Madrid of Leonardo da Vinci.* New York: Dia Center for the Arts, 1998.

Rose, Bernice, and Ann Temkin. *Thinking Is Form: The Drawings of Joseph Beuys*. Philadelphia: Philadelphia Museum of Art; New York: The Museum of Modern Art, 1993.

MEL BOCHNER

Cummings, Paul. "Interview: Mel Bochner Talks with Paul Cummings." *Drawing* 10, no. 1 (May/June 1988): 9–13.

Field, Richard S., ed. *Mel Bochner: Thought Made Visible, 1966–1973*. New Haven, Conn.: Yale University Art Gallery, 1995.

Mel Bochner: Twenty-five Drawings, 1973–1980. With a statement by Bochner. Dallas: University Gallery, Meadows School of the Arts, Southern Methodist University; Cleveland: The New Gallery of Contemporary Art, 1981.

Richardson, Brenda. *Mel Bochner: Number and Shape*. Baltimore: The Baltimore Museum of Art, 1976.

Schwabsky, Barry, and Mel Bochner. *Mel Bochner. Drawings, 1966–1973*. With a text by Bocher. New York: Lawrence Markey, 1998.

LEE BONTECOU

De Salvo, Donna. "Inner and Outer Space: Bontecou's Sculpture through Drawing." In *Lee Bontecou: A Retrospective*, Elizabeth A. T. Smith et al., 212–23. Chicago: Museum of Contemporary Art; Los Angeles: Armand Hammer Museum of Art and Cultural Center, University of California, in association with Harry N. Abrams, 2003.

Del Deo, Frank, and Ann Freedman. *Lee Bontecou: Drawings, 1958–1999*. New York: Knoedler and Company, 2004.

Field, Richard S. *Prints and Drawings by Lee Bontecou*. Middletown, Conn.: Davison Art Center, Wesleyan University Press, 1975.

Jones, Leslie. "Lee Bontecou's Sublime Drawings." *Art on Paper* 8, no. 4 (March–April 2004): 50–53.

LOUISE BOURGEOIS

Bernadac, Marie-Laure, and Elisabeth Bronfen. *Louise Bourgeois: The Insomnia Drawings*. Zurich: Daros, 2000.

Bourgeois, Louise. *Louise Bourgeois: Drawings and Observations*. Berkeley: University Art Museum and Pacific Film Archive, University of California, 1995.

Gorovoy, Jerry, and John Cheim, eds. *Louise Bourgeois Drawings*. New York: Robert Miller and Daniel Lelong, 1988.

MARCEL BROODTHAERS

Buchloh, Benjamin H. D., ed. *Marcel Broodthaers: Writings, Interviews, Photographs*. Cambridge, Mass.: The MIT Press, 1988.

Compton, Michael, et al. *Marcel Broodthaers*. Minneapolis: Walker Art Center, 1989.

David, Catherine, et al. *Marcel Broodthaers*. Paris: Galerie nationale du Jeu de Paume, 1991.

CHRIS BURDEN

Ryskamp, John. *Post-Performance Paintings and Drawings*. San Francisco: The Farm, 1980.

Schimmel, Paul, et al. *Chris Burden. A Twenty-Year Survey*. Newport Beach, Calif.: Newport Harbor Art Museum, 1988.

JAMES LEE BYARS

James Lee Byars. The Perfect Moment. Valencia: Generalitat Valenciana, Conselleria de Cultura, 1995.

Ottoman, Klaus. *James Lee Byars: Life, Love, and Death*. Ostfildern-Ruit, Germany: Hatje Cantz, 2004.

JOHN CAGE

Cage, John. *M: Writings 1967–1972*. Middletown, Conn.: Wesleyan University Press, 1974.

d'Harnoncourt, Anne, et al. *John Cage: Rolywholyover a Circus*. Los Angeles: Museum of Contemporary Art; New York: Rizzoli International Publications, 1993.

Lebeer, Irmeline. "La vie peut être tellement excellente: Entretien avec John Cage." *Cahiers du musée national d'art moderne* 52 (summer 1995): 114–35.

Sylvester, David. "Points in Space." In Susan Sontag, ed., *Dancers on a Plane: Cage, Cunningham, Johns*, 47–52. London: Anthony d'Offay Gallery, 1989.

VIJA CELMINS

Celmins, Vija. Interview by Chuck Close. In William S. Bartman, ed., *Vija Celmins*, 5–54. New York: A.R.T Press, 1992.

———. *Vija Celmins: Drawings of the Night Sky*. London: Anthony d'Offay Gallery, 2001.

Chandès, Hervé, and Robert Storr. *Vija Celmins*. With interview of Celmins by Jeanne Silverthorne. Paris: Fondation Cartier pour l'art contemporain, 1995.
Larsen, Susan C. "Vija Celmins." In Betty Turnbull, *Vija Celmins: A Survey Exhibition*, 19–33. Los Angeles: Fellows of Contemporary Art, 1979.
Relyea, Lane. *Vija Celmins*. London: Phaidon, 2004.
Tannenbaum, Judith. *Vija Celmins*. Philadelphia: Institute of Contemporary Art, University of Pennsylvania, 1992.

CHRISTO and **JEANNE-CLAUDE**
Alloway, Lawrence, et al. *Christo and Jeanne-Claude. Early Works, 1958–69*. Cologne: Taschen, 2001.
Christo. [Statement, July 1983.] In Frank Gettings, *Drawings, 1974–1984*, 53–54. Washington, D.C.: Hirshhorn Museum and Sculpture Garden, Smithsonian Institution, 1984.
Donovan, Molly. *Christo and Jeanne-Claude in the Vogel Collection*. With interview of Christo by Molly Donovan. Washington, D.C.: National Gallery of Art, 2002.
Fineberg, Jonathan. *Christo and Jeanne-Claude: On the way to "The Gates," Central Park, New York City*. New Haven, Conn., and London: Yale University Press in association with The Metropolitan Museum of Art, 2004.
Hammacher, A. M., et al. *Dessins, Collage, Photographs*. With interviews of Christo by Marcel Daloze and Dominique Verhaegen. Braine-L'Alleud, Belgium: Centre d'Art Nicolas de Staël, 1987.
Objects, Collages, and Drawings, 1958–84. London: Juda-Rowan Gallery, 1984.

CHUCK CLOSE
Close, Chuck. [Statement, July 1983.] In Frank Gettings, *Drawings, 1974–1984*, 61–64. Washington, D.C.: Hirshhorn Museum and Sculpture Garden, Smithsonian Institution, 1984.
———. *Keith: Six Drawings*. New York: Lapp Princess Press, 1979.
Engberg, Siri, Madeleine Grynsztejn, and Doug Nickel. *Chuck Close: Self-Portraits, 1967–2005*. San Francisco: San Francisco Museum of Modern Art; Minneapolis: Walker Art Center, 2005.
Finch, Christopher. *Chuck Close: Dot Drawings, 1973–75*. Austin: Laguna Gloria Art Museum, 1975.
Pillsbury, Edmund P. *Chuck Close: Works on Paper*. Houston: Contemporary Arts Museum, 1985.
Storr, Robert, et al. *Chuck Close*. New York: The Museum of Modern Art, 1998.

BRUCE CONNER
Boswell, Peter W. "Theater of Light and Shadow." In Boswell, Bruce Jenkins, and Joan Rothfuss, *2000 BC: The Bruce Conner Story Part II*, 25–82. Minneapolis: Walker Art Center, 1999.
Cummings, Paul. "Interview: Bruce Connor Talks with Paul Cummings." *Drawing* 16, no. 3 (September/October 1994): 55–59.
Garver, Thomas H. *Bruce Conner: Drawings, 1955–1972*. San Francisco: Fine Arts Museum of San Francisco, 1974.
Hirsch, Faye. "Up Above My Head: Consciousness and Habitation in the Graphic Work of Bruce Conner." *Parkett*, no. 28 (1996): 122–23.
Schwabsky, Barry. *Looking for Mushrooms: Bruce Conner Drawings, 1960 to 1968*. Los Angeles: Kohn Turner Gallery, 1999.
Storr, Robert. "Bruce Conner." In *Disparities and Deformations: Our Grotesque*, 44–45. Santa Fe: SITE Santa Fe, 2004.

JOSEPH CORNELL
Hartigan, Lynda Roscoe, Richard Vine, and Robert Lehrman. *Joseph Cornell: Shadowplay, Eterniday*. New York and London: Thames & Hudson, 2003.
Hauptman, Jodi. *Joseph Cornell: Stargazing in the Cinema*. New Haven, Conn., and London: Yale University Press, 1999.
Joseph Cornell: Collages, 1931–1972. New York: Castelli, Feigen, Corcoran, 1978.

HANNE DARBOVEN
Burgbacher-Krupka, Ingrid. *Hanne Darboven: Konstruiert, Literarisch Musikalisch/Constructed, Literary, Musical: The Sculpting of Time*. Ostfildern, Germany: Cantz Verlag, 1994.
Doherty, Brigid, and Peter Nisbet. *Hanne Darboven: Works 1969/1972/1983*. Cambridge, Mass.: Busch-Reisinger Museum, 1999.
Kaak, Joachim. "Hanne Darboven." In Kaak and Corinna Thierolf, *Hanne Darboven/John Cage*, 12–39. Munich: Staatsgalerie Moderner Kunst, 1997.

JORGE DE LA VEGA
Casanegra, Mercedes. *Jorge de la Vega*. Buenos Aires: Alba, 1991.

Martín-Crosa, Ricardo. "Jorge de la Vega." In Gabriel Levinas, ed., *Arte argentino contemporáneo*, 134–37. Madrid: Editorial Ameris, 1979.
Pacheco, Marcelo. *Jorge de la Vega obras 1961–1970*. Buenos Aires: Centro Cultural Borges, 1995.
Pacheco, Marcelo, et al. *Jorge de la Vega: A contemporary artist*. Buenos Aires: Editorial El Ateneo, 2003.

AGNES DENES

Deecke, Thomas. *Agnes Denes – Sculpture of the Mind – Philosophical Drawings*. Berlin: Amerika Haus, United States Cultural Center, 1978.
Hartz, Jill, ed. *Agnes Denes*. With texts by Denes. Ithaca, N.Y.: Herbert F. Johnson Museum of Art, Cornell University, 1992.
Mills, Dan, ed. *Agnes Denes: Projects for Public Spaces. A Retrospective*. With texts by Denes. Lewisburg, Pa.: Samek Art Gallery, Bucknell University, 2003.

ANTONIO DIAS

Dias, Antonio, and Wanda Lemanczyk, eds. *Antonio Dias. Trábahos, Arbeiten, Works, 1967–1994*. Ostfildern-Ruit, Germany: Hatje Cantz, 1994.
Duarte, Paulo Sergio. *Antonio Dias*. Rio de Janeiro: Edição FUNARTE, 1979.
Friedel, Helmut, and Ronaldo Brito. *Antonio Dias: Arbeiten auf Papier/Trabalhos sobre papel, 1977–1987*. Berlin: Staatliche Kunsthalle, 1988.

RICHARD DIEBENKORN

Eitner, Lorenz. *Drawings/Richard Diebenkorn*. Stanford, Calif.: Stanford University, 1965.
Elderfield, John. *The Drawings of Richard Diebenkorn*. New York: The Museum of Modern Art, 1988.
Nordland, Gerald. *Richard Diebenkorn: Ocean Park, Paintings on Paper*. San Francisco: Hackett-Freedman Gallery, 2000.

SARI DIENES

Hochhausen, Bill, and David Weinrib. *Sari Dienes: Retrospective*. Sparkill, N.Y.: Thorpe Intermedia Gallery, 1986.
Sari Dienes: 1950–1970. Paris: Galerie J & J Donguy, 1991.
"Tombstone Tracery: Artist Records Shadowy Images of Cemetery Art." *Life* 37 (November 15, 1954): 133–34, 136.

JIM DINE

Brodie, Judith. *Drawings of Jim Dine*. Washington, D.C.: National Gallery of Art; Göttingen, Germany: Steidl, 2004.
Glenn, Constance. *Jim Dine Drawings*. New York: Harry N. Abrams, 1985.
Rogers-Lafferty, Sarah. *Jim Dine, Drawings 1973–1987*. Cincinnati: Contemporary Arts Center, 1988.

ÖYVIND FAHLSTRÖM

Ekbom, Torsten. *Öyvind Fahlström. A Monograph*. Stockholm: Bonniers, 1967.
Martin, Henry, et al. *Öyvind Fahlström. Samlad grafik och multiplar*. Norrköpings, Sweden: Norrköpings konstmuseum, 2000.
Öyvind Fahlström. Paris: Centre Georges Pompidou, Musée national d'art moderne, 1980.

LEÓN FERRARI

Amaral, Aracy A. "León Ferrari: A invenção e a maquina." In *Arte e meio artistico entre a feijoada e o x-burguer*, 336–38. São Paulo: Livraria Nobel, 1982.
Camnitzer, Luis. *León Ferrari: Politiscripts. Drawing Papers* 48. New York: The Drawing Center, 2004.
Ferrari, León. *La Bondadosa Crueldad*. Buenos Aires: Editorial Argonauta, 2000.
Giunta, Andrea, et al. *León Ferrari. Retrospectiva. Obras 1954–2004*. With texts by Ferrari. Buenos Aires: Centro Cultural Recoleta y Malba-Colección Costantini, 2004.

DAN FLAVIN

Drawn Along the Shores, 1959–1976. Yonkers, N.Y.: The Hudson River Museum, 1979.
Govan, Michael, and Tiffany Bell. *Dan Flavin: A Retrospective*. New York: Dia Art Foundation in association with Yale University Press, 2004.
Rauh, Emily S., and Dan Flavin. *Drawings and Diagrams by Dan Flavin, 1963–72*. Vol. 1. St. Louis: St. Louis Art Museum, 1973.

LUCIO FONTANA

Billeter, Erika. "Lucio Fontana: Between Tradition and Avant-Garde." In *Lucio Fontana 1899–1968: A Retrospective*, 13–20. New York: Solomon R. Guggenheim Museum, 1977.

Crispolti, Enrico. *Fontana. Catalogo generale*. Milan: Electa, 1986.

Garberi, Mercedes, and Paolo Fossati. *Fontana/disegni. Opere donate alle Collezioni civiche di Milano*. Milan: Electa, 1977.

Gualdoni, Flaminio. *Lucio Fontana. Il disegno*. Modena, Italy: Palazzina dei Giardini, 1990.

Peterson, Stephen. "From Matter to Light: Fontana's Spatial Concepts and Experimental Photography." *Art on Paper* 4, no. 4 (March–April 2000): 52–57.

Tognon, Paola. "Lucio Fontana's Drawings: Notes for a History." In Enrico Crispolti and Rosella Siligato, eds., *Lucio Fontana*, 108–14. Milan: Electa, 1998.

SAM FRANCIS

Hoyer, Anneliese. *Sam Francis: Exhibition of Drawings and Lithographs*. San Francisco: San Francisco Museum of Art, 1967.

Prokopoff, Stephen. *Sam Francis: Works on Paper. A Survey, 1948–1979*. Boston: Institute of Contemporary Art, 1980.

Sam Francis, Prints and Drawings, 1957–1989. New York: Associated American Artists, 1990.

LUCIAN FREUD

Feaver, William. *Lucian Freud*. London: Tate Publishing, 2002.

Mantura, Bruno, Agnes Cook, and Lucian Freud. *Lucian Freud: Dipinti e opere su carta*. Milan: Mondadori, 1991.

Penny, Nicholas, and Robert Flynn Johnson. *Lucian Freud: Works on Paper*. London: South Bank Board in association with Thames & Hudson, 1988.

Smee, Sebastian. *Lucian Freud: Drawings, 1940*. New York: Matthew Marks, 2003.

GEGO

Figarella, Mariana. *Gego: Dibujos sin papel*. Caracas: Museo de Bellas Artes, 1984.

Pérez-Oramas, Luis. "Gego and the Analytical Context of Cinetismo." In Mari Carmen Ramírez and Héctor Olea, eds., *Inverted Utopias: Avant-Garde in Latin America*, 255–61. New Haven, Conn., and London: Yale University Press, 2004.

Peruga, Iris, et al. *Gego: Obra Completa, 1955–1990*. Caracas: Fundación Cisneros, 2003.

Peruga, Iris, and Mauricio Vilas, eds. *Gego, 1955–1990*. Caracas: Fundación Museo de Bellas Artes, 2000.

Ramírez, Mari Carmen, and Theresa Papanikolas, eds. *Questioning the Line: Gego in Context*. Houston: The Museum of Fine Arts, 2003.

Sierra, Eliseo. *Gego: Dibujos, grabados, tejeduras*. Caracas: Fundación Gego, 1996.

ALBERTO GIACOMETTI

Carluccio, Luigi. *Giacometti: A Sketchbook of Interpretive Drawings*. New York: Harry N. Abrams, 1967.

de la Beaumelle, Agnès. *Alberto Giacometti: Le dessin à l'œuvre*. Paris: Centre Georges Pompidou, Musée national d'art moderne, 2001.

Giacometti, Alberto, et al. *Giacometti: Sculptures, Paintings, Drawings*. London: Arts Council Gallery, 1980.

Klemm, Christian, et al. *Alberto Giacometti*. New York: The Museum of Modern Art; Zurich: Kunsthaus Zürich, 2001.

Lord, James. *Alberto Giacometti Drawings*. Lausanne: Paul Bianchini, 1971.

Omer, Mordechai. *Alberto Giacometti: Drawings and Prints*. Tel Aviv: Tel Aviv Museum of Art, 2003.

Schneider, Angela, and Lucius Grisebach. *Alberto Giacometti: Sculpture, Paintings, Drawings*. Munich: Prestel, 1994.

ARSHILE GORKY

Billeter, Erika. *Arshile Gorky: Œuvres sur papier, 1929–1947*. Lausanne: Musée cantonal des beaux-arts, 1990.

Karmel, Pepe. "Arshile Gorky: Anatomical Blackboard." *Master Drawings* 40, no. 1 (spring 2002): 9–23.

Lee, Janie C., and Melvin P. Lader. *Arshile Gorky: A Retrospective of Drawings*. New York: Whitney Museum of American Art, 2003.

Rylands, Philip, and Matthew Spender. *Arshile Gorky: Works on Paper*. Venice: Peggy Guggenheim Collection, 1992.

Spender, Matthew, and Barbara Rose. *Arshile Gorky and the Genius of Abstraction: Drawings from the Early 1930s*. Princeton, N.J.: Princeton University Art Museum, 1994.

PHILIP GUSTON

Ashton, Dore. "Impassioned Quest." *Art International*, no. 5 (winter 1998): 101–03.

Barañano, Kosme María de. *Philip Guston: La raiz del dibujo/Roots of Drawing*. Bilbao: Sala de Exposiciones Rekalde, 1993.

Coolidge, Clark, and Philip Guston. *Baffling Means: Writings/Drawings by Clark Coolidge and Philip Guston*. New Haven, Conn.: Eastern Press, 1991.

Dabrowski, Magdalena. *The Drawings of Philip Guston*. New York: The Museum of Modern Art, 1988.

Philip Guston: Drawings, 1947–77. With a statement by Guston. New York: David McKee Gallery, 1978.

RICHARD HAMILTON

Richard Hamilton: Collected Words, 1953–1982. London: Thames & Hudson, 1982.

Richard Hamilton: Prints, Multiples, and Drawings. Manchester, England: Whitworth Art Gallery, 1972.

Richard Hamilton. Retrospective: Paintings and Drawings, 1937–2002. Cologne: Walther König, 2003.

Schwarz, Dieter. *Richard Hamilton: exteriors interiors objects people*. Winterthur, Switzerland: Kunstmuseum Winterthur, 1990.

EVA HESSE

Brown, David. *Eva Hesse 1936–1970: A Retrospective of Works on Paper*. London: The Mayor Gallery, 1979.

Johnson, Ellen H. *Eva Hesse. A Retrospective of the Drawings*. Oberlin, Ohio: Allen Memorial Art Museum, Oberlin College, 1982.

Shearer, Linda. "Eva Hesse: Last Works." In Linda Shearer and Robert Pincus-Witten, *Eva Hesse. A Memorial Exhibition*, unpag. New York: Solomon R. Guggenheim Foundation, 1972.

Sussman, Elizabeth. *Eva Hesse*. San Francisco: San Francisco Museum of Modern Art; New Haven, Conn., and London: Yale University Press, 2002.

DAVID HOCKNEY

Hockney, David. *72 Drawings by David Hockney/Chosen by the Artist*. New York: The Viking Press, 1971.

———. *Hockney's Pictures. The Definitive Retrospective. Compiled and with a Commentary by D. Hockney*. New York and Boston: Bulfinch Press, 2004.

Luckhardt, Ulrich, and Paul Melia. *David Hockney: A Drawing Retrospective*. London: Royal Academy of Arts, 1995.

Spender, Stephen, ed. *Hockney's Alphabet. Drawings by David Hockney*. New York: Random House, 1991.

JASPER JOHNS

Foster, Carter E. "Technique and the Tradition of Modern Drawing in Jasper Johns's Numbers." In Roberta Bernstein and Carter E. Foster, *Jasper Johns: Numbers*, 34–43. Cleveland: The Cleveland Museum of Art, 2004.

Rosenthal, Mark. *Jasper Johns: Drawings, The Menil Collection*. Houston: The Menil Foundation, 2003.

Rosenthal, Nan, and Ruth E. Fine. *The Drawings of Jasper Johns*. Washington, D.C.: National Gallery of Art, 1990.

Sweet, Christopher, ed. *Jasper Johns: Drawings, 1954–1984*. New York: Harry N. Abrams, 1984.

Varnedoe, Kirk, ed. *Jasper Johns: Writings, Sketchbook Notes, Interviews*. New York: The Museum of Modern Art, 1996.

RAY JOHNSON

Bourdon, David. *Works by Ray Johnson*. Roslyn Harbor, N.Y.: Nassau County Museum of Fine Art, 1984.

De Salvo, Donna M., and Catherine Gudis. *Ray Johnson: Correspondences*. Columbus, Ohio: Wexner Center for the Arts, The Ohio State University; Paris: Flammarion, 1999.

Ray Johnson, a Memorial Exhibition. New York: Richard L. Feigen & Co., 1995.

DONALD JUDD

Haskell, Barbara. *Donald Judd*. New York: Whitney Museum of American Art in association with Norton, 1988.

Kellein, Thomas, and Matthew Drutt. *Donald Judd: Das Frühwerk/The Early Work 1955–1968*. Bielefeld, Germany: Kunsthalle Bielefeld; Houston: The Menil Collection, 2002.

Koepplin, Dieter. *Donald Judd: Zeichnungen/Drawings, 1956–1976*. Basel: Kunstmuseum Basel; New York: New York University Press, 1976.

Serota, Nicholas, ed. *Donald Judd*. London: Tate Publishing, 2004.

ALEX KATZ

Alex Katz. Drawings 1944–1981. New York: Marlborough Gallery, 1982.

Schweizer, Paul D., and Carter Ratcliff. *Alex Katz. A Drawing Retrospective*. With interview of Katz by Paul D. Schweizer. Utica, N.Y.: Museum of Art, Munson-Williams-Proctor Institute, 1991.

Scott, Sue. *Alex Katz: Paintings, Drawings, and Cutouts*. Orlando: Orlando Museum of Art, 1990.

ELLSWORTH KELLY

Bois, Yve-Alain. *Ellsworth Kelly, Tablet 1948–1973*. New York: The Drawing Center, 2002.

Bois, Yve-Alain, ed. *The Early Drawings 1948–1955*. Cambridge, Mass.: Harvard University Art Museums; Winterthur, Switzerland: Kunstmuseum Winterthur, 1999.

Cooper, Harry. *An Intense Detachment: Ellsworth Kelly's Line Form Color*. Cambridge, Mass.: Harvard University Art Museums, 1999.

Labrusse, Rémi, and Éric de Chassey. *Henri Matisse-Ellsworth Kelly: Plant Drawings*. Paris: Centre Georges Pompidou, Musée national d'art moderne, 2002.

Upright, Diane. *Ellsworth Kelly: Works on Paper*. New York: Harry N. Abrams, 1987.

Waldman, Diane. *Ellsworth Kelly: Drawings, Collages, Prints*. Greenwich, Conn.: New York Graphic Society, 1971.

YVES KLEIN

Berggruen, Olivier, Max Hollein, and Ingrid Pfeiffer, eds. *Yves Klein*. Ostfildern-Ruit, Germany: Hatje Cantz, 2004.

Bozo, Dominique, et al. *Yves Klein, 1928–1962: A Retrospective*. Houston: Institute for the Arts, Rice University, 1982.

Charlet, Nicolas. *Yves Klein*. Paris: Adam Biro, 2000.

Ledeur, Jean-Paul. *Yves Klein*. Paris: Éditions Guy Pieters, 2000.

FRANZ KLINE

Anfam, David. *Franz Kline: Black and White, 1950–1961*. Houston: The Menil Collection, 1994.

Ashton, Dore, et al. *Franz Kline, 1910–1962*. Rivoli, Italy: Castello di Rivoli, Museo d'Arte Contemporanea, 2004.

Franz Kline: A Retrospective. London: Whitechapel Gallery in association with The Museum of Modern Art, 1964.

Hess, Thomas B. *Franz Kline: Works on Paper*. London: Mayor Gallery, 1977.

WILLEM DE KOONING

The Artist's Hand: Willem de Kooning Drawings, 1937 to 1954. New York: Mitchell-Innes & Nash, 2002.

Butler, Cornelia H., and Paul Schimmel. *Willem de Kooning: Tracing the Figure*. Los Angeles: Museum of Contemporary Art, 2002.

Hess, Thomas B. *Willem de Kooning: Drawings*. Greenwich, Conn.: New York Graphic Society, 1972.

Kertess, Klaus. *Willem de Kooning: Drawing Seeing/Seeing Drawing*. Santa Fe: Arena Editions, 1998.

Rosenblum, Robert. *Willem de Kooning: Mostly Women, Drawings and Paintings from the John and Kimiko Powers Collection*. New York: Gagosian Gallery, 2000.

Shiff, Richard. "With Closed Eyes: de Kooning's Twist." *Master Drawings* 40, no. 1 (spring 2002): 73–88.

YAYOI KUSAMA

Moos, David. *Yayoi Kusama. Early Drawings from the Collection of Richard Castellane*. Birmingham, Ala.: Birmingham Museum of Art, 2000.

Munroe, Alexandra, et al. *Love Forever: Yayoi Kusama, 1958–1968*. Los Angeles: Los Angeles County Museum of Art, 1998.

Yayoi Kusama: The 1950s and 1960s. Paintings, Sculptures, Works on Paper. New York: Paula Cooper Gallery, 1996.

JACOB LAWRENCE

Nesbett, Peter T., and Michelle DuBois. *Jacob Lawrence: Paintings, Drawings, and Murals, 1935–1999. A Catalogue Raisonné*. Seattle: University of Washington Press, 2000.

Van Keuren, Philip. *After Vesalius: Drawings by Jacob Lawrence*. Dallas: Division of Art, Southern Methodist University, 1996.

Wolfe, Townsen. *Jacob Lawrence: Drawings, 1945 to 1996*. New York: DC Moore Gallery, 1996.

BARRY LE VA

Holler, Wolfgang. *Barry Le Va: Zeichnungen von 1967 bis 1996*. Dresden: Kupferstich-Kabinett, Staatliche Kunstsammlungen Dresden, 1998.

Kertess, Klaus. "Between the Lines: The Drawings of Barry Le Va." In *Barry Le Va, 1966–1988*, 25–29. Pittsburgh: Carnegie Mellon Art Gallery, Carnegie Mellon University Press, 1988.

Ligare, David. *Barry Le Va: Drawings, 1967–77*. Salinas, Calif.: Hartnell College Gallery, 1978.

Tucker, Marcia. *Barry Le Va: Four Consecutive Installations and Drawings*. New York: The New Museum, 1978.

SOL LEWITT

Fuchs, Rudi, and Franz W. Kaiser. *Sol LeWitt: Drawings, 1958–1992.* The Hague: Haags Gemeentemuseum, 1992.

Garrels, Gary, ed. *Sol LeWitt: A Retrospective.* New Haven, Conn., and London: Yale University Press, 2000.

Harvey, Michael. *Notes on the Drawings of Sol LeWitt.* Geneva: Ecart Publications, 1977.

Rose, Bernice. "Sol LeWitt and Drawing." In Alicia Legg, ed., *Sol LeWitt*, 31–42. New York: The Museum of Modern Art, 1978.

Singer, Susanna. *Sol LeWitt Wall Drawings, 1968–1984.* Amsterdam: Stedelijk Museum, 1984.

ROY LICHTENSTEIN

Abadie, Daniel. *Roy Lichtenstein: Dessins sans bandes.* Paris: Centre national d'art contemporain, 1975.

Holm, Michael Juul, Martin Caiger-Smith, and Paul Erik Tojner, eds. *Roy Lichtenstein: All About Art.* Humlebæk, Denmark: Louisiana Museum of Modern Art, 2004.

Rose, Bernice, and Elizabeth Richebourg Rea. *The Drawings of Roy Lichtenstein.* New York: The Museum of Modern Art, 1987.

Waldman, Diane. *Roy Lichtenstein, Drawings and Prints.* New York: Chelsea House Publishers, 1970.

RICHARD LONG

Brettell, Richard R., and Dana Friis-Hansen. *Richard Long: Circles Cycles Mud Stones.* Houston: Contemporary Arts Museum, 1996.

Fuchs, Rudi. *Richard Long.* New York: Solomon R. Guggenheim Museum, 1986.

Long, Richard, and Martina Giezen. *Richard Long in Conversation.* Noordwijk, the Netherlands: MW Press, 1985.

Moorhouse, Paul. *Richard Long: Walking the Line.* London: Thames & Hudson, 2002.

LEE LOZANO

Kinmont, Ben, and Lee Lozano. *Project Series: Lee Lozano.* New York: Antinomian Press, 1998.

Rondeau, James. *Lee Lozano.* Brochure. Hartford, Conn.: Wadsworth Atheneum, 1998.

ROBERT MANGOLD

Howard, Jan. *Drawing Now: Robert Mangold.* Baltimore: The Baltimore Museum of Art, 1987.

Rattemeyer, Volker, et al. *Robert Mangold: Träger des Alexej von Jawlensky-Preises. Gemälde und Zeichnungen, 1984–1997.* Wiesbaden, Germany: Museum Wiesbaden; Nuremberg, Germany: Verlag für moderne Kunst, 1998.

Shiff, Richard. *Robert Mangold.* London: Phaidon Press, 2000.

Verna, Gianfranco, and Robert Mangold. *Robert Mangold. Works on Paper.* Zurich: Galerie Annemarie Verna, 1988.

PIERO MANZONI

Battino, Freddy, and Luca Palazzoli. *Piero Manzoni: Catalogue raisonné.* Milan: Edizioni di V. Scheiwiller, 1991.

Costache, Irina. "Piero Manzoni." *Art and Text*, no. 52 (September 1995): 88–89.

Gualdoni, Flaminio. *Le carte di Piero Manzoni.* Milan: Charta, 1995.

Ruiz, Alma, and Angela Vettese. *Piero Manzoni: Line Drawings.* Los Angeles: Museum of Contemporary Art; Ravenna, Italy: Danilo Montanari Editore, 1995.

BRICE MARDEN

Bell, Tiffany. *Drawing the Line: A Retrospective of Drawings by Brice Marden.* Brochure. Lynchburg, Virginia: Maier Museum of Art, Randolph-Macon Woman's College, 2001.

Codognato, Mario, ed. *Brice Marden: Works on Paper, 1964–2001.* Rome: Instituto Nazionale per la Grafica, Calcografia, 2001.

Keller, Eva, ed. *Brice Marden: Drawings and Paintings 1964–2002.* With an interview of Marden by John Yau. Zurich: Daros Collection and Scalo Publishers, 2003.

Kern, Hermann, and Klaus Kertess. *Brice Marden: Zeichnungen/Drawings 1964–1978.* With a statement by Marden. Munich: Kunstraum, 1979.

Kertess, Klaus. *Brice Marden: Paintings and Drawings.* New York: Harry N. Abrams, 1992.

Lee, Janie C. *Brice Marden Drawings: The Whitney Museum of American Art Collection.* With an interview of Marden by Janie C. Lee. New York: Whitney Museum of American Art, 1998.

Schwarz, Dieter, and Michael Semff, eds. *Brice Marden: Work Books 1964–1995.* Munich: Staatliche Graphische Sammlung, 1997.

AGNES MARTIN

Agnes Martin: Works on Paper. Santa Fe: Museum of Fine Arts, Museum of New Mexico, 1998.

Ashton, Dore, and Agnes Martin. *Agnes Martin: Paintings and Drawings, 1957–1975*. London: Arts Council of Great Britain, 1977.

Fer, Briony. "Drawing Drawing: Agnes Martin's Infinity." In Catherine de Zegher and Hendel Teicher, eds., *3 x Abstraction: New Methods of Drawing by Hilma af Klint, Emma Kunt, and Agnes Martin*. New York: The Drawing Center; New Haven, Conn.: Yale University Press, 2005.

Haskell, Barbara, et al. *Agnes Martin*. New York: Whitney Museum of American Art, 1992.

Schwarz, Dieter, ed. *Agnes Martin: Writings/Schriften*. Winterthur, Switzerland: Kunstmuseum Winterthur; Stuttgart: Edition Cantz, 1991.

HENRI MATISSE

Bois, Yve-Alain. "Matisse and 'Arche-drawing.'" In *Painting As Model*, 3–63. Cambridge, Mass.: The MIT Press, 1990.

Carlson, Victor I. *Matisse As a Draughtsman*. Baltimore: The Baltimore Museum of Art, 1971.

Elderfield, John. *The Cut-Outs of Henri Matisse*. New York: George Braziller, 1978.

———. *The Drawing of Henri Matisse*. New York: The Museum of Modern Art, 1992.

Flam, Jack. "Drawings by Matisse." In *Henri Matisse: A Survey of Drawings*, unpag. New York: C & M Arts, 1996.

Labrusse, Rémi, and Éric de Chassey. *Henri Matisse-Ellsworth Kelly: Plant Drawings*. Paris: Centre Georges Pompidou, Musée national d'art moderne, 2002.

Matisse, Henri. "Notes of a Painter on His Drawing." In Jack Flam, ed., *Matisse on Art*, 80–82. 1973. Reprint, Berkeley and Los Angeles: University of California Press, 1994. Originally published as "Notes d'un peintre sur son dessin," *Le Point* 4, no. 21 (July 1939): 104–10.

GORDON MATTA-CLARK

Breitweiser, Sabine, Pamela M. Lee, and Peter Fend. *Reorganizing Structure by Drawing through It: Zeichnung bei Gordon Matta-Clark*. Vienna: Generali Foundation, 1997.

Diserens, Corinne, ed. *Gordon Matta-Clark*. London: Phaidon Press, 2003.

Gordon Matta-Clark. Valencia: IVAM Centre Julio Gonzáles, 1992.

Jacob, Mary Jane, et al. *Gordon Matta-Clark: A Retrospective*. Chicago: Museum of Contemporary Art, 1985.

MARIO MERZ

Celant, Germano, et al. *Mario Merz*. New York: Solomon R. Guggenheim Museum; Milan: Electa, 1989.

Haenpein, Carl Albrecht, and Mario Merz. *Mario Merz: Disegni/Arbeiten auf Papier*. Hannover: Kestner Gesellschaft, 1982.

Krane, Susan, and Robin Dodds. *Mario Merz: Paintings and Constructions and Drawings*. With a statement by Merz. Buffalo, N.Y.: Albright-Knox Art Gallery, 1984.

Mario Merz: Opere su carta. With a statement by Merz. Turin: Galleria In Arco, 1988.

Mundici, Cristina, ed. *Mario Merz. Terra elevata o la storia del disegno*. With a conversation between Beatrice Merz and Mario Merz. Rivoli, Italy: Castello di Rivoli, Museo d'Arte Contemporanea, 1990.

HENRI MICHAUX

Comment, Bernard, and Claire Stoullig. *Henri Michaux: Frottages*. Toulouse: Musée des abattoirs; Geneva: Musées d'art et d'histoire, 2001.

Henri Michaux. With a statement by Michaux. Trans. John Ashbery. London: Robert Fraser Gallery, 1963.

Henri Michaux. With statements by Michaux. Trans. Michael Fineberg. New York: Solomon R. Guggenheim Museum, 1978.

Spira, Anthony, ed. *Henri Michaux, 1899–1984*. London: Whitechapel Art Gallery, 1999.

Zegher, Catherine de, and Raymond Bellour. *Untitled Passages by Henri Michaux*. New York: The Drawing Center, 2000.

Zegher, Catherine de, ed. *Henri Michaux: Emergences/Résurgences*. Drawing Papers 14. New York: The Drawing Center, 2000.

ROBERT MORRIS

Berger, Maurice. *Labyrinths: Robert Morris, Minimalism and the 1960's*. New York: Harper & Row, 1989.

Krauss, Rosalind, et al. *Robert Morris: The Mind/Body Problem*. New York: The Solomon R. Guggenheim Foundation, 1994.

Krens, Thomas. *The Drawings of Robert Morris.* Williamstown, Mass.: Williams College Museum of Art, 1982.

Morris, Robert. *Continuous Project Altered Daily: The Writings of Robert Morris.* Cambridge, Mass.: The MIT Press, 1993.

ROBERT MOTHERWELL

Carmean, E. A. *The Collages of Robert Motherwell: A Retrospective Exhibition.* Houston: The Museum of Fine Arts, 1972.

Flam, Jack. *Robert Motherwell Drawings: A Retrospective.* Houston: Janie C. Lee Gallery, 1979.

O'Hara, Frank. *Robert Motherwell.* New York: The Museum of Modern Art, 1965.

Rosand, David, ed. *Robert Motherwell on Paper: Drawings, Prints, Collages.* New York: Harry N. Abrams, 1997.

BRUCE NAUMAN

Bruggen, Coosje van. *Bruce Nauman.* New York: Rizzoli, 1988.

Bruggen, Coosje van, Dieter Koepplin, and Franz Meyer. *Bruce Nauman: Drawings, 1965–1986.* Basel: Museum für Gegenwartskunst, 1986.

Livingston, Jane, and Marcia Tucker. *Bruce Nauman: Work from 1965 to 1972.* Los Angeles: Los Angeles County Museum, 1972.

Simon, Joan, and Jean-Christophe Amman. *Bruce Nauman.* London: Whitechapel Art Gallery, 1986.

Simon, Joan, ed. *Bruce Nauman.* Minneapolis: Walker Art Center, 1994.

BARNETT NEWMAN

Newman, Barnett. "'Frontiers of Space.' Interview with Dorothy Gees Seckler." In John P. O'Neill, ed., *Barnett Newman: Selected Writings and Interviews,* 247–51. New York: Alfred A. Knopf, 1990.

Richardson, Brenda. *Barnett Newman: The Complete Drawings, 1944–1969.* Baltimore: The Baltimore Museum of Art, 1979.

Shiff, Richard, Carol C. Mancusi-Ungaro, and Heidi Colsman-Freyberger. *Barnett Newman: A Catalogue Raisonné.* New York: Barnett Newman Foundation; New Haven, Conn., and London: Yale University Press, 2004.

Strick, Jeremy. *The Sublime Is Now: The Early Work of Barnett Newman. Paintings and Drawings.* Minneapolis: Walker Art Center, 1994.

Zweite, Armin. *Barnett Newman: Paintings, Sculptures, Works on Paper.* Trans. John Brogden. Ostfildern-Ruit, Germany: Hatje Cantz, 1999.

JIM NUTT

Adrian, Dennis. "The Metaphysics of Perception in the Drawings of Jim Nutt." *Drawing* 15, no. 2 (July–August 1993): 25–29.

Andera, Margaret, et al. *Jim Nutt.* Milwaukee: Milwaukee Art Museum, 1994.

Halstead, Whitney. *Jim Nutt.* Chicago: Museum of Contemporary Art, 1974.

Jim Nutt/Portraits. Chicago: Museum of Contemporary Art, 1999.

Johnson, Ken. "Jim Nutt's Human Comedy." *Art in America* 80 (February 1992): 84–91.

HÉLIO OITICICA

Brett, Guy, Catherine David, and Chris Dercon, eds. *Hélio Oiticica.* Minneapolis: Walker Art Center; Rotterdam: Witte de With, 1992.

Figuereido, Luciano. *Hélio Oiticica: Cor, imagem, poética.* Rio de Janeiro: Centro de Arte Hélio Oiticica, 2003.

Hélio Oiticica: Grupo Frente e Metaesquemas. São Paulo: Galeria São Paulo, 1989.

CLAES OLDENBURG

Baro, Gene. *Claes Oldenburg: Drawings and Prints.* London and New York: Chelsea House, 1969.

Lee, Janie C. *Claes Oldenburg Drawings in the Whitney Museum of American Art.* New York: Whitney Museum of American Art, 2002.

Oldenburg, Claes. "Notes by the Artist on Selected Drawings." In *Proposals for Monuments and Buildings, 1965–1969,* 155–68. Chicago: Big Table Publishing Company, 1969.

———. "Chronology of Drawings." *Studio International* 179, no. 923 (June 1970): 249–52.

Rose, Barbara. "The World Is Not a Drawing." In *Claes Oldenburg,* 154–67. New York: The Museum of Modern Art, 1970.

Wilde, Eddy de, and Coosje van Bruggen. *Claes Oldenburg: Tekeningen, Aquarellen En Grafiek*. Amsterdam: Stedelijk Museum, 1977.

SIGMAR POLKE

Gachnang, Johannes. *Sigmar Polke: The Early Drawings, 1963–1969*. Bern and Berlin: Verlag Gachnang and Springer, 1991. Originally published as *Sigmar Polke: Zeichnungen, 1963–1969*. Bern and Berlin: Verlag Gachnang and Springer, 1987.

Rowell, Margit, ed. *Sigmar Polke. Works on Paper, 1963–1974*. New York: The Museum of Modern Art, 1999.

Schmidt, Katharina, and Gunter Schweikhart. *Sigmar Polke: Zeichnungen, Aquarelle, Skizzenbucher, 1962–1988*. Bonn: Kunstmuseum Bonn, 1988.

JACKSON POLLOCK

Cernuschi, Claude. *Jackson Pollock: "Psychoanalytic" Drawings*. Durham, N.C.: Duke University Museum of Art, 1992.

Davidson, Susan, David Anfam, and Margaret Holben Ellis. *No Limits, Just Edges: Jackson Pollock Paintings on Paper*. New York: Solomon R. Guggenheim Foundation, 2005.

Krauss, Rosalind. "Jackson Pollock's Drawings." In Pepe Karmel, ed., *Jackson Pollock: Interviews, Articles, and Reviews*, 176–79. New York: The Museum of Modern Art, 1999. Originally published in *Artforum* 9, no. 5 (January 1971): 58–61.

Rose, Bernice. *Jackson Pollock: Works on Paper*. New York: The Museum of Modern Art, 1969.

———. *Jackson Pollock: Drawing into Painting*. New York: The Museum of Modern Art, 1980.

Rosenthal, Nan, Katharine Baetjer, and Lisa Mintz Messinger. *The Jackson Pollock Sketchbooks in The Metropolitan Museum of Art*. New York: The Metropolitan Museum of Art, 1997.

ARNULF RAINER

Arnulf Rainer: An Exhibition. New York: Solomon R. Guggenheim Museum, 1989.

Arnulf Rainer: Zeichnungen, 1949–1985. Munich: Verlag Fred Jahn, 1988.

Dahlem, Franz, Arnulf Rainer, and Antonio Saura. *Arnulf Rainer: Young Cross*. Houston: The Menil Collection, 1992.

ROBERT RAUSCHENBERG

Alloway, Lawrence. *Robert Rauschenberg: Drawings, 1958–1968*. New York: Acquavella Contemporary Art, 1986.

Hopps, Walter. *Robert Rauschenberg: The Early 1950s*. Houston: The Menil Collection and Houston Fine Art Press, 1991.

Hopps, Walter, et al. *Robert Rauschenberg: A Retrospective*. New York: Solomon R. Guggenheim Museum, 1997.

Ratcliff, Carter. "Rauschenberg's Solvent-Transfer Drawings." *Print Collector's Newsletter* 18, no. 2 (May–June 1987): 49–51.

Robert Rauschenberg: Paintings, Drawings, and Combines. London: Whitechapel Art Gallery, 1964.

BRIDGET RILEY

Bridget Riley: Works 1959–78. London: British Council, 1978.

Hickey, David. *Bridget Riley: Paintings 1982–2000 and Early Works on Paper*. New York: PaceWildenstein, 2000.

Licht, Jennifer. *Bridget Riley: Drawings*. New York: The Museum of Modern Art, 1966.

Moorhouse, Paul, ed. *Bridget Riley*. London: Tate Publishing, 2003.

Moorehouse, Paul, et al. *Bridget Riley: Paintings and Drawings, 1961–2004*. London: Ridinghouse, 2004.

DOROTHEA ROCKBURNE

Marlais, Michael. *Dorothea Rockburne. Drawing: Structure and Curve*. New York: John Weber Gallery, 1978.

Olson, Roberta. "An Interview with Dorothea Rockburne." *Art in America* 66 (November–December 1978): 142.

Stoops, Susan L., and Carl Belz. *Dorothea Rockburne*. Waltham, Mass.: Rose Art Museum, Brandeis University, 1989.

DIETER ROTH

Dobke, Dirk, ed. *Dieter Roth. Unique Pieces*. London: Hansjorg Mayer, 2003.

Hofmann, Werner, Hanna Hohl, and André Kambe. *Dieter Roth, Zeichnungen*. Hamburg: Hamburger Kunsthalle, 1987.

1234 Schnellstzeichnungen von Dieter Roth/1234 Most Speedy Drawings by Dieter Roth. Stuttgart: Edition Hansjorg Mayer, 1987.

Vischer, Theodora, and Bernadette Walter eds. *Roth Time: A Dieter Roth Retrospective*. New York: The Museum of Modern Art; Baden, Switzerland: Lars Müller Publishers, 2004.

EDWARD RUSCHA

Hopper, Dennis. *Edward Ruscha: Powders, Pressures, and Other Drawings*. San Francisco: John Berggruen Gallery, 2000.

Marshall, Richard. *Edward Ruscha: Los Angeles Apartments 1965*. New York: Whitney Museum of American Art, 1990.

Rowell, Margit, ed. *Cotton Puffs, Q-Tips, Smoke, and Mirrors: The Drawings of Ed Ruscha*. New York: Whitney Museum of American Art, 2004.

Ruscha, Ed. *They Called Her Styrene*. London: Phaidon Press Limited, 2000.

Schjeldahl, Peter. *Guacamole Airlines and Other Drawings by Edward Ruscha*. New York: Harry N. Abrams, 1980.

Wakefield, Neville, and Dave Hickey. *Ed Ruscha: New Paintings and a Retrospective of Works on Paper*. London: Anthony d'Offay, 1998.

LUCAS SAMARAS

Glenn, Constance W., and Jack Glenn, eds. *Lucas Samaras: Sketches, Drawings, Doodles, and Plans*. New York: Harry N. Abrams, 1987.

Glimcher, Mildred. *Lucas Samaras: Pastels*. New York: Pace Gallery, 1993.

Prather, Marla, and Donald Kuspit. *Unrepentant Ego: The Self-Portraits of Lucas Samaras*. New York: Whitney Museum of American Art, 2003.

Schjeldahl, Peter, and Dianne Vanderlip. *Samaras: Pastels*. Denver: Denver Art Museum, 1981.

Vanderlip, Dianne Perry, ed. *Lucas Samaras: Objects and Subjects, 1969–1986*. New York: Abbeville Press, 1988.

FRED SANDBACK

Ahrens, Carl, Carl Haenlein, and Fred Sandback. *Fred Sandback: Diagonal Constructions/Broken Lines. Skulpturen und Zeichnungen*. Hannover: Kestner Gesellschaft, 1987.

The Art of Fred Sandback. A Survey. Champaign: Krannert Art Museum, University of Illinois at Urbana-Champaign, 1985.

Sandback, Fred. *Ten Isometric Drawings for Ten Vertical Constructions*. New York: Lapp Princess Press, 1977.

———. "Lines of Inquiry." Interview with Joan Simon. *Art in America* 85, no. 5 (May 1997): 88.

MIRA SCHENDEL

Herkenhoff, Paulo. "Mira Schendel and the Shaping of the Inexpressible." In Lori Ledis, Robert Flam, and Mary Sabbatino, *Art from Brazil in New York*, unpag. New York: The Drawing Center, 1995.

Kautz, Willy, and Rodrigo Naves. *Mira Schendel: Continuum amorfo*. Mexico City: Fundación Olga y Rufino Tamayo/ Museo Tamayo Arte Contemporáneo, 2004.

Marques, Maria Eduarda. *Mira Schendel*. São Paulo: Cosac & Naify, 2001.

Salzstein, Sônia, and Paulo Venancio Filho. *Mira Schendel a forma volátil*. Rio de Janeiro: Centro de Arte Hélio Oiticica, 1997.

Salzstein, Sônia, ed. *No vazio do mundo. Mira Schendel*. São Paulo: Editora Marca D'Agua, 1996.

JAN SCHOONHOVEN

Courtney, David. *Jan Schoonhoven: A Retrospective*. Boca Raton, Fla.: Ritter Art Gallery, 1987.

Fuchs, Rudi, and Beat Wismer. *Jan Schoonhoven*. New York: Paula Cooper Gallery, 1999.

Graevenitz, Antje V. *J. J. Schoonhoven: Zeichnungen/ Tekeningen, 1940–1975*. Düsseldorf: Städtische Kunsthalle, 1975.

J. J. Schoonhoven. Amsterdam: Stedelijk Museum, 1971.

Jan Schoonhoven Retrospectief: Tekeningen En Reliëfs/ Jan Schoonhoven Retrospektiv: Zeichnungen und Reliefs. The Hague: Haags Gemeentemuseum, 1984.

RICHARD SERRA

Aukeman, Anastasia, ed. *Richard Serra: Weight and Measure Drawings*. New York: The Drawing Center, 1994.

Janssen, Hans, ed. *Richard Serra: Drawings/Zeichnungen 1969–1990*. With a statement by Serra. Bern: Benteli Publishers, 1990.

Pauseback, Michael. *Richard Serra: Skulpturen und Zeichnungen, 1967–1983*. Berlin: Reinhard Onnasch Ausstellungen, 1983.

Rosenthal, Mark. *Richard Serra: Drawings and Etchings from Iceland*. With an interview with Serra. New York: Matthew Marks Gallery, 1992.

Schlieker, Andrea, et al. *Richard Serra. Drawings*. Düsseldorf: Richter Verlag, 1993.

Serra, Richard, and Lizzie Borden. "About Drawing: An Interview." In *Richard Serra: Tekenigen/Drawing '71–'77*. Amsterdam: Stedelijk Museum, 1977. Reprinted in Richard Serra, *Interviews, Etc. 1970–1980*, ed. Clara Weyergraf, 76–87. Yonkers, N.Y.: The Hudson River Museum, 1980.

DAVID SMITH

Clark, Trinkett. *The Drawings of David Smith*. Washington, D.C.: The International Foundation, 1985.

Cummings, Paul. *David Smith: The Drawings*. New York: Whitney Museum of American Art, 1979.

Dabrowski, Magdalena. "David Smith: Identity and Creative Vision." In *David Smith. Related Clues: Drawings, Paintings, and Sculpture 1931–1964*, 7–16. New York: Gagosian Gallery, 2004.

Day, Holliday T. *David Smith, Spray Paintings, Drawings, Sculpture*. Chicago: Arts Club of Chicago, 1983.

Lauterbach, Ann. *David Smith: Ink Drawings from 1957*. Los Angeles: Margo Leavin Gallery, 2000.

McCoy, Garnett, ed. *David Smith*. With excerpts from Smith lecture "Drawing" delivered at a forum at Tulane University, New Orleans, on March 21, 1955. New York and Washington, D.C.: Praeger, 1973.

Merkert, Jörn, Hannelor Kersting, and Rachel Kirby. *David Smith, Sculpture and Drawings*. Munich: Prestel, 1986.

Wilkin, Karen. "David Smith: A Sculptor Draws." *Master Drawings* 40, no. 1 (spring 2002): 43–56.

TONY SMITH

Kertess, Klaus, and Joan Pachner. *Tony Smith: A Drawing Retrospective*. New York: Matthew Marks Gallery, 1995.

Meschede, Friedrich, et al. *Tony Smith: Skulpturen und Zeichnungen/Sculptures and Drawings, 1961–1969*. Münster, Germany: Westfälisches Landesmuseum für Kunst und Kulturgeschichte, 1988.

Storr, Robert. *Tony Smith: Architect, Painter, Sculptor*. New York: The Museum of Modern Art, 1998.

ROBERT SMITHSON

Ginsburg, Susan, and Joseph Masheck. *Robert Smithson: Drawings*. New York: New York Cultural Center, 1974.

Meschede, Friedrich, et al. *Robert Smithson: Drawings from the Estate*. Münster, Germany: Westfälisches Landesmuseum für Kunst und Kulturgeschichte, 1989.

Tsai, Eugenie. *Robert Smithson Unearthed: Drawings, Collages, Writings*. New York: Columbia University Press, 1991.

Tsai, Eugenie, ed. *Robert Smithson*. Los Angeles: Museum of Contemporary Art in association with University of California Press, 2004.

FRANK STELLA

Frank Stella: Working Drawings, 1956–1982. Kitakyushu, Japan: Kitakyushu Municipal Museum of Art, 1982.

Geelhaar, Christian. *Frank Stella: Working Drawings/Zeichnungen, 1956–1970*. Basel: Kunstmuseum Basel, 1980.

Goldman, Judith. *Frank Stella, Fourteen Prints: With Drawings, Collages, and Working Proofs*. Princeton, N.J.: The Art Museum, Princeton University, 1983.

Rubin, Lawrence. *Frank Stella : A Catalogue Raisonné*. 1st ed. New York: Stewart, Tabori & Chang, 1986.

Verspohl, Franz-Joachim, ed. *The Writings of Frank Stella*. Cologne: Walter König, 2001.

MYRON STOUT

Myron Stout. Edinburgh: Inverleith House, Royal Botanic Garden, 1998.

Schwartz, Sanford, et al. *Myron Stout*. New York: Whitney Museum of American Art, 1980.

MARK TOBEY

De Baranano, Kosme, et al. *Mark Tobey*. Madrid: Museo Nacional Centro de Arte Reina Sofía, 1997.

Mark Tobey: Works on Paper. Stanford, Calif.: Stanford University Museum of Art, 1990.

Roberts, Colette. *Mark Tobey: Drawings*. New York: Grove Press, 1960.

Taylor, Joshua C. *Tribute to Mark Tobey*. Washington, D.C.: Smithsonian Institution Press, 1974.

ANNE TRUITT

Carmean, E. A. *Anne Truitt*. With a text by Truitt. Charlottesville: University of Virginia, 1976.

Hopps, Walter. *Anne Truitt: Sculpture and Drawings, 1961–1973*. Washington, D.C.: Corcoran Gallery of Art, 1974.

Meyer, James, and Margaret Shufeldt. *Anne Truitt. Early Drawings and Sculpture, 1958–1963*. Atlanta: Michael C. Carlos Museum, Emory University, 2004.

Truitt, Anne. *Dayboo: The Journal of an Artist*. New York: Pantheon Books, 1982.

RICHARD TUTTLE

Grynsztejn, Madeleine, et al. *Richard Tuttle: A Retrospective*. San Francisco: San Francisco Museum of Modern Art, forthcoming.

Haldemann, Matthias. *Richard Tuttle: Replace the Abstract Picture Plane*. Zug, Switzerland: Hatje Cantz Verlag, 2001.

Netter, Maria, and Richard Tuttle. *Richard Tuttle: 100 Zeichnungen und Aquarelle, 1968–1976*. Basel: Kunsthalle Basel, 1977.

Poetter, Jochen, and Margrit Franziska Brehm. *Richard Tuttle: Chaos, die Form*. Baden-Baden, Germany: Staatliche Kunsthalle, 1993.

Tucker, Marcia. *Richard Tuttle*. New York: Whitney Museum of American Art, 1975.

Verna, Gianfranco, et al. *List of Drawing Material of Richard Tuttle & Appendices*. With a text by Tuttle. Zurich: Gianfranco and Annemarie Verna, Robert Krauthammer, Alfred Gutzwiller, and Richard Tuttle, 1979.

CY TWOMBLY

Barthes, Roland. *Cy Twombly: Paintings and Drawings, 1954–1977*. New York: Whitney Museum of American Art, 1979.

Bastian, Heiner, and Franz Meyer. *Cy Twombly: Zeichnungen, 1953–1973*. Basel: Kunstmuseum Basel, 1973.

Boehm, Gottfried. "Remembering, Forgetting: Cy Twombly's Works on Paper" (1987). In Nicola Del Roscio, *Writings on Cy Twombly*, 180–90. Munich: Schirmer/Mosel, 2002.

Delehanty, Suzanne. "The Alchemy of Mind and Hand." In *Cy Twombly: Paintings, Drawings, Constructions, 1951–1974*, 10–32. Philadelphia: Institute of Contemporary Art, 1975.

Lambert, Yvon. *Cy Twombly: Catalogue raisonné des œuvres sur papier de Cy Twombly*. Milan: Multhipla, 1979.

Larsen, Susan C. *Cy Twombly: Works on Paper 1954–1976*. Newport, R.I.: Newport Harbour Art Museum, 1981.

Sylvester, Julie. *Cy Twombly: Fifty Years of Works on Paper*. New York: Whitney Museum of American Art, 2005.

JACQUES DE LA VILLEGLÉ

Catalogue thématique des affiches lacérées de Villeglé. 6 vols. Paris: Marval, 1988–96.

Felgine, Odile. *Villeglé*. Neuchâtel, Switzerland: Ides et Calandes, 2001.

Jacques Villeglé: Buenos Aires. Buenos Aires: Centre culturel de la Recoleta, 2003.

Lamarche-Vadel, Bernard. *Villeglé. La présentation en jugement*. Paris: Marval, 1990.

Piriou, Françoise. *La natura del manifesto strappato*. Livorno, Italy: Galleria Peccolo, 1990.

ANDY WARHOL

Andy Warhol. Drawings and Related Works. New York: Gagosian Gallery, 2003.

Baume, Nicholas. *About Face: Andy Warhol Portraits*. Cambridge, Mass.: The MIT Press, 1999.

Breidenbach, Tom. *Andy Warhol: Still Life Drawings, 1954–1985*. New York: Paul Kasmin Gallery, 2002.

Crone, Rainer. *Andy Warhol: The Early Work, 1942–1962*. New York: Rizzoli, 1987.

Francis, Mark, and Dieter Koepplin. *Andy Warhol: Drawings, 1942–1987*. New York: Bulfinch Press, 1998.

McShine, Kynaston, ed. *Andy Warhol. A Retrospective*. New York: The Museum of Modern Art, 1989.

Vartanian, Ian. *Andy Warhol: Drawings and Illustrations of the 1950s*. Milan: Charta, 2000.

LAWRENCE WEINER

Alberro, Alexander, et al. *Lawrence Weiner*. London: Phaidon Press, 1998.

Beeren, Wim. *Lawrence Weiner: Works From the Beginning of the Sixties Towards the End of the Eighties*. Amsterdam: Stedelijk Museum, 1988.

Lawrence Weiner: Displacement. New York: Dia Center for the Arts, 1991.

Weiner, Lawrence. [Statement on Drawing.] *White Walls*, no. 13 (1986): 52.

H. C. WESTERMANN

Barrette, Bill, ed. *Letters from H. C. Westermann*. New York: Timken Publishers, 1988.

"H. C. Westermann." In Christiaan Braun, ed. *Eye Infection*, 165–205. Amsterdam: Stedelijk Museum, 2001.

H. C. Westermann: Sculpture and Drawing. New York: Lennon Weinberg, 1988.

Haskell, Barbara. *H. C. Westermann*. New York: Whitney Museum of American Art, 1978.

"Sincerely, Cliff": H. C. Westermann. Madison: Madison Art Center, 1996.

Storr, Robert. "The Devil's Handyman." In Lynne Warren, ed., *H. C. Westermann*, 16–33. Chicago: Museum of Contemporary Art in association with Harry N. Abrams, 2001.

JOSEPH YOAKUM

DePasse, Derrel B. *Traveling the Rainbow: The Life and Art of Joseph E. Yoakum*. New York: Museum of American Folk Art; Jackson: University Press of Mississippi, 2001.

Joseph Yoakum, 1886–1972. New York: Hirschl & Adler Modern, 1985.

CREDITS

Individual works of art appearing herein may be protected by copyright in the United States of America or elsewhere, and may not be reproduced in any form without the permission of the rights holders. In reproducing the images contained in this publication, the Museum obtained the permission of the rights holders whenever possible. In those instances where the Museum could not locate the rights holders, notwithstanding good faith efforts, it requests that any contact information concerning such rights holders be forwarded, so that they may be contacted for future editions.

© 2005 Vito Acconci: 188; © 2005 Artists Rights Society (ARS), New York/ADAGP, Paris: 33 top, 78, 81, 83, 122; © 2005 Artists Rights Society (ARS), New York/DACS, London: 112; © 2005 Artists Rights Society (ARS), New York/SABAM, Brussels: 193; © 2005 Artists Rights Society (ARS), New York/SIAE, Rome: 146; © 2005 Artists Rights Society (ARS), New York/VG Bild-Kunst, Bonn: 2, 21, 75–77, 195; © 2005 Richard Artschwager/Artists Rights Society (ARS), New York: 110; © 2005 Jo Baer: 155; © 2005 Georg Baselitz: 32, 33 bottom, 136, 137; © 2005 Lee Bontecou/courtesy Knoedler & Co., New York: 144; © 2005 Louise Bourgeois: 69; © 2005 Chris Burden: 189; © 2005 Waltercio Caldas: 183; © 2005 Vija Celmins: 187; © 2005 Christo: 113; © 2005 Chuck Close: 186; © 2005 Hanne Darboven: 167; © 2005 Ernesto Deira: 34; © 2005 Agnes Denes: 182; © 2005 Antonio Dias: 130; © 2005 Richard Diebenkorn: 134; © 2005 Jim Dine/Artists Rights Society (ARS), New York: 114; © 2005 Artists Rights Society (ARS), New York/ADAGP, Paris/Estate of Marcel Duchamp: 38, 39; © 2005 León Ferrari: 48 bottom, 143; © 2005 Estate of Dan Flavin/Artists Rights Society (ARS), New York: 156, 157; © 2005 Fondazione Lucio Fontana: 74; © 2005 Estate of Sam Francis/Artists Rights Society (ARS), New York: 71; © 2005 Lucien Freud: 82; © 2005 Gego: 48 top, 141; © 2005 Estate of Arshile Gorky/Artists Rights Society (ARS), New York: 55; © 2005 The Estate of Philip Guston: 35 bottom, 65, 132, 133; © 2005 Reproduced with the permission of the Estate of Eva Hesse. Galerie Hauser & Wirth, Zurich: 45, 162, 163; © 2005 David Hockney: 111; © 2005 Jasper Johns/Licensed by VAGA, New York: 27, 94–97; © 2005 Alex Katz: 115; © 2005 Ellsworth Kelly: 86–89; © 2005 The Franz Kline Estate/Artists Rights Society (ARS), New York: 64; © 2005 The Willem de Kooning Foundation/Artists Rights Society (ARS), New York: 15, 17 top, 57, 60, 61, 135; © 2005 Yayoi Kusama: 80, 151; © 2005 The Jacob and Gwendolyn Lawrence Foundation: 138; © 2005 Sol LeWitt/Artists Rights Society (ARS), New York: 41 bottom, 170, 171; © 2005 Estate of Roy Lichtenstein: 28, 102–05; © 2005 Richard Long: 192; © 2005 Robert Mangold/Artists Rights Society (ARS), New York: 169; © 2005 Brice Marden/Artists Rights Society (ARS), New York: 22, 180; © 2005 Succession H. Matisse, Paris/Artists Rights Society (ARS), New York: 85; © 2005 Estate of Gordon Matta-Clark/Artists Rights Society (ARS), New York: 184; © 2005 Robert Morris/Artists Rights Society (ARS), New York: 44, 177; © 2005 Bruce Nauman/Artists Rights Society (ARS), New York: 161; © 2005 Barnett Newman Foundation/Artists Rights Society (ARS), New York: 19, 63; © 2005 Jim Nutt: 123; © 2005 Claes Oldenburg: 116–19; © 2005 Projeto Lygia Pape: 46; © 2005 Estate of Pablo Picasso/Artists Rights Society (ARS), New York: 25; © 2005 Pollock-Krasner Foundation/Artists Rights Society (ARS), New York: cover, 17 bottom, 20, 56, 59; © 2005 Arnulf Rainer: 190; © 2005 Bridget Riley: 165; © 2005 Dorothea Rockburne/Artists Rights Society (ARS), New York: 179; © 2005 Estate of Dieter Roth: 191; © 2005 Edward Ruscha: 30, 106–09; © 2005 Estate of Fred Sandback: 172; © 2005 Estate of Mira Schendel: 142; © 2005 Jan J. Schoonhoven: 150; © 2005 Richard Serra/Artists Rights Society (ARS), New York: 181; © 2005 Estate of Tony Smith/Artists Rights Society (ARS), New York: 70; © 2005 Frank Stella/Artists Rights Society (ARS), New York: 159; © 2005 Anne Truitt: 154; © 2005 Richard Tuttle: 168; © 2005 Cy Twombly: 24, 72, 73; © 2005 Estate of Jorge de la Vega: 35 top, 131; © 2005 Andy Warhol Foundation for the Visual Arts/Artists Rights Society (ARS), New York: 29 bottom, 98–101; © 2005 Lawrence Weiner/Artists Rights Society (ARS), New York: 166

PHOTOGRAPH CREDITS:

CNAC/MNAM/Dist. Réunion des Musées Nationaux/Art Resource, New York, photography by Philippe Migeat: 33; Sheldan C. Collins, © 2001 Whitney Museum of American Art, New York: 15; Gamma One Conversions, Inc., New York: 35 bottom; Archivio Fundación Gego. Photograph: Paolo Gasparini, © Fundación Gego: 48 top; Gianfranco Gorgoni: 18, 29; Rick Hall, Jack S. Blanton Museum of Art: 35 top; Martha Holmes/Time Life Pictures/Getty Images: 12 left; courtesy LA Louver, Venice, California: 111; © 1983 The Metropolitan Museum of Art, New York: 17; Digital Imaging Studio, © 2005 The Museum of Modern Art, New York: 17 top, 24, 25, 27, 28, 30, 36, 39, 41, 42, 44–46, 55, 58–64, 66, 67, 74–77, 80–85, 92, 93, 95, 97, 101, 102, 105–07, 114, 116–19, 122, 124, 125, 127, 130, 131, 134, 136, 139–42, 144, 151, 161, 162, 175, 183, 186, 187, 193, 195; Digital Imaging Studio, © 2005 The Museum of Modern Art, New York, photography by Thomas Griesel: 56, 68, 69, 71–73, 88–90, 99, 109, 110, 113, 115, 121, 123, 132, 133, 135, 137, 138, 143, 148, 149, 154, 165, 170, 171, 179–81, 184, 185, 189–92, 194; Digital Imaging Studio, © 2005 The Museum of Modern Art, New York, photography by Paige Knight: 48 bottom, 78, 79, 86, 87, 98, 103, 104, 112, 120, 128, 129, 145–47, 150, 152, 153, 155, 156, 158, 163, 164, 166–68, 172, 174, 176, 182, 188; Digital Imaging Studio, © 2005 The Museum of Modern Art, New York, photography by John Wronn: cover, 2, 20, 34, 70; © 1991 Hans Namuth Estate, Collection Center for Creative Photography, The University of Arizona: 19; courtesy P.S.1 Contemporary Art Center, Long Island City, New York: 47; courtesy Michael Werner Gallery, New York and Cologne: 32; Via Wynroth, courtesy Ronald Feldman Fine Arts, New York: 12 right; Dorothy Zeidman: 94